Education and Alienation
in the Junior School

Education and Alienation Series

Series Editor: Neville Jones, Principal Educational Psychologist, Oxfordshire

Education and Alienation in the Junior School

Edited by

Jim Docking

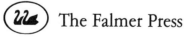 The Falmer Press
(A member of the Taylor & Francis Group)
London • New York • Philadelphia

UK   The Falmer Press, Rankine Road, Basingstoke, Hants RG24 0PR

USA   The Falmer Press, Taylor & Francis Inc., 1900 Frost Road, Suite
          101, Bristol, PA 19007

First published 1990

British Library Cataloguing in Publication Data

Docking, Jim
    Education and alienation in the junior school. –
(Education and alienation series).
    1. Great Britain. Primary schools. Students. Social
adjustment
    I. Title   II. Series
    372'.241'0941

    ISBN 1–85000–571–0
    ISBN 1–85000–572–9 pbk

Library of Congress Cataloging-in-Publication Data

Education and alienation in the junior school/edited by
    Jim Docking
        p.   cm.
    Includes index.
    ISBN 1–85000–571–0. — ISBN 1–85000–572–9 (pbk.)
    1. School children—Great Britain—Attitudes. 2. Problem
children—Education—Great Britain. 3. Elementary schools—
Great Britain.   I. Docking, Jim.
    LB1117.E28   1990
    372.18'1'0941—dc20   90–36085 CIP

Jacket design by Caroline Archer

Typeset in 10/12 Garamond by
Chapterhouse, The Cloisters, Formby L37 3PX

*Printed in Great Britain by
Redwood Burn Limited, Trowbridge, Wiltshire*

Contents

Preface

The books in this series are published as part of the work being carried out on the Disaffected Pupil Programme in Oxfordshire (DPP). The Programme is essentially about learning and personal development in primary and secondary schools, and the social context within which teachers and pupils are engaged in the process of education. Given that schools are the context in which disaffection finds expression and where solutions to pupils' alienation have to be found, the focus of the Programme and these books is on effective school management, skilled and imaginative teaching, and appropriate curriculum for all pupils.

The approach to pupil disaffection being taken is that schools do matter and do make a difference in the way pupils grow and develop during early childhood and adolescence. This is a positive philosophy that has to be developed by all teachers in all our schools, taking account of what early learning experiences all children bring to their learning in school. Essential to the task of preventing educational disaffection is that every pupil should be engaged in purposeful learning and should be seen positively as a potential learner. The Programme, therefore, aims to look at what can be achieved in ordinary schools by virtue of good practice.

The books in this series examine both those factors that prevent positive learning taking place and the good practice that enhances a pupil's experience of schooling irrespective of previous background experience and learning. This volume, which is concerned with pupils at a particular stage in their education, is one of a series that ranges from when pupils are prepared for schooling in playgroups, day centres and nurseries, through primary and secondary schooling, to further and adult education. Each volume attempts to identify those factors which encourage disaffection at a particular stage in education. The series has been planned in recognition of the fact that there are strands of disaffection — attitudinal, management, teaching and curriculum — that thread themselves throughout the education service. These affect pupils in a variety of ways, depending both on individual susceptability and the characteristic features of school organisation and management. Disaffection is, therefore, a multi-dimensional phenomenon.

The continuities that thread their way through the different phases of education include attitudes towards ability and achievement, gender, disability and race, together with those attitudes which tend to determine how we structure our education system, establish its aims and goals, and determine its casualties. So at each stage in the education process there are characteristic features of school management, teaching techniques, and curriculum design which provide for each pupil, and sometimes member of staff, a basis for disenchantment even when this is not positive disaffection.

A starting point for much of this is in the way pupils become marginalised into learning groups (classes we call them, sometimes special) which make pupils feel outsiders, determine their success at school, and pervasively erode self-esteem — the basis of all effective learning. Sometimes the system of marginalising is a structural process within schools, arising from ways in which pupils are grouped, and how facilities are made available for some pupils and not others, but sometimes pupils are marginalised out of normal schooling altogether, into units and special institutions. When the latter occurs there is a plethora of professional administrators, peripatetic support services, research and inspection, all of which support the marginalising process, but in doing so, offer a bewildering array of approaches and practices on how to educate such pupils once they are marginalised. This is not to say that a proportion of our school population is not without an educational approach that requires action to be taken to minimise disaffection where it occurs. But it is the contexts, the aims, and the practices that come into play that determine whether disaffection is part and parcel of the learning (and making mistakes) process, or whether it is a self-determining creation of the way we organise our schools which in outcome secures certain pupils in modes of alienation that they can do little about. The aim should be that all pupils feel normal, valued, and achieving.

Disaffection is, however, a normal experience for both adults and children. It has a positive aspect when it acts as an incentive for self-appraisal, for it can be a spur towards setting new goals. Yet there are circumstances when for certain pupils the strong feelings of disaffection can be damagingly pre-occupying, adversely affecting learning and a sense of accomplishment. If this occurs during the time a pupil is at secondary school then its effect may be heightened as pupils cope with the turmoils of adolescent growth. A peak in disaffection is also noticeable as young pupils begin to approach school-leaving age, appraise their circumstance, and reflect on prospects for work and a career.

The response of a pupil to disaffection can vary considerably, depending on past experiences, the manner in which these have been coped with successfully, and the nature and extent of existing precipitating factors. How well a pupil is able to cope with new frustrations is very difficult to predict. The need, however, is for an awareness of those school experiences which place pupils under extra strain and which some pupils find intolerable, leading to a devaluing of the self and lower self-esteem.

If a pupil feels devalued then there can be ample opportunities during a school day for this to be reflected in disaffected behaviour which becomes pervading and entrenched. This is more likely to happen when the pupil discovers there is no resolution to feelings of disaffection either through personal effort or the efforts of others. Pupils then begin to look away from support by parents and teachers, seeking friendship and mutual support from peers or experiencing various forms of social isolation. It is at this point that feelings of disaffection become translated into characteristic patterns of disaffected behaviour in either active or passive forms.

In the active form, pupils behave in ways that have a tendency to exacerbate their feelings of disaffection. These behaviours are usually categorised according to the style of management or resources available to cope with the disaffected behaviour. These categories of behaviour used to have their roots in medical typology: now they are administrative descriptions. The behaviours are disruption, vandalism, maladjustment, absenteeism, and truancy. In the passive form, the characteristic behaviour is that of educational underachievement and simply opting out of ordinary school activities. The active form of disaffection creates more problems for teachers while the pupils are in school. The passive form is possibly more insidious, having implications beyond school-life, may be throughout the life of the pupil, and can be overlooked by teachers. Both active and passive disaffection may be part of a matrix of home and family conditions. All carry implications for recurrent family cycles of resistance to schooling. For whatever the cause of pupil disaffection, whether arising from home or school factors, there is always the risk that the pupil, finding no solution to problems, may become educationally alienated.

Although disaffected pupils are open to negotiation about their problems, alienation becomes a state of mind where a pupil is highly resistant to help or support, believing that there are no solutions. For such pupils this legitimizes aggression, aggravation towards teachers and other pupils, and sometimes the vandalism of school property.

Research in recent years has revealed the extent to which pupils, not always wittingly, negotiate their own learning. They do this with their peer group and often with the classteachers as part of trading off work and obligations. In one sense alienation can be seen as a breakdown in these negotiations with teachers, and maybe with peers. Where there is conflict there is in the majority of schools no 'ACAS facility' to bring the conflicting sides together. Indeed, where there is significant alienation in a school this can highlight the absence of 'ACAS-minded' teachers! Alienation becomes symptomatic when the maintenance of discipline and dignities have to be upheld and other channels of resolving conflict are closed.

Alienated pupils increasingly find themselves in a position where negotiable options have ceased to exist, either as a process of learning or as negotiation out of difficult circumstances. Where this has happened pupils have crossed a threshold of acceptable or non-acceptable behaviour. These thresholds are not always clear for either pupils or staff. They become activated when problems arise but are always present as 'hidden' factors of the ethos of a school. It is usually the case that it is the staff who have the prerogative in deciding whether to maintain a threshold or not. They may be related to pupil-teacher relationships but also can be a function of the administrative procedures like class streaming, setting and banding, or the existence of special classes or units within a school. Sometimes the thresholds centre round such issues as school uniform, the use and maintenance of lockers, and homework. Thresholds differ considerably from school to school, within staff groups, and in classroom practices. Every child has to learn the threshold matrix of every given staff member and there are no lessons or tutorials to help. Because of this, the extent to which an alienated pupil can engage in negotiation about his or her feelings of disaffection is often not clear. This is part of the problem that makes management and restitution so difficult. Yet thresholds need not be constant factors but can be open to review from time to time. Indeed in some schools such review procedures involve pupils as part of the progress of re-negotiating thresholds. In these circumstances, pupils can take a part in creating the ethos of the school in which they are to learn and grow and the risk of alienation is thereby reduced.

By definition, disaffected pupils invariably feel in some respect devalued persons. Not all devalued pupils express their sense of worthlessness through disaffected behaviour nor become alienated; sometimes there is passive acceptance of the status quo. However expressed, devaluing processes are both historical and endemic in state education. Indeed ordinary education is occasionally defined by such practices.

An example is where schools practice discrimination by virtue of categorising ability. Many schools systematically group children for learning purposes according to some criteria of ability. This happens in nursery and primary schools as much as in secondary education, though in secondary schools the procedure may be formalised in methods of streaming, setting and banding. It is not the exercise of grouping pupils that is at fault so much as the criteria used for determining how the learning group shall be constituted and the style of relationships which this engenders. What is beginning to be questioned is the appropriateness of always having pupils in age-related groups for learning purposes, and that classes should be of given size irrespective of the subject matter being taught. The notion of a school 'class' is an educational concept whose validity rests on administrative convenience rather than effective education. There is no special requirement that all learning has to take place in classes or even in an institution or building that we call a school. A school intent on doing something about pupil disaffection will take a hard look at the way it groups its pupils especially if this is related to some criteria of deficiency.

Attitudes and prejudice are rooted in discriminatory policies and practices in three other areas of school management: firstly the issues of sexism both in respect of female staff and pupils; secondly, the growing recognition of widespread racial attitudes; and thirdly, attitudes that discriminate against class groups in society. In all these areas there is an assault on personal status and self-esteem, accompanied by feelings of devaluation. But these are all part of what is currently regarded as the normal fabric of our education system.

Neville Jones, Series Editor
1989

Introduction

Jim Docking

To be alienated is to feel estranged from others and powerless to bring about a change in relationships. Although primary schools generally appear to be friendly places, some pupils can still feel socially isolated and believe that they cannot be successful on the school's terms, no matter how hard they try. Consequently they feel depersonalized, lacking in status and self-respect, divorced from the life around them, disabled and ineffectual because their sense of personal worth is constantly under threat. They may withdraw within themselves or, more noticeably and threateningly to teachers and other pupils, become difficult to handle and display disruptive behaviour.

Some of the contexts in which pupils aged 7 to 11 years may develop feelings of alienation are explored in the contributions to this book. Whilst each author adopts a distinct perspective, there is a shared assumption that alienation is less a term about 'problem pupils' and more one about 'pupils who have problems' which can be alleviated through improving the quality of relationships in school. As each contributor illustrates, feelings of alienation are less likely in those schools where staff are prepared to reflect critically on their practices, to make changes, and to monitor their effectiveness. This means regularly appraising school policies, styles of decision-making, pupil management, assessment procedures, teaching methods, and relationships with parents.

Any discussion of alienation must begin by addressing the problems of self-esteem and personal responsibility. The first two chapters which comprise Part 1 of this book therefore focus on ways in which primary school pupils might be helped to develop a sense of personal worth and agency. Peter Gurney argues that pupils' levels of self-esteem are enhanced or diminished by the manner in which teachers show regard for each individual and afford opportunities for all pupils to experience success and friendship. After discussing the features of various measures of self-concept, Gurney examines a variety of strategies by which teachers can encourage all children, and not just those experiencing failure, to think more positively about their own achievements.

Colin Rogers then considers the problem of pupil disaffection from the perspective of attribution theory. This is concerned with ways in which individuals explain events, including their personal successes and failures. It is during the primary years that children gradually develop attributional styles which affect their feelings about school, possibly laying the seeds for disaffection in secondary school, if not the later junior years. Drawing on a rich source of research studies, Rogers shows how teachers can unwittingly discourage children from developing feelings of agency, yet also how, through an awareness of the effect of their actions, they can try to help children to view themselves as responsible for their own learning and capable of improvement.

Part 2 is concerned with social relationships and pastoral care. Jacquie and David Coulby begin their discussion by noting how the term 'alienation', as applied in schools, appears to function as a successor to 'disruption' (where responsibility was too easily placed at the door of the 'disruptive pupil') and 'disaffection' (where rebelliousness was often seen as the manifestation of anger directed towards the unacceptable face of 'isms' which have their origins outside school). The authors argue that the use of the term 'alienation' is helpful in so far as it focuses squarely on the contribution which the school can make to improve the quality of relationships between pupils and teachers. Hence their chapter is concerned with strategies of intervention: whole-school policies which respect children's rights and individuality; curricular intervention to improve classroom atmosphere and behaviour; and a positive approach to classroom management which provides for individual needs whilst also encouraging a collaborative approach to learning.

Collaborative learning is also a major theme of the next chapter. In discussing approaches to the promotion of positive relationships and pro-social behaviour in the primary school, Peter Kutnick argues that teachers must take responsibility not only for the structure of relationships between pupils and teacher but also among the pupils. Too much teacher-pupil interaction, he suggests, is functional and ritual. Many teachers try to humanize traditional management styles by promoting a caring atmosphere in the classroom, giving greater opportunity for pupils to engage in consensual acts. This is frequently successful in keeping control in a way which children find acceptable, not least because it gives them a sense of security. However it does little to break down the pupil's dependency on the teacher's authority. Kutnick believes that more creative interaction is possible in classrooms where the teacher facilitates genuinely collaborative learning experiences. This approach makes even more planning demands on staff, but is less likely to produce an atmosphere of competition and concomitant feelings of alienation, and is more likely to promote trust, cooperation, self-responsibility and positive self-esteem.

Drawing on his experiences as a junior school head, David Winkley then turns to the child presenting persistent social and emotional difficulties, who, in contrast to the normal 'naughty' child, has problems in internalizing rules and accepting constraints. For the teacher, the behaviour of such children 'disturbs calm, threatens the thin plaster of the ego, undermines order and disorientates convenience'. The appropriate response, Winkley suggests, lies in a range of strategies which cultivate feelings of success in both the child and the teacher. The practical implications of this policy are sympathetically explored not only in relation to classroom management but also whole-school policies and home-school liaison.

The importance of staff reviewing policies and practices is also emphasized by Peter Lang, who urges primary schools to incorporate into their thinking the central concepts of planned 'pastoral care', a term whose employment unfortunately still tends to be confined to secondary education. Lang insists that there is a need for a broad, positive framework in which the affective development of all pupils is promoted — an objective which he considers will assume even greater significance as the pressures of the National Curriculum build up. He rejects the defence of 'Oh-I-already-do-that', and supplies detailed guidance for appraising current practices and developing strategies by which schools can help pupils to achieve a sense of belonging and personal identity.

Part 3 of the book focuses on the problem of alienation in relation to pupil achievement and assessment. It begins with a detailed report by Pamela Sammons and Peter Mortimore, whose recent Junior School Project is the largest and most sophisticated study of school effectiveness yet undertaken in this country for the 7–11 age-range. Through an analysis of the information collected in 50 London schools, many aspects of the academic progress and social development of nearly 2,000 children were monitored over four years, taking account of the pupils' background, their initial attainment, and school processes. Both cognitive and non-cognitive outcomes were found to be related to pupil's age, social class, sex and race. Of these, the age factor is perhaps less generally recognized as significant. For instance, when judging pupils' ability in the three Rs, teachers in this study did not seem to take account of age variations within a year group, thus prejudicing judgements (and presumably the expectations?) of summer-born children, who have less infant school experience. Attitudes to school in general and to mathematics in particular were significantly less favourable among these children compared with those born in the autumn. Yet what also emerged from the Junior School Project was a clear demonstration of the ability of some schools to reduce the related risks of under-achievement and pupil alienation. The authors discuss some implications of these findings in terms of teacher-awareness and school policies.

The possibility that the introduction of national assessments will exacerbate the problem of alienation in schools is a fear held by many in the teaching profession. In his chapter on primary school assessment, Colin Conner feels that the outcome could be just the opposite, and for two main reasons. First, provided the emphasis is on formative rather than summative assessment as the Task Group stressed, teachers will be given the means to develop skills in observing children's progress more closely in feeding the knowledge gained back into teaching. Secondly, benefits are likely to accrue during the course of the moderation exercises when teachers in groups of schools get together to share and compare perceptions of children's work and to discuss standards of achievement. Only time will tell whether the mechanisms involved in national testing will, in fact, reduce the problem of pupil alienation; but at least, as Conner shows, a conceptual framework and set of procedures have been developed to maximize the chances of the assessments becoming an educational tool and not simply an accountability device.

After tracing the historical influence (or lack of it) of educational psychology in primary schools, Neville Jones argues that too often educational psychologists have failed to respond to the needs of ordinary primary schools as perceived by the teachers who work in them. Rather than playing a central role in helping primary teachers to manage pupil learning effectively and thereby reduce the risk of pupil alienation, educational psychologists, with some important exceptions, have tended to operate in a service mainly concerned with segregated special education and the assessment and remediation of individual pupils who have failed in main-stream education. Although some primary teachers have welcomed the EP's inter-vention when this has resulted in the removal of a 'difficult' child from their care, the role of the school psychological service has not been generally regarded as sup-portive in developing whole-school policies and proactive strategies which attend to the needs of all pupils. Jones feels that opportunities thrown up by recent legis-lation have been missed or misused by EPs, and fears the same may happen with provisions in the 1988 Act. He warns educational psychologists of the dangers of becoming entrapped in 'statementing' for special needs and in assessing under the National Curriculum, and urges them instead to develop an active partnership with heads and teachers in areas which are of central concern to them. These include curriculum planning, classroom management, communication skills, work with parents and in-service activities.

In Part 4, consideration is given to children who can experience alienation as a consequence of social disadvantage or giftedness. Paul Widlake discusses the first group in the context of recent education legislation. He argues that, for all its short-comings, this has given parents long overdue rights to participate in school govern-ment, stimulated greater interest in education, and provided opportunity to raise the standards of achievement of working-class children. But rights are sterile if right-holders do not possess the requisite skills to make the best use of their new powers. Referring to schemes which have involved parents and teachers working together in learning projects and school activities, Widlake argues that it is in this kind of collaborative endeavour — 'bringing the community into the school' — that the real power lies for working-class parents to improve educational standards. He also suggests that in information technology teachers have a new resource to improve the educational opportunities of disadvantaged children.

John Welch importantly reminds us that the problem of pupil alienation is by no means confined to slow learners but may arise in gifted children. Like their less-able peers, they too can experience a discrepancy between their personal needs and what the schools have to offer, and perceive the system as a threat to their security, self-respect and self-development. This, argues Welch, is less of a problem amongst the exceptional performers since these children are generally admired in our society; but alienation is common among those who are gifted in social leadership, intelligence and creativity, attributes which can be a source of confrontation between pupils and teachers. Welch describes the kinds of everyday school situ-ations which thwart children who are gifted in one respect or another. He points to many practical ways in which teachers can respond more sympathetically and con-structively to their needs, concluding that 'a rich, varied and demanding curriculum is the best defence against the possibility of alienation in junior schools'. As in all cases of special need, teachers must be prepared to change their institutional practices if they are to care for gifted children effectively and humanely.

I would like to express my gratitude to all the contributors for their cooperation and forebearance during the preparation of this volume. I am also greatly indebted to Neville Jones, the series editor, whose inspiration this book was and whose continuous support and advice have been invaluable.

1
The Enhancement of Self-Esteem in Junior Classrooms

Peter Gurney

Introduction

It was half-past four. The pottery club had been under way for three quarters of an hour. I was unpacking the coil pots which had been fired two days earlier at my home by Darren and three other pupils. The second pot out of the box was his. 'Cor! Sir!' was all Darren could manage. This eleven year old boy who usually struggled through his school work during the day, and looked perpetually miserable, was now smiling. 'It's good, Darren', I said, 'really good. One of the best we've ever had.' Darren beamed!

Although usually a low achiever, Darren had succeeded at something new. His self-esteem had been boosted which went some way to off-set his poor academic performance. Even after Darren transferred to the comprehensive school I saw him for two more years as a regular member of the Junior School Pottery Club. He became technically very competent for his age. Just before he finally moved away we talked about the importance of this experience for him — how it had been a 'bright corner' in his life which had made other events less grey, although he did not put it in these particular words.

This brief case study illustrates the importance of success to a failing child, a fact understood by all teachers. What perhaps is less well understood is the interaction with feelings of self-worth, or self-esteem, which form the substance of this chapter. I intend to discuss its importance as a concept in the classroom process and to outline how it may be enhanced in all junior children, not just those who are experiencing failure.

It is important to begin by defining the terms self-concept and self-esteem. The self-concept is the picture of ourselves which we carry around and incorporates all those things which are important to us — relative and friend relationships, status, job, material possessions, other skills and hobbies. It is learned in detail as we grow up and glean information from what others do or say to us. 'Significant others' — other people whom we respect, like and are important to us — are a crucial source. Normally such persons are our parents, grandparents and friends.

Teachers will also be significant others particularly for young children and, in this role, they can influence pupils' self-concepts in either a positive or a negative way.

It is often argued that the self-concept has an important function in guiding our behaviour, making it more probable in a given situation that we will do one thing rather than another. Such a feature clearly makes the self-concept important. Since it is also argued that the self-concept is learned, it is crucially important to young children, not only in influencing their behaviour but also because it is still in the process of being learned and crystallized. It is vital, therefore, that early experiences are predominantly positive and that children come to see themselves as accepted, loved and successful. They are then in a better position to love and accept others.

When children have developed a rudimentary self-concept, they also begin to evaluate it in terms of their acceptability as a person to other people. This concept of overall worthiness is termed self-esteem. Coopersmith (1967) defined self-esteem as 'the evaluation which the individual makes and customarily maintains with regard to himself — it expresses an attitude of approval and disapproval, and indicates the extent to which the individual considers himself to be capable, significant, successful and worthy' (pp. 4–5). Our level of self-esteem makes us more likely to behave in one way than another and therefore has important behavioural consequences. This is the reason why it is so important to maintain positive self-evaluations in children and to actively intervene, where appropriate, both to counter negative self-evaluations and to change behaviour.

How is behaviour influenced by the self-concept? If a pupil does not see a school subject as central to his self-concept, then he will not want to work hard on that subject, and may drop it if it becomes a voluntary element in the curriculum. A central element in the self-concept, on the other hand, will be highly motivating. Self-esteem also affects behaviour in that a pupil who develops low self-esteem will lose confidence and take the blame for failure (even though it may not be his fault!).

A clear example of a longer term association between self-esteem and behaviour concerns school performance. There is a substantial body of evidence to suggest that school achievement is positively associated with the level of self-esteem (Simon and Simon, 1975). Gill (1969), in summarizing a similar trend in his research, stated that the results of his work supported the association between self-esteem and school achievement with such convincing uniformity that the importance of self-esteem in the educational process, 'seems to need more emphasis than is presently given to it' (p. 6).

It is important to note here that the effect of comments from parents and teachers on children's self-esteem should never be under-estimated. There is ample research evidence that young children are particularly affected by the comments on them made by significant others, who of course include their peers. Because the self-concept may only be partially formed such comments may be particularly formative. In middle childhood the pupil's self-concept is crystallized to a greater extent and is, in effect, now seeking evidence to confirm itself. In children who have low self-esteem, negative comments may be more readily accepted than in those with high self-esteem. The latter group will, however, accept positive or praise statements more readily.

The reader will no doubt be able to confirm this point from practical experience. Arrange for a failing child to achieve success in a task and what is he likely to say? 'It was a fluke' or 'I was lucky'. The evidence of success is likely to be rejected because it is discrepant with his self-concept. It can take a long time to convince such a child that success can be typical of his performance in some areas of school work.

The remainder of this chapter will examine the development of the self-concept, research on self-esteem and achievement, the assessment of self-esteem and methods of enhancing self-esteem in junior pupils.

The development of the self-concept

Our self-concept has to be learned from perceptions which we derive from our environment as we grow up. The child's self-concept can be said to pass through three broad stages of Primitive Self, Exterior Self and Interior Self.

Primitive self

In the first stage, the infant is learning about his surroundings and the various objects within them. He gradually becomes aware that he is a separate entity, a person in his own right. One has to rely on observation of children in these early months to provide data on the development of the self-concepts since verbalization is either not present or is too primitive. An important milestone is the use of the personal pronoun which appears first as, 'Peter do it', then 'Me do it', then 'I do it'. We can regard this point as marking the end of the stage of the primitive self, occurring as it does between 18 and 30 months, with the average being around 24 months.

Exterior self

The exterior self stage is present from two to thirteen years approximately and relates therefore to the period of middle childhood. Study of the self-concept becomes easier because children can now give us information verbally in response to simple questions. Many students of the self-concept argue that once it is formed, it will become increasingly differentiated by means of new data but also evaluated in a form which becomes positive or negative overall. It is very important therefore that parents and teachers are as positive as is possible towards children at this stage. They will assist in determining the basic view that the child has of himself which will be resistant to change once it is established.

The pre-school child conceives his self in physical terms as being a part of the body, inside the head or the chest. Self, mind and body are generally confused and the child may state that a plant can have a self and a mind. Discrimination of self from peers is carried out by using physical attributes, by focusing, for example, upon hair colour or height.

As the child approaches eight years old, on average, he shows an increasing ability to separate mind from body and the beginning of an understanding that some of his differences from peers derive from internal processes also. The increasing awareness of the difference between mental and physical attributes helps children to understand the subjective nature of self. Guardo and Bohan (1971) noted that almost all children in their study expressed belief in their own humanity, sexuality, individuality and continuity during middle childhood. Their investigation revealed a significant trend however. Six and seven-year-olds used evidence from physical and behavioural features to support their beliefs in the four dimensions, while eight to nine-year-olds utilized psychological explanations as well. Secord and Peevers (1974) also note a shift during this developmental period from the absolute to the comparative. 'I can swim now' becomes 'I can swim better than John', thus indicating an additional and more complex way of differentiating oneself from others.

Selman (1980) noted a further change towards the end of this stage which is shown when children can observe self as both agent and object at the same time and therefore adopt the *generalized other* position. Perhaps the awareness of others as both agent and object leads to an understanding of this dual process in themselves.

Harter (1982) studied children's understanding of emotion labels to monitor changes in the affective component of self-awareness as revealed by terms 'ashamed' and 'proud'. The first adequate definitions were found between five and seven years and they related to how *others* might feel: 'My dad was proud of me when I caught a fish last week.' However, it was not until eight years and older that children in Harter's sample were able to describe how you could be ashamed or proud of *yourself*. This shift from learning about others to learning about self was commented upon earlier, showing how important good modelling and discussion are to the child's development of self-awareness. This argument does not imply that younger children cannot experience the emotions of shame and pride but shows that they cannot stand back and make affective judgements about the self until about eight years or older. A greater self-consciousness begins to emerge and there is a growing ability for self-evaluation.

The final sub-stage of the 'exterior self' is shown between nine and thirteen years, on average, in a shift towards a more internal form of reference within self-awareness. In this period the child becomes increasingly aware of internal processes in adults and peers which he comes to appreciate may be causal in their behaviour. As children move towards adolescence it is possible to observe a growing recognition of these internal processes in their selves and how they may function to influence their own behaviour.

Since the concern of this chapter is with Junior School pupils it is not the intention to discuss the final developmental stage of the 'interior self' but, as the label implies, the adolescent conceives his self as being predominantly subject to internal psychological processes. Appreciation of this difference from middle childhood is helpful in understanding the differences in discipline problems and management procedures between the junior school stage and that of the comprehensive school.

Developmental aspects of self-esteem

It is not possible to examine self-esteem itself on a developmental basis in the same sense that we can study the self-concept. It is possible, however, to study trends and factors at various ages which appear to contribute to general levels of self-esteem. In relation to children of junior school age the work of Coopersmith has been particularly useful. Coopersmith (1967) reported studies on self-esteem with a sample of pre-adolescent children, comprising 1,748 10-year-olds and utilizing a 58-item self-report inventory, the Coopersmith Self-Esteem Inventory (SEI), together with a Behaviour Rating Form (BRF) for use by observers in identifying children who exhibit different levels of self-esteem in their behaviour.

Coopersmith (1967) carried out a review of previous writing and research concerned with self-esteem and concluded that four major factors contribute to the development of self-esteem. These factors are:

i. the amount of respectful, accepting and concerned treatment that an individual received from 'significant others' in his/her life;
ii. the history of an individual's successes and the status that he/she holds in the community;
iii. the way experiences are interpreted and modified in accord with the individual's values and aspirations; and
iv. the manner in which the individual responds to evaluation (p. 37).

Since the junior school teacher will be one of the 'significant others' in the pupil's life, her behaviour towards that pupil will be crucial.

Research on general self-esteem and achievement in junior age children

Trowbridge (1972) related children's scores on Coopersmith's SEI with achievement levels in reading and reported correlations ranging from 0.35 to 0.45. Simon and Simon (1975) studied self-esteem levels as measured on the SEI with achievement levels in basic skills for boys and girls aged 10 years and reported a correlation of 0.33. Chang (1976) noted a significant correlation between teachers' ratings of pupil self-esteem and achievement levels. Both Purkey (1970) and West and Fish (1973) emphasize the association between self-esteem and academic achievement in school children. Purkey (1970, p. 15) noted that, 'Overall the research evidence clearly shows a persistent and significant relationship between the self-concept and academic achievement'.

A key issue relates to the direction of causality between self-esteem and academic achievement. Does enhanced self-esteem create improved academic performance or does improvement in school achievement function to enhance self-esteem? Various research findings provide evidence that effective remedial help will enhance self-esteem (Coley, 1973; McCormick and Williams, 1974). Despite a widespread belief that enhancing self-esteem will also serve to improve academic performance, it is difficult to find direct evidence to support this view. The work of Lawrence (1973) is an exception, where counselling of infant children to improve self-esteem as readers also improved reading skills. Calsyn and Kenny (1977) attempted to throw some light on this question by analysing eight previous studies using a statistical method to identify cause and effect features. They considered that there was evidence for improvement in academic achievement acting to enhance self-esteem, but not for the reverse effect. Sweet and Burbach (1977) used a more complex form of the same statistical method to analyse previously published studies of academic achievement and self-esteem and were of the opinion that self-esteem enhancement had preceded academic achievement.

For the practising junior school teacher it appears valid to assume that influence in both directions is possible and that improving both self-esteem and academic achievement concurrently is the best approach. There is no doubt in my mind, however, that some children who have very low self-esteem do require help in boosting their self-confidence and self-esteem as a prerequisite to other learning.

Assessment of self-esteem

Techniques for assessment are varied and include self-rating scales, in the form of questionnaire, checklist, Q sort, open-ended response method, projective approach, and interview and observation instruments, which may be based on any of the above types of assessment, but will involve inferential judgements to a degree. The author's intention here is to select a few representative examples of general self-esteem instruments for classroom use from the questionnaire or inventory type of self-rating scale. The criteria for selection are that each instrument has reasonable reliability and validity, has been used fairly widely in most cases, has 'back-up' in terms of a manual or set of instructions, and is appropriate for schoolchildren within the Junior School age range.

Self-esteem inventory (Coopersmith, 1967)

This is a 58-item scale (including eight lie scale items) which is intended for use with children from 10 to 16 years. Items were either written by the author or derived from the Butler-Haigh Q sort (1954). The fifty self-esteem items, both positively and negatively worded, contribute to a global self-esteem score out of 100 with the subject endorsing 'like me' or 'unlike me'. Coopersmith recorded a test-retest reliability of 0.88 over a five-week period.

Children's self-concept scale (Piers and Harris, 1964)

This is an 80-item scale designed for the age-group 8 to 16 years. Children are asked to endorse 'yes' or 'no' to items drawn originally from Jersild's (1952) survey. Positively and negatively worded items are equally balanced, and test-retest reliability over an eight-week period was 0.77.

Canadian self-esteem inventory (Battle, 1976)

This 60-item scale is intended for use with 8 to 11-year-olds and contains a lie scale of ten items. Items were provided by the author or drawn from Gough and Heilbron (1965) and Coopersmith (1967). The scale is 'balanced' with an equal number of positive and negative items, each requiring one of two responses. Test-retest correlations exceeded 0.72, but only over a two-day period. A short form comprising 30 items only is also available. The reader should note that evidence for validity has yet to be provided.

LAWSEQ (Lawrence, 1981)

Less widely used, but more appropriate for use with British pupils because it was developed in the UK, this self-esteem questionnaire has the merit of being relatively short, as it has only 16 items. The scale comprises both positively and negatively worded items, but they are not equal in number. Hart (1985) reported a reliability coefficient of 0.64 over a four-month period.

Self-description questionnaire (Marsh et al., 1983)

Although not yet widely used, this Australian instrument merits inclusion because it is recent and has been carefully developed with documented evidence for its validity and reliability. The scale has 72 items and is designed to measure the seven dimensions of the self-concept proposed by Shavelson *et al.*, (1976).

It must be noted that all measures of self-esteem are suspect to a degree, as they are less valid and reliable than tests of intelligence. Provided this fact is borne in mind, they can be a useful tool, particularly when used qualitatively with individual pupils. Teachers often find that discussion with the pupil about his responses to individual items after taking a self-esteem test is very revealing both of self-attitudes and degree of self-awareness.

A junior school's own rating scale or checklist should not be despised since it may also help to identify pupils who are low in self-esteem and may require special help. An additional bonus is that the process of designing and evaluating the school's own self-esteem checklist can be a valuable staff development exercise. The reader is referred in this connection to the author's own checklist of behaviours considered to be indicative of low self-esteem (Gurney, 1988, pp. 47–49).

Enhancing self-esteem in junior school children

There are three general areas that need to be considered in terms of self-esteem enhancement. These are: (a) indirect effects from general school factors (b) school and classroom strategies and (c) practical activities.

Indirect effects from school factors

In this first category we find school factors such as the impact of the current curriculum, the system of rewards and punishments used in the school, the degree of democracy in school government, the extent to which pupils are used for peer or cross-age tutoring, the amount of parent involvement and the teacher's own self-esteem and attitudes towards her pupils. Since the length of this chapter does not permit detailed examination of the above points, the reader is referred to the author's recent book (Gurney, 1988, Ch. 5) for further reading.

School and classroom strategies to enhance self-esteem

The author suggests the following strategies as useful both in the classroom and within the school as a whole. They are: counselling and relationships, extra-curricular activities, increasing the frequency of positive self-referent verbal statements, positive feedback and success experiences.

Counselling and relationships

There is a widespread view that effective counselling and pastoral care support in schools increase self-confidence and enhance self-esteem. While this view is also held by the author it must be said that the research evidence in support of this belief is very thin indeed. Pigge (1970) carried out an investigation into the effects of group counselling on fourth grade pupils' self-esteem. Self-esteem levels were raised but not significantly when compared with a control group. Brookover (1965) found that the most effective counselling method was to involve the pupil's parents as significant others in praising their children at home for achievements in school. Brookover (1965) stated that, 'Strategies to enhance self-concept will be most effective when they involve helping students with low self-evaluations to perceive that their parents, or other significant others, have raised their evaluation of them as students' (p. 209). Lawrence (1971), however, did report significant effects on both self-esteem and reading performance in beginning readers which resulted from time spent on counselling as compared with time spent on improving reading skills.

The author wishes to endorse the concept of counselling practised by all teachers, not solely by trained counsellors. The value of time spent *individually* with a child in discussing a problem cannot be over-emphasized and the school organization should be arranged to allow it to happen easily.

The teacher-pupil relationship is a fundamental element both in the learning process and in the development of self-esteem in school. Researchers have understandably found difficulty in assessing its influence from an experimental point of view because it is both complex and partly hidden. The teacher herself is of course aware how important this relationship is for all children and that it is an element that must be created where it does not already exist.

There are a number of elements which characterize the approach of the teacher who will be effective in creating sound, positive relationships with her pupils. The first element is *respect for pupils as persons*. As Peters (1966) has stated, there is an important distinction to be made between liking pupils and respecting them as persons. This respect requires that teachers will encourage pupils to gradually take more responsibility for their own behaviour, to become eventually 'agents of their own destiny'. Docking (1980) writes that, 'Knowledge which a teacher has of children's developmental levels and of their ability to cope with freedom should enable teachers to provide for choice making in a deliberate and progressive way' (p. 100). It sometimes appears to be the case that this aspect of teachers' knowledge is not sufficiently developed to be effective in this sense and that the teacher does not have sufficient time to be reflective about the issues relating to self-management. A substantial increase in full-time and part-time courses of in-service training for teachers would be potentially very helpful in this respect.

The second element is *positive regard* which is generated by increased interaction and greater knowledge of each other's problems. Positive regard is useful in avoiding the tendency for either pupil or teacher to think the worst of each other and to infer deliberate intent as being behind unacceptable behaviour.

The third element is that of *commitment*, to the other person, to any task in hand, and to the mutually agreed goals. This will create a persistence in the direction of behaviour which will carry the teacher or pupil through any short-term difficulties or disagreements and induce an attitude to reconcile such problems.

The fourth element is that of *mutual support*, both of each other as people and in terms of challenges and goals which have to be adopted. This aspect is particularly crucial because a real challenge automatically creates the possibility of failure. The pupil's view of that failure, if it occurs, is crucial and whether the child has a second attempt will depend very largely on the degree of support available from the teacher at that time.

The final element of the valid teacher-pupil relationship relates to the dynamic aspect, that both parties should *learn and grow together*. In the case of the pupil this relates to the quality of the education received from the teacher who is helping the children both to feel significant and to *be* significant. It is here that the teacher's special skills, knowledge and attitudes become particularly important.

Extra-curricular activities

This area of school life is one which is potentially rich in opportunities for the enhancement of junior school pupils' self-esteem. There are a number of obvious reasons which include the fact that the pupil is a volunteer and therefore wants to learn, the atmosphere is more relaxed, group size is usually smaller and teachers may be keener! Control and discipline issues therefore become less obvious, often irrelevant. Extra-curricular activities can therefore provide a valuable arena for self-esteem enhancement in individual junior school pupils. It is one way in which teachers derive considerable job satisfaction. If a junior school is not providing any such activities it does raise a serious question about its educational philosophy.

Activities which take children beyond the confines of the school in terms of visits, expeditions, weekends, camping weeks and the like are even more promising arenas because pupils throw off their customary attitudes and behaviour and become more open to change. Children who are failing in most of their school subjects and experiencing low self-esteem often need an opportunity for a fresh start in a new and interesting activity somewhat removed from academic work. The teacher often finds that the extra-curricular activity programme will provide that important opportunity.

Increasing the frequency of positive self-referent verbal statements

Felker and Thomas (1971) investigated the view that the statements a pupil makes about himself are a valid indicator of self-esteem level. The experiment involved 13 white fourth-grade children and showed that their self-esteem correlated positively with the frequency of positive self-referent statements (PSRVS) made by them. Hauserman *et al.* (1976) reported an attempt to enhance children's self-esteem by prompting and reinforcing PSRVS, following a success experience amongst 40 elementary children receiving remedial help. These subjects all had low self-esteem and were randomly allocated to experimental and control groups. During a 40-day treatment period the experimental group subjects were asked to note a successful experience in the classroom and to make a positive self-referent comment on it. They then received immediate positive social reinforcement from their teacher. Post-test analysis revealed a highly significant difference between the experimental and control groups in self-esteem.

Gurney (1987) worked intensively on a daily basis over a six-week period with a small group of maladjusted boys aged between ten and twelve years. He used behaviour modification techniques within the experimental group of pupils in an effort to increase the frequency of their PSRVS and thereby to enhance their self-esteem. Post-test comparisons between the experimental and control pupils revealed a significant difference in overt behaviour related to self but not in terms of verbal self-esteem scores. A significant increase in the latter within both groups was evident and clearly was not related to the procedures confined only to the experimental group. Gurney concluded that other procedures experienced by both groups could have been responsible and these included the daily interviews on a one-to-one basis, together with maintaining a diary of positive behaviours and achievements. Gurney (1979) suggests how a PSRVS might be discriminated by the teacher and how children with special needs might be encouraged to produce them with increasing frequency. 'I did well in Maths today' should replace the teacher's praise comment and the pupil should be rewarded when he makes a statement of this kind. The teacher's praise is therefore not used solely to reinforce good work and effort but also to shape self-reinforcing behaviour on the part of the pupil.

The work discussed, together with other studies, suggests that increasing the frequency of PSRVS can be a useful intervention strategy for self-esteem enhancement.

Positive feedback

Willey (1987), a first school headteacher in the ILEA, described how pupils' errors in her school were treated neutrally as useful feedback to assist in improving performance. This approach is a part of her teacher strategy of Encouraging Competence, Independence and Self-Determination (ECID). The strategy is intended to increase intrinsic motivation in children but also appears of value in enhancing pupil self-confidence and self-esteem. The ECID strategy resembles in some respects the teaching style identified by Galton and Simon (1980) in terms of formative feedback and the work of De Charms (1976) in his attempts to make children better initiators of their own behaviour. The latter advocated warm acceptance of children, with the longer term aim of reducing external control and encouraging self-directed behaviour. Overall, the work of these authors bears a close relationship to the findings of Coopersmith (1967) in identifying parental behaviours which are conducive to the development of high self-esteem in children. The similarities give us additional information about strategies likely to enhance self-esteem in junior school pupils in terms of warm acceptance, consistency, democratic rule setting, enforcing rules with respect for the pupil and encouraging self-management.

Success experiences

As teachers we all know how powerful success can be in its effect on a pupil but it is often a problem to determine the criteria for success in a particular task. In a lesson concerned with creative language what constitutes a successful product? Is the teacher clear? Do the pupils understand? Junior teachers need to clarify the position on success criteria and make sure that they are appropriate and understood by each pupil. In this way we can reduce the frequency of failure and help pupils to select sensible targets for themselves. As La Benne and Greene (1969, pp. 29–30) say, 'To help a child develop a positive self-concept, one must help him select experiences which provide a challenge, and at the same time help him maximize his opportunities for success'. Similarly, Purkey (1978, p. 32) has argued for an invitational approach to teaching in order to ensure success stating that, 'These invitations to learning are most likely to be accepted and acted upon if students see them as personally meaningful and self-enhancing'.

Failure tends to breed further failure. More seriously, pupils lose heart and begin to incorporate failure into their self-concepts. Self-esteem is lowered and then behavioural consequences follow, e.g. the pupil stops trying or avoids that subject area altogether.

Practical classroom activities related to self-esteem enhancement

The following are some of the practical activities which may be used effectively in the Junior classroom to help pupils develop positive self-esteem. It is by no means an exhaustive list but these have been personally tried and tested! Nor is it claimed that these activities will enhance self-esteem directly. They should certainly increase self-awareness and often bring to the surface fact or feeling which may be used in an individual counselling session on a later occasion.

Diary of 'good things'

Memory of successes and positive experiences is fleeting in younger pupils and can be short-lived in teachers! I have found it to be very worthwhile indeed to give junior age children diaries in which they can enter anything positive which they have done. These items can range from helping as a classroom monitor to improving previous performance in solving mathematics problems. Teacher or pupil can record but pupil entries need to be verified by an adult. In my experience these diaries are highly valued and carefully preserved when full so that parents can read them. There is every reason of course why school and home should both be involved in this activity.

The value of these diaries is apparent in day-to-day work when children are concerned about errors, failure or lack of progress. The diary can then be reviewed as a reminder of those events that have been positive.

There are other by-products also. In dealing with a behaviour problem I have found it useful to review the diary immediately. It appears to act as the pupil's advocate and put the behaviour into context as 'inappropriate'. It provides a brief space in which the junior teacher can calm down and reflect, so improving the validity of any sanction which may be imposed. The diary also provides valuable discussion material for self-esteem enhancement sessions and individual counselling.

In my work with junior age maladjusted children I found this to be a powerful procedure and regretted that I had not employed it with my own sons when they were younger!

Expressing feelings

The expression of strong feelings, both positive and negative, in a form which is both appropriate and socially acceptable, is a social skill which has to be learned.

Our culture normally expects children and adults to conceal such feelings, which is unhelpful. Pupils often feel frightened or guilty of their strong negative feelings towards, say, a sibling or a parent. These can be progressively aired over a period of time, initially on a generalized basis. The junior teacher can help considerably by discussing her own feelings and personal memories of strong feelings experienced as a child. Pupils are then more likely to discuss strong negative feelings openly with their teacher or in front of each other. It is necessary to emphasize that trust must be built up in any group sessions and that the teacher should proceed sensitively.

This classroom activity can be conducted in various ways but one valid approach is to ask junior pupils to write out two lists, one headed 'What makes me happy is . . . ' and the other 'What makes me sad / angry is . . . '. These items can then be utilized in individual or class sessions, depending on the teacher's judgement.

Friends

Any activity which focuses on personal relationships must be used with great care. The teacher must be sensitive to individual differences amongst her pupils because some will not have close friends or indeed, may have none at all. Accordingly one can begin by asking the class what the word 'friend' means. Their responses can be listed on an overhead projector so that the transparency can be photocopied and displayed if required. Pupils can then be asked to paint either a real friend or an ideal one which helps to avoid the problem of poor social relationships. The pupils' work can be displayed and some could be asked why they chose that peer or what qualities they would seek in an ideal friend. Some discussion of friendship is also useful in terms both of how friendships can be started and also maintained. 'What do you do for your friend?' is a productive question to ask of pupils in middle childhood, some of whom may still be very egocentric.

My assets

Some pupils do not perceive their strengths as assets at all. In this case they are losing an opportunity to use material to support their self-esteem. The classroom teacher therefore should pick up these points and assist the pupil towards a reassessment. The activity is one in which pupils are encouraged to list their strengths or assets by asking the question, 'What do you think you do well?' Older junior pupils might also be asked to put them into rank order. The lists provide fertile ground for discussion, not only in terms of the items which are recorded but also in terms of those that are *omitted*.

The lists have a continuing function even after discussion has taken place. They can be pasted into a child's workbook, pinned inside a desk lid or placed in a work tray. Pupils should be encouraged to read the list each time they see it. When events are going against them they can be reminded to review it. The value of this activity for children who are low in self-esteem cannot be over-estimated. It also provides another procedure by which teachers can attempt to modify pessimistic or destructive self-comment in junior pupils.

Personal 'coat of arms'

This activity uses the idea of replacing traditional heraldic devices by symbols which have a strong meaning for the pupil. The class can paint or draw the coat of arms but with younger or slower learning children it may be necessary to show some examples of previous work as a guide. Some writers argue that this kind of activity, involving a personal coat of arms, flag or shield, strengthens identity. While this assumption may be questioned, the activity certainly appears to increase self-awareness and it is also enjoyable. It is my experience that discussion during and after the work is both lively and stimulating. Displays in the corridor create inter-class discussion also.

Personal profile

The word profile refers to an historical log of past events in a pupil's life which he wishes to record. These events may be joyful, sad, traumatic or mundane but will be important and personally relevant to that pupil. Once again parents can usefully be involved in the discussion to check dates and to provide encouragement. The profile will act as a summary of where the pupil has come from and raise questions about the present and the future. The profile is rich in opportunities to talk about normal life, with its mixture of success and failure. It also allows the teacher to encourage the pupil to focus on the positive and the successful outcomes. Related activities which are often recommended are drawing up a family tree or completing a 'time-line', i.e. listing in chronological order important personal events over a period of years.

Portraits

As part of an Art or Creative Work period, pupils can be encouraged to paint their own portraits from memory or from a mirror. The degree of skill is irrelevant but the opportunity for self-comment and discussion by the teacher is potentially substantial. In an atmosphere of trust and security pupils could discuss each others' products, with the criteria being determined by the teacher. Discussion is appropriately directed towards the individual elements that distinguish Tracey from Sharon rather than the degree of their artistic prowess.

Photographs

The visit of the school photographer, or the availability of a polaroid camera and film, presents an opportunity to display and discuss personal photographs. In a safe, controlled discussion, interesting and reassuring feedback can be obtained. 'I think my nose is awful!' 'I don't. It's rather nice — better than mine!' Photographs can be displayed in the classroom against the names for monitorial duties and in the corridor for those pupils who, say, will be assisting at School Assembly in the following week. These pupils will find other children in the school picking them out and talking to them about their achievements or duties.

Success sessions

A regular time needs to be set aside for this opportunity for pupils and teacher to share each others' successes. Initially pupils are invited to report their own achievements during the day: nothing negative can be mentioned. The teacher is also expected to add comments on her own behaviour during the day. Sometimes it can act as a reminder to the teacher that even bad days are good in parts. Later in the session, if some pupils have not contributed, peers are invited to speak for each other on any successes that they have observed.

It is important to realize that the term 'success' in this context should be defined very broadly and at a basic level, particularly for some pupils. It may include helping another child who has fallen in the playground and being cheerful when in some pain: it must not be confined simply to classroom work.

The home base lesson in the junior school is probably the most appropriate time. Some small village schools use their Assembly for this purpose and some special schools build it into their timetable day. One has only to watch children's faces during these sessions and listen to their conversations afterwards to be convinced of their value.

Older children may appear to find these sessions uncomfortable initially but this feeling soon disappears, particularly if the teacher joins in on an equal basis and acts as a model. It is, of course, possible to provide alternative forms of contributing which may include posting comments slips in a box or recording them in the class newspaper. I prefer to see these latter methods combined with, and linking to, the success session itself.

Conclusion

The foregoing discussion does not require summary here but I should like to conclude by making three points:

Alienation

The reader will be clear that self-esteem offers a clear central model to explain how pupils become alienated from their school and either abscond or become disruptive. Imagine yourself in a marriage where your partner constantly criticized you, where none of your skills seemed adequate or appropriate and everything seemed to be going wrong. You would feel a failure and certain to become alienated from your partner. If schools lay too great emphasis on academic achievement then personal qualities are devalued and many pupils will be seen as failures. Their self-esteem will be lowered and to preserve what is left of it they will 'withdraw' from those classroom experiences they find damaging. Pupils can withdraw physically or mentally; either or both are disastrous. Schools need to pay more attention to the *absent* alienated pupil and to plan ahead for the impact of the National Curriculum, with its age level tests, on pupils' self-esteem!

Teachers' self-esteem

It is clear to all who work in schools or alongside teachers that salary battles, additional work and constant denigration from the Secretary of State for Education has damaged the self-esteem of teachers as a professional body. It is therefore even more important that teachers organize themselves to actively enhance their own self-esteem. They will benefit and so will their pupils.

All that has been stated in this chapter about pupils' self-esteem applies equally to teachers. Junior school head teachers can use a number of these strategies with their teachers on school-based INSET courses. It is equally important for heads to encourage an atmosphere of security and warm acceptance amongst their staff members and to clarify the criteria for success in teaching.

School environment

It is vital for pupils, parents and teachers that their school has a positive psychological environment in which to work and learn. Once again, headteachers have a key role to play but it does require staff cooperation as well. The junior school needs to be a caring and productive community in which individual differences are fostered, development towards independence is encouraged and self-esteem is enhanced. Only in this way can teachers and children both flourish and 'grow', with alienation being kept at a minimum.

References

Battle, J. (1976) 'Test-retest reliability of the Canadian Self-esteem Inventory for Children', *Psychological Reports*, 38, pp. 1343–5.

Brookover, W.B. (1965) *Improving Academic Achievement through Students' Self-concept Enhancement: Self-concept of Ability and School Achievement II*, Michigan State University, East Lansing, Michigan, U.S. Office of Education.

Butler, J.M. and Haigh, G.V. (1954) 'Changes in the relationship between self-concepts consequent upon client-centered counselling', in Rogers, C.R. and Dymond, R.F. (Eds) *Psychotherapy and Personality Change*, Chicago, University of Chicago.

Calsyn, R.J. and Kenny, D.A. (1977) 'Self-concept of ability and perceived evaluation of others: cause or effect of academic achievement?', *Journal of Educational Psychology*, 69, pp. 136–45.

Chang, T.S. (1976) 'Self-concepts, academic achievement and teachers' ratings', *Psychology in the Schools*, 13, pp. 111–13.

Coley, J.D. (1973) 'The relationship of self-concept growth to reading quotient, cognitive style and teacher assessment of pupil progress for boys who are remedial readers', University of Maryland, unpublished PhD thesis.

Coopersmith, S.A. (1967) *The Antecedents of Self-esteem*, San Francisco, W.H. Freeman.

De Charms, R. (1976) *Enhancing Motivation*, New York, Irvington Publishers.

Docking, J.W. (1980) *Control and Discipline in Schools: Perspectives and Approaches*, London, Harper and Row.

Felker, D.W. and Thomas, S.B. (1971) 'Self-initiated verbal reinforcement and positive self-concept', *Child Development*, 42, pp. 1285–7.

Galton, M. and Simon, B. (1980) *Progress and Performance in the Primary Classroom*, London, Routledge and Kegan Paul.

Gill, M.P. (1969) *Patterns of Achievement as Related to the Perceived Self*, Washington, DC., American Educational Research Association.

Gough, H.G. and Heilbron, A.B. (1965) *Adjective Check List Manual*, Palo Alto, Consulting Psychologists Press.

Guardo, C.J. and Bohan, J.B. (1971) 'Development of a sense of self-identity in children', *Child Development*, 42, pp. 1909–21.

Gurney, P.W. (1979) 'The use of Behaviour Modification to increase the level of self-esteem in maladjusted boys', University of Exeter, unpublished PhD dissertation.

Gurney, P.W. (1987) 'The use of operant techniques to raise self-esteem in maladjusted children', *British Journal of Educational Psychology*, 57, pp. 87–94.

Gurney, P.W. (1988) *Self-Esteem in Children with Special Educational Needs*, London, Routledge.

Hart, J.G. (1985) 'LAWSEQ: its relation to other measures of self-esteem and academic ability', *British Journal of Educational Psychology*, 55, pp. 167–9.

Harter, S. (1982) 'Children's understanding of multiple emotions: a cognitive-developmental approach', in Overton, W.F. (Ed.) *The Relationship Between Social and Cognitive Development*, Hillsdale, New Jersey, Lawrence Erlbaum.

Hauserman, N., Miller, J.S. and Bond, F.T. (1976) 'A behavioural approach to changing self-concept in elementary school children', *Psychological Record*, 26, pp. 111–6.

Jersild, A.T. (1952) *In Search of Self*, New York, Teachers' College, Columbia University.

La Benne, W.D. and Greene, B.I. (1969) *Educational Implications of Self-concept Theory*, Pacific Palisades, California, Goodyear.

Lawrence, D. (1971) 'The effects of counselling on retarded readers', *Educational Research*, 13, pp. 119–24.

Lawrence, D. (1973) *Improved Reading Through Counselling*, London, Ward Lock.

Lawrence, D. (1981) 'The development of a self-esteem questionnaire', *British Journal of Educational Psychology*, 51, pp. 245–51.

McCormick, M.K. and Williams, J.H. (1974) 'Effects of a compensatory program on self-report, achievement and aspiration level of disadvantaged High School students', *Journal of Negro Education*, 43, pp. 47–52.

Marsh, H.W., Parker, J.W. and Smith, I.D. (1983) 'Pre-adolescent self-concept: its relation to self-concept as inferred by teachers and to academic ability', *British Journal of Educational Psychology*, 53, pp. 60–78.

Peters, R.S. (1966) *Ethics and Education*, London, Allen and Unwin.

Piers, E.V. and Harris, D. (1964) 'Age and other correlates of self-concept in children', *Journal of Educational Psychology*, 55, pp. 91–5.

Pigge, F.L. (1970) 'Children and their self-concepts', *Childhood Education*, 47, pp. 107–8.

Purkey, W.W. (1970) *Self-concept and School Achievement*, New York, Prentice-Hall.

Purkey, W.W. (1978) *Inviting School Success*, Belmont, Wadsworth.

Secord, P. and Peevers, B. (1974) 'The development of attribution of person concepts', in Mischel, T. (Ed.) *Understanding Other Persons*, Oxford, Blackwell.

Selman, R. (1980) *The Growth of Interpersonal Understanding*, New York, Academic Press.

Shavelson, R.J., Hubner, J.J. and Stanton, G.C. (1976) 'Self-concept: validation of construct interpretations', *Review of Educational Research*, 46, pp. 407–41.

Simon, W.E. and Simon, M.G. (1975) 'Self-esteem, intelligence and standardised academic achievement', *Psychology in the Schools*, 12, pp. 97–9.

Sweet, A.E. and Burbach, H.J. (1977) 'Self-esteem and reading achievement', Paper presented at the Annual Meeting of AERA (New York, April 1977) ERIC (ED 137 756, September 1977).

Trowbridge, N. (1972) 'Socio-economic status and self-concept of children', *Journal of Teacher Education*, 23, pp. 63–5.

West, R.C. and Fish, J.A. (1973) 'Relationships between self-concept and school achievement: a survey of empirical findings', ERIC, Clearinghouse on Early Childhood Education, (ED 092 239).

Willey, M.M. (1987) 'A strategy for motivation in the inner city primary school classroom', University of Exeter, unpublished MPhil dissertation.

2
Disaffection in the Junior Years: A Perspective from Theories of Motivation

Colin Rogers

Introduction

The aim of this chapter is to provide the reader with an introduction to some current thinking about the processes of motivation in the junior school context. The work will centre on the contribution provided by attribution theory, but other perspectives will also be examined.

Some recent research (Mortimore *et al.*, 1988 and this volume) tends to reinforce the commonly held view that the junior school pupil is generally positive in his/her attitude towards school and schooling. The common conception of the secondary school pupil is a less positive one. As will be seen later, this decline in enthusiasm has its counterpart in motivational terms. By introducing these terms and some of the debate that has helped to develop them it is hoped to provide the reader with a set of conceptual tools for the analysis of junior school issues of the kind discussed elsewhere in this volume.

The last decade or so has seen a marked growth in the amount of attention being paid by psychological and educational researchers to motivational issues. The literature is growing at a steady pace and the interested reader is directed to the following in order to obtain a more detailed introduction than can be given here: Ames and Ames, 1984 and 1985; Atkinson and Raynor 1974 and 1978; Deci and Ryan 1985; Fyans 1980; Rogers 1982 and 1987; and Weiner 1979, 1983 and 1984.

At the present stage of development the field is characterized by a healthy proliferation of different theories, each competing for the researcher's attention. Again the interested reader will have to look elsewhere in order to follow through these detailed differences. The present discussion is necessarily selective but more detail of the approaches to be emphasized here will follow below. At the outset, the initial intention is to present some of the common themes that run through these different accounts and to highlight ways in which these themes can be useful to those concerned with the notion of alienation in the early years of schooling.

Conceptualizing motivation

Ask for definitions of a well-motivated pupil from groups of experienced teachers (this is an exercise that I have carried out a number of times at the beginning of INSET courses) and the chances are that the responses will be largely teacher centred in their concerns. That is, the well motivated pupil is described in terms that are derived from direct observation by the teacher and that reflect the concerns and value system of the teacher. Thus, the well-motivated pupil is one who 'gets on', is well-behaved, shows interest, keeps on-task and is not too demanding of teacher time. The well-motivated pupil and the 'ideal-type' pupil (Hargreaves, 1977) have a lot in common.

Many things could be said about this picture of the well-motivated pupil; two will suffice here. First, the definition is given from the teachers' point of view: it is a definition from the outside looking in. There are no references to the perceptions, values, feelings (in short the cognitions) of the pupil. Well-motivated pupils are, by definition, those that are going to do largely what the teacher wants.

Second, the definition is essentially quantitative. The points of reference that it utilizes are to do with such concepts as time-on-task, remaining in seat when supposed to be and so on. Again there are no references to the more qualitative aspects of the experience of engaging in work within the school setting.

In many respects, the main concern of current work in pupil motivation has been to change this definition. As summarized by Ames (1987) current conceptions of motivation emphasize the qualitative aspects of the concept and, in addition, move towards a definition that places an emphasis upon process rather than state or trait. This last point is an important one for present purposes and will be returned to later. For the moment, let it suffice to say that this emphasis assumes that the motivational state of an individual is not entirely determined by the personality traits or characteristics that the individual brings into the situation. Being a well-motivated pupil is not just a matter of having the right kind of personality. Rather, 'good' motivation arises from the interactions that take place between the individual and the situation within which that individual has to operate. As Ames (1987) points out, one immediate implication of this conception is that poor motivation cannot simply be accounted for by reference to the unfortunate or even undesirable characteristics of the individual concerned, but rather need to be understood as the joint product of that individual and the situation. As teachers and school managements are very much part of the situation, poor motivation cannot be used by them as a ready excuse for poor performance.

The theoretical approach that will underpin this chapter is that provided by attribution theory. The following sections of this chapter will outline the concerns of this approach. However, it is useful to precede this with a brief account of some earlier work into motivation that helps to set the scene for a consideration of the attribution theorists' own contributions.

The dynamics of motivation

Atkinson (Atkinson and Raynor, 1974, 1978) and his associates were in part responsible for the current increase in interest in the study of motivational processes. Their studies of motivation helped to bring the term 'achievement motivation' into current thinking. Atkinson was concerned to explore the specific motivational dynamics that come into play when an individual is confronted with an achievement-related setting. By this is meant any setting where it is possible to succeed or fail by either reaching or not reaching some predetermined standard of excellence. Such a standard could be set by oneself or somebody else.

The first and most fundamentally important distinction that Atkinson utilized was that between intrinsic and extrinsic motivation. Intrinsic motivation is that part of the motivational process that is driven by the individual's own personal desire to engage in, or avoid, the task. Hobby activities are usually good examples of tasks that are motivated intrinsically. Generally we are not concerned about what others might think of our performance when engaged in a hobby pursuit; neither are we looking for monetary or other tangible rewards. The standards of excellence set are those that, by and large, we ourselves determine. The focus of attention for the intrinsically motivated individual is upon the task itself. Engagement in, and not the completion of the task is often the reward. Extrinsic motivation, on the other hand, is concerned with most of the other factors that might determine our performance. Financial reward, threats of punishment for non-completion, the need to obtain or keep the approval of others are all examples of factors that can be extrinsically motivating. The highly extrinsically motivated individual will often have more of an eye on the consequences of success and failure than on the engagement in the task itself. Atkinson's approach assumes that both intrinsic and extrinsic motivation will operate at the same time. Clearly, however, both can operate at different strengths. Low motivation of one type can be compensated for by strength in the other.

At this point it might seem that the potential victim of growing disaffection is the individual who is primarily extrinsically motivated. In some respects, as will be argued in more detail later, this would seem to be the case. The highly intrinsically motivated person is one who would be expected to show a high level of task engagement, to be absorbed in the work and to find the activity rewarding in its own right. However, the matter is more complicated than this, and Atkinson's contribution is notable for his attempt to show that intrinsic motivation need not always operate in a positive manner.

In essence, Atkinson claims that there are at least two types of intrinsic motivation, each to be found within all of us and operating concurrently. The first is a positive force, referred to as the Motive to Achieve Success while the second is characterized as a negative force, the Motive to Avoid Failure. The former is concerned with the strength of the individual's capacity to experience positive emotions consequent upon success. Success makes us all feel good but some apparently feel better about it than others. The greater this capacity, the greater will be the individual's desire to engage in achievement-related tasks simply in order to provide themselves with the prospect of success and the good experiences that will bring. The latter, the

Motive to Avoid Failure, is concerned with the capacity of the individual to experience bad feelings in connection with failure and therefore to experience anxiety when faced with the possibility of failure. Both of these are intrinsic forces and are not concerned with our feelings about the reactions of others, only with our personal reaction to what takes place.

Our behaviour is determined, as far as intrinsic motivation is concerned, by the relative strength of these two opposing forces. Each achievement related task presents us with a classic approach/avoidance conflict. Our motive to achieve success draws us into the task for if we do not engage in it we cannot experience the (intrinsic) rewards of success. But to engage is to run the risk of failure. The possibility of failure provokes the anxieties related to the Motive to Avoid Failure which steers us away from engagement, for the lack of engagement ensures that we cannot fail.

Atkinson's theory, then, suggests that the world may be considered to be made up of two different types of people. The first have a stronger motive to succeed than motive to avoid failure, and, left to their own intrinsic devices would always choose to engage in achievement related tasks. All such tasks are seen, first and foremost, as opportunities to succeed, to demonstrate to oneself what one can do. (The theory also has things to say about which task would be chosen if more than one were available, but that goes beyond our present concerns.) Others are dominated by the Motive to Avoid Failure and for them all achievement related tasks are seen as opportunities to fail, to demonstrate, to themselves, what they cannot do. For these people, no achievement related task will be attractive in itself.

It follows, therefore, that the second type of individual, dominated by fear of failure and feelings of anxiety, will only engage in achievement related activities if extrinsic motivators are sufficiently powerful to overcome the intrinsic desire to keep away from the task. Thus are the seeds of disaffection sown.

In short, the dynamics of motivation as set out by Atkinson, indicate that the positively motivated individual is likely to find him/herself at home in the school environment. Extrinsic motivators, ranging from signs of teacher approval and disapproval to the passing and failing of examinations, will be working in harmony with the individual's own intrinsic desire to engage in achievement related activity. But the individual driven by the Motive to Avoid Failure finds that the school's extrinsic systems are all designed so as to work against his/her own intrinsic desire to keep away from achievement related tasks. Such individuals only engage in achievement related tasks if the extrinsic motivators are sufficiently powerful to outweigh the intrinsic ones.

Atkinson's theory then suggests that pupils with the 'wrong' type of motivational dynamic will find themselves increasingly in situations where they have to resort to a number of strategems in order to avoid the worst of their own fears while at the same time keeping those in authority over them, who tend also to be the people who control the extrinsic reward systems, happy. One would predict, therefore, that as the young child made his/her way through the primary school the chance of becoming alienated from the school's official practices, aims and values would grow ever higher.

While these ideas are of considerable interest, it is fair to say that in the form set out by Atkinson, they have made relatively little impression upon the educational community and the process of schooling. There are many reasons for this, but there are two that ought to be highlighted here.

First, the theory is presented as an algebraic model that is not readily located within the constructs employed by teachers in their own thinking about classroom processess. The extent to which a psychological theory can mesh with the established thinking of practitioners, while at the same time provoke new ways of thinking and acting will determine crucially the degree to which that theory will help to influence practice. By contrast, the approach of the attribution theorists, to be introduced below, seems well equipped in this respect. Second, Atkinson's work has assumed that a large role is played by relatively enduring personality traits located within the child, traits that are unlikely to be readily changed by the child's school experiences. As with other research into trait/treatment interactions (Child, 1986) the results are interesting but the practical implications far from obvious.

The role of attributions

Weiner (1979, 1984) has been the dominant figure in establishing an approach to the study of motivation based upon attribution theory. Attribution theory is a collection of ideas and hypotheses that attempts to account for aspects of human behaviour by looking at the ways in which people arrive at their own explanations for events. It is rooted in the study of 'naïve' psychology (Heider, 1958); that is, the generally implicit ideas that we all use in our everyday lives in an attempt to make sense of what we see others, and ourselves, getting up to. An example from the achievement domain will illustrate the main points.

Having undertaken a task and having failed to reach the required standards (set by the self or others) an individual has, of course, experienced a failure. The psychological meaning of this failure is, however, still far from clear. Many factors will determine how the individual responds. How important was the task? What was at stake? Are there important things that the individual now cannot do (e.g. go to University, get a job as a lorry driver)? Such issues are concerned with the consequences of the failure and involve the inter-relationships between the value system of the individual and the nature of the attempted task, together with the social structures of which that task is a part. As these are consequences of the failure, they are all to do with looking forward. Attribution theory directs our attention to factors that are related to the individual's own consideration of the past, the antecedents or causes of the failure.

Weiner has examined the types of causes that might be considered as possible explanations of success and failure. The list of all potential causes would be almost infinite and some researchers (Little, 1985; Whitley and Frieze, 1985) have drawn attention to the range that might actually be employed. Weiner has argued that what is important is the nature of the cause to which a success or failure might be attributed. Causes have been classified on a number of different dimensions. The most commonly employed dimensions are stable-unstable and internal-external, followed by global-specific, controllable-uncontrollable and intentional-unintentional. It is not possible to enter into a full discussion of the claimed characteristics of all of these here, but the following offers a brief summary and hopefully serves to illustrate the main features of the claims that are made about the roles played by different types of causes.

If a success or failure is attributed to an internal cause, the individual making the attribution is, in a sense, accepting or claiming some degree of responsibility for what took place. If I fail because I lack the ability or did not make the necessary effort, that has more to do with me than a failure due to the difficulty of the task. The last cause is an external one, the former two internal. Some causes are believed to be transient in their effects or to be variable in terms of the level at which they operate. Effort, for example, will tend to be positively related to outcomes, but the level of effort put into different tasks at different times is believed to vary. A lack of ability, on the other hand, will generally reduce one's chances of being successful but the assumption that one lacks ability now is likely to be accompanied by the belief that one will continue to lack ability (and therefore be likely to continue to fail) in the future. Ability is therefore generally held to be a stable cause, while effort is seen to be an unstable one.

The next step for Weiner to take now seems apparent. Failures attributed to different types of causes are likely to have different types of perceived consequences. The failure attributed to a stable cause presents a different prognosis from the one attributed to an unstable cause. This is all the more so if the unstable cause is also judged to be controllable. If I fail due to lack of effort, I might still predict failure as I see my lack of effort as being something that I cannot control. If, however, I believe that I could try harder if I wanted to, then the combination of instability and controllability in the perceived cause of my failure is likely to lead to a relatively positive prediction.

The other dimensions also have similar effects. A failure attributed to a global cause can give rise to a very poor prognosis (Seligman, 1975; Dweck, 1975) as one will begin to believe that future failure is not only to be expected on this task but on most others as well. In other situations a failure in say, mathematics, may be attributed to a specific cause that will have no implications for how well one might perform in the next school football match. The final dimension of intentional-unintentional probably has greater implications for the attributions that we might make about the causes of someone else's activities rather than our own (I will be more upset if I think that you *meant* to tread on my toe) and this dimension will be returned to later when the attributions of teachers for their pupils are looked at.

The details of Weiner's work, and that of his colleagues, have been concerned with examining the antecedents and consequences of different types of attributions. The suggested consequences follow from the classification of causes along the various dimensions introduced above. At the heart of the attributional approach to the study of motivation is the idea that it is the subjective experience of failure or success to which an individual responds, and not the objective result as it might be understood by some impartial third party observer.

Central to this analysis is the role of causes located at either end of the stability dimension. Attributions to stable causes are likely to produce expectations for more of the same. A failure attributed to a stable cause gives rise to more confident predictions of future failure than does a failure attributed to an unstable cause. Failure at a test that is attributed to the stable cause of ability is a failure that one is likely to expect to be repeated. It was my stupidity that caused the failure, and as I will still be stupid tomorrow further failure must be expected. A failure perceived to have been caused by a bad hangover, however, will not give rise to the same expectation of future failure (as long as being hungover is not a regular condition!).

Following from this arises the notion of attributional or motivational style. The notion of style arises from some of the earliest work by attribution theorists (Kelly, 1972; Jones *et al.*, 1972) who sought to establish a number of principles that guided the ways in which attributions were made. One of the principles, or rules of thumb that has received extensive empirical backing (Ames and Ames, 1984 and 1985) is that expected events are more likely to be attributed to stable causes than are unexpected ones. Early attributions play a part in determining what level of performance is to be expected, and therefore help to determine the attributions that will be made to explain those later events when they do take place.

In as much as pupils develop typical styles of attributing success and failure, so they can be seen to be likely to develop typical ways of responding to situations where success or failure is possible. If success on a series of mathematics tests is attributed by a pupil to his or her ability (a factor that is judged to be both stable and internal) but any failures are attributed to the poor selection of test items in terms of their correspondence to the work done in class (a factor that is judged to be external because this is somebody else's responsibility, and unstable because it is not always the case that items are inappropriate) the theory predicts that the pupil will become increasingly more optimistic and confident about his or her future performance. However, if failure is attributed to internal and stable factors (such as the lack of ability) and success to external and unstable ones (such as help from the teacher) then the outlook becomes increasingly bleak and the confidence of the pupil declines. Under circumstances where behaviour was not con strained by others one might expect such pupils to seek other areas of endeavour to engage in.

The great majority of published research that has concerned itself with attributions for success and failure has examined the role of effort and ability as causal factors. Ability has been taken to be an example of a stable cause, while effort has been taken to be an example of an unstable cause (see Weiner, 1979). While these factors may have only been put forward as examples of a type in the first place by Weiner, it is now clear that they are causes that are frequently used by individuals to explain their own (and indeed other people's) successes and failures. Differences in the use that is made of ability and effort as causes of success and failure are held to be important components of attributional style. In particular, pupils who make repeated attributions to lack of ability to explain failure are thought to be more likely to develop motivational strategies that will be considered as maladaptive by the school system. Such pupils are, after all, being constantly asked to attempt work that they have already decided they lack the ability to complete to other people's (and indeed their own) satisfaction.

The work of Dweck (1975, 1985) is important here. Drawing on previous work (Seligman, 1975) Dweck has explored the attributional differences between children characterized by learned helplessness and those who are described as being mastery oriented. Learned helplessness, in attributional terms, is a state that follows from determining that one's lack of success is caused by stable, global and uncontrollable causes. With this diagnosis it is hardly surprising that such children come to assume that they will always be unsuccessful and that there is little or nothing that they can do about it. Mastery-oriented children do not make such attributions and maintain a much more positive and less fearful approach to learning. For these children, failures represent opportunities to further one's learning, rather than signs that one has reached the end of the road. It is clearly the learned helpless child who is likely to become disaffected with schooling.

One of the more important aspects of Dweck's work is the claim that attributions are not merely the cause of the different orientations of children but are part of a broader pattern. The learned helpless child seems to be disposed to accept the fact of failure. The belief that the failure was caused by stable and generalizable causes carries the clear implication that future failure is to be expected. The mastery-oriented child, however, responds quite differently. While the failure is still acknowledged and recognized, it is not to be seen as an indicator of the child's limits. The latter child's prime concern remains with the eventual mastery of the material. The present failure is understood to mean that mastery has not yet been achieved, not that it will never be achieved. The mastery-oriented child is therefore less concerned with understanding the causes of the failure than with looking for ways of moving forward. The most important point is that attributions are being seen here to be part of a broader motivational system, rather than being the cause of the system itself. Rather than accepting that attributions cause motivation, Dweck is arguing that more basic motivational concerns determine whether or not attributions are made at all.

Increasingly, this and other work (Covington, 1984) points to the view that attributions are themselves motivated. The early conceptions of people like Kelley (1972), referred to above, assumed that the process of making attributions was an essentially logical one. The models produced to account for the ways in which attributions are made assumed that there is a close similarity between the reasoning processes formally adopted by the scientist and those normally adopted by the 'naïve psychologist'. These are information processing models that imply that differences between people in the attributions that they make are due to differences in the information that has been available initially to them. So the child who experiences early success will be more likely to attribute any particular success to a stable cause (as it is in line with previous experience) and therefore more likely to expect further success. As future success is now expected it, too, is likely to be attributed to stable causes when it occurs. The very logic of the situation impels those who get off to a good start to make more favourable patterns of attributions than those who do not. The alternative view (most frequently expressed by Covington, although he has tended to base his work on research with students at undergraduate level) is that the process of making attributions is itself motivated.

The essential motivating ingredient here is the preservation and elevation of self-esteem. Covington's argument is based on the assumption that there exists a culturally determined desire to maintain a view of oneself that includes the belief that one has a high level of ability. As such a view has to be kept in line with available evidence, there is a built-in tendency to interpret success and failure experiences, particularly the latter, in such a way as to maintain the highest possible estimate of our own ability. A failure attributed to a lack of effort is less threatening than one attributed to a lack of ability, as the former attribution allows us to accept the fact of the failure but refute the allegation that it implies a lack of competence on our part. Covington's work suggests that, at the undergraduate level at least, the motivational force underlying the attributional process can produce situations where individuals begin to engage in learning strategies that appear as counter-productive to the outsider in order to maintain the possibility of making ego-protecting attributions. Many teachers at most levels of the educational system have observed individuals playing down the amount of effort that they have put into a task, which the pupils are clearly concerned to complete successfully, even to the point of actually producing a lower level of effort than would have been desirable and possible. Clearly if one has publicly displayed a high level of effort it will then be difficult to make an attribution for failure to a lack of effort, and if a lack of effort cannot explain the failure then the chances are increased that a lack of ability will. So the student most anxious about failing becomes the one who might be least willing to make the effort to succeed. The notion is, of course, similar to that developed some years ago by Atkinson in his discussions of the Motive to Avoid Failure. Covington is now not only claiming that it is the implications of that failure for the individual's own self-concept that are important (rather than the failure itself), but also that the link between failure and self-concept is provided by the attributions that the individual makes.

Covington's work implies that teachers need to maintain a vigilant view of the relationship between their policies for encouraging effort and rewarding success. Under a system where the pupil is constantly encouraged to try harder, but rewards tend to be limited only to those who succeed in competitive terms (by performing at a higher level than most others) the need to protect self-esteem from the conse-quences of failures is maximized. Covington suggests that the pupils' preferred tactic, the reduction of effort, will bring them into direct conflict with the espoused values of their teachers and the school system as a whole.

Non-attributional approaches

Before finally turning our attention to the particular implications of all of this for the issue of disaffection in the junior years, there is one more particular theoretical position that it would be helpful to examine. Deci and Ryan (1985) have developed a comprehensive theory of motivation that ascribes only a very limited role, if any, to attributions as typically understood by the attribution theorists (although Covington's work seems to have more in common with their developments). Deci and Ryan declare the classic attribution theory approach to be too limited by its commitment to an information processing model. For them, the notion that one has to acquire an understanding of one's own motivational (and other) states through the process of deductive attributing, implies that personal causation, and thereby true freedom to act in accordance with one's true self, has already been lost. Theirs is very much a 'motivational' theory in which it is assumed that the human organism contains inherent tendencies to strive for a situation in which it can be self-determining. The parallels, at this superficial level at least, to the ideas of Carl Rogers (1984) may well seem clear.

Their complete theoretical framework is a multifaceted one and only one small part of it will be discussed here. Deci and Ryan are concerned with the processes involved in the interactions between the individual, with his/her own particular dispositions acquired through experience, and the situation in which he/she operates at any given time. It is to be stressed that it is the environment as perceived by the individual that is of importance. Three kinds of environments can be identified. (There are also corresponding types of people and it is ultimately people, for example teachers, who determine the nature of the environment.) The working environment can be seen to be informational, controlling or amotivating.

The essential differences are simple, although the full account gets more complex. Informational environments provide the individual with feedback that enables him/her to make decisions about how to best make their own next move. Feedback informing the individual that he/she has failed is informational in as much as it contains within it information that enables him/her to understand the nature of and reasons for the failure. The individual might then begin to plan how to overcome the difficulty. Such an environment is likely to help to encourage self-determining individuals who are likely to remain involved with their work and to see it as being related to their own desires and objectives.

A controlling environment, as the title suggests, provides a context in which the participant comes to see others as having the ability to determine outcomes and activities. The goals and objectives belong to other people not to oneself. One works for them, not in order to accomplish one's own goals. Such environments can, seemingly, be all too readily created in educational settings.

Finally, amotivating circumstances operate when the individual is led to believe that they lack the requisite ability for success. A belief that one has sufficient competence for the task seems to be an essential ingredient of self-determining behaviour. The lack of it destroys the highest forms of motivation and leaves individuals in something akin to the pawn-like state identified by De Charms (1968, 1984). In considering the consequences of different types of classroom environments for young pupils, it will be helpful to bear these sketches of different types of motivational influences in mind.

The most immediate, and perhaps the most important practical implication of these accounts concerns the role of assessment. For Deci and Ryan the ideal form of assessment would be one that encouraged the pupil to be involved in the making of decisions about the objectives they were to work to. It would also ensure that the feedback provided drew attention both to progress that had been made and to areas where extra attention was needed. Systems that simply inform the pupil that they have failed to reach a target established by someone else, and also carry the implication that the pupil is unlikely to be able to make the target at all (and this easily occurs when the target is to be in the top band), are to be avoided.

Motivation and development in the junior classroom

At this stage, the main contribution of the attribution theorists' work for a consideration of classroom processes lies in the provision of a set of conceptual tools that can be used to analyse a number of different types of practice. The final section of this chapter will attempt to do this by making reference to a few areas of research that have particular relevance to the question of the development of disaffection in the junior school years.

The first of these areas involves work that is directly concerned with the development of attributional processes in primary school aged children. A consistent finding by motivational researchers (Nicholls, 1984) has been that young children during the first few years of schooling are unlikely to suffer adverse effects of failure. They clearly prefer to succeed rather than to fail but they do not tend to assume, as many older people do, that failures imply an inability to ever complete the task to the required standard. The reasons for the existence of this state of affairs, and just as importantly the reasons for its loss, are only imperfectly understood. But some observations can be made. Stipeck (1984) produces evidence to show that wishful thinking is involved. Children are not incapable of making judgements that place themselves at the bottom of a hierarchy and deducing from this that they are unlikely to progress from this position; they simply prefer not to.

Nicholls (Nicholls, 1983; Nicholls and Miller, 1984) has offered another account that contains within it the somewhat gloomy suggestion that there is perhaps something inevitable about this decline in optimism. It will be recalled that the attribution theorists have put some store by the importance of attributions to ability to explain success and failure, especially the latter. The significance of ability as a cause comes partly from the culturally value-laden aspects of the concept (as discussed by Covington) and partly from the claim that it is seen to be a stable factor. Failures caused by a lack of ability give rise to a poor prognosis as the cause of the problem is seen to be enduring. It follows, therefore, that if ability is *not* regarded by some as being a stable cause, then attributions to ability to explain success and failure will not carry the same implications. This, according to Nicholls, may well be the case with young children.

In a fascinating series of studies, Nicholls has shown that young children (approximately up to the age of eight) do not share the adult view of the stable nature of ability. Indeed, Nicholls argues that younger children do not fully differentiate between cause and effect at all. Success, hard work and ability necessarily go together as they are all good characteristics of people (see Rogers, 1978, and Livesley and Bromley, 1973, for accounts of the general nature of this tendency in young children to see people in all good or all bad terms). There is a similar expectation to find failure, sloth and stupidity linked together. Young children would find it difficult to imagine someone who worked hard but still failed, or who was stupid but successful.

At a later stage children come to see cause and effect relationships more clearly, but they still have a different view from older children and adults about the nature of some of the causes. In particular, they see ability as a plastic entity. A lack of ability cannot simply be compensated for by extra effort, which is held to be the adult view; it can actually be altered. Children who work harder do better and get cleverer. A lack of ability at a given task does not, therefore, imply a lack of ability at the same task in the future.

It is only during the final year or so of primary schooling and the early years of secondary that the child comes to acquire the adult view of ability as something that is stable and that sets a limit upon what one can reasonably expect to achieve. The more sophisticated the child becomes in his/her understanding of the nature of one of the assumed major causes of success and failure, the more fearful that child will become of concluding that he or she lacks ability. The defensive strategies that Covington and others discuss in relation to the undergraduate would be unlikely to apply to the young primary school child. Covington in one of his research papers (Covington and Omelich, 1979) referred to effort as a 'double-edged' sword, in that the lack of effort made failure more likely but its application made its consequences more serious by implying a lack of ability. For the young primary child effort cuts only one way; by the end of the primary years this is less likely to be the case.

It is important to note that while Nicholls bases his argument on notions to do with the process of cognitive development itself, it is also possible to argue that age-related changes in the organization of formal school-based learning environments will also play a part. Eccles *et al.* (1984) have outlined the means by which the different treatment that a child could expect to receive as a function of age can be seen to bring about changes in the child's approach to learning. These changes involve a move away from a positive and self-determining approach towards a negative, fearful and more controlled one.

So far, it would appear that at face value the primary school teacher has relatively little to be concerned about. The predisposition of the younger child is such as to incline him/her to remain optimistic and, in a sense, well-motivated, while the typical primary school mode of operation is held to be better suited to the facilitation of intrinsic and self-determining styles of motivation than that which characterizes the secondary school. However, it is important to note that it is during the primary years that children will be acquiring attributional habits which, while not immutable, will be difficult to change (Maehr and Kleiber, 1987). A continuing research programme by the present author (Rogers, 1986) is examining the ways in which young children come to acquire beliefs about the specific causes of success and failure in specific areas of the primary school curriculum.

For example, this research shows that there are not only variations between children at different stages in primary schooling in the use that they make of ability, but also that there are differences within an age group according to the subject matter that they are discussing. A concept of 'general ability' is more likely to be used to account for success in a mathematics test than it is to account for success at reading. Perhaps, more significantly, the results also show that children will be influenced in their use of the ability concept by the teaching methods employed within a subject area as well as by the subject area itself. When success in mathematics was defined in terms of performance on whole class tests, children were more inclined to believe that success requires a high level of general ability than when mathematics was defined in terms of work on an individualized scheme. This work is still in its early stages, but it is likely that the attitudes that a child develops concerning the degree to which ability is a necessary requirement for success in a particular domain may well depend on how that subject matter was initially presented.

Similar findings have been much more clearly established with respect to the use of competition and cooperation in the classroom. Ames (1981, 1984) and Slavin (1983) have reviewed much of this research but the broad conclusion is that the more children are exposed to overtly competitive learning environments, the more likely they are to attribute success and failure to ability or the lack of it. Competition is also likely to make children more concerned with adopting self-defensive strategies designed to protect them from the worst consequences of failure (the assumption that one lacks the necessary level of ability) and less likely to be mastery-oriented (concerned with gaining their best level of understanding of the requirements of the task at hand).

Both of these areas of research suggest that developments during the primary years may well be significant for the 'sleeper effects' that they have. That is, a child may be acquiring the view that ability is particularly significant in respect to certain curriculum areas, and also becoming more concerned about his or her own standing relative to others. Yet, due to the child's early developmental stage in respect to the understanding of the concept of ability itself, the full effects of these developing beliefs do not make themselves clear until later, perhaps not until the early years of secondary school. It is interesting to note that some of the more dramatic differences between the sexes in terms of academic performance do not begin to materialize until this time, but that it is also possible to argue that a similar 'sleeper effect' is in operation (Nicholls, 1980; Rogers, 1986).

The processes alluded to above concern the overall organization of the classroom and the school. The particular teaching methods adopted and the relative emphasis placed on competition or cooperation are matters that will affect the whole class and are often determined at the school rather than the classroom level. It is also the case, however, that details of interactions between teacher and pupil will be relevant to the developing attributions of the young child.

There have been some attempts to investigate these effects, and reviews can be seen in the following: Bar-Tal, 1982; Eccles and Wigfield, 1985; Brophy, 1987. One study that has close relevance to the concerns of this present chapter is that of Rohrkemper and Brophy (1983).

The concern here was with the attributions that teachers made for various aspects of their pupils' behaviour. There are a number of important features to this data but the one that concerns us is that the kind of attributions that teachers made varied according to the degree to which the behaviour of the pupil could be considered to be causing problems for the teacher. Aspects of pupil behaviour that were problematic in this way were more likely than others to be attributed to the pupil so as to suggest that the pupil was able to control the behaviour and that the behaviour was also intentional. At the same time the researchers found that the teachers had pessimistic prognoses for these types of behaviour and tended to deal with the situation by making recourse to short-term desists that were designed to bring about an immediate, but temporary, alleviation of the problem.

The important feature of this study is that an examination of the attributions made by teachers for typical classroom events enabled an analysis to be made of some of the dynamics associated with those events. Somewhat similar concerns have also been expressed by Cooper (1985) in an analysis of the processes involved in the communication of teacher expectations. In brief, Cooper's model suggests that teachers will wish to exert greater control over pupils whom they regard as being academically weak. Although well-intentioned (the teachers believed that they would be better able to assist the pupil by maintaining close control over their interactions with him/her) the effects of this strategy were to deny such pupils opportunities to demonstrate what they were capable of doing in front of their classmates. Any contributions that such pupils did make would be less likely to be taken up and made use of by the teacher.

Again, similar concerns are demonstrated by Deci and Ryan and co-workers (Deci and Ryan, 1985; Deci *et al.*, 1981) in their investigations of the differences between teachers in the degree to which they were willing and/or able to create classroom environments that provided the pupils with informational environments. Such environments, it will be recalled, are believed to be associated with the degree to which the pupils themselves will develop self-determining motivational styles.

In each case, from a variety of standpoints, the point made by the theorist carries the same application. Under certain circumstances, and for the best of reasons, teachers of young children will help to create environments that begin to direct the pupil away from a self-determining motivational style in which they, the pupils, will see themselves as being reponsible for their own learning and capable of effecting positive change. It is important to stress that these tendencies will often arise with response to pressures and restrictions placed upon teachers themselves. With the advent of the National Curriculum, and its associated forms of assessment, it is possible that more teachers will aim to produce the required results by imposing greater control and thereby reducing the informational nature of their classrooms. A drive for short-term results can often produce longer term problems.

Another point that this chapter has stressed is that the effects of these processes may well not be apparent while the pupil is still at the primary stage of their schooling. The combination of the child's own cognitive development, together with the organizational changes that accompany the transfer from primary to secondary schooling will lead to the generation of observable disaffection from the cognitive structures already in place.

The final concluding point is to concede that neither the attributional nor any of the other theories of motivation have yet developed a sufficient corpus of classroom based data to enable the production of convincing sets of 'tips for teachers' designed to ensure trouble-free primary schooling. It does, however, seem clear that a grounding in the theory sufficient to enable classroom teachers to make analyses of the attributional patterns made by themselves, their colleagues and their pupils can help to illuminate otherwise obscure, but important, classroom processes.

We know that schools can make a difference to levels of disruptive behaviour (Galloway *et al.*, 1982; Mortimore *et al.*, 1988) but it is not yet clear just how this happens. Collective introspection by the school into its own practices will almost certainly be helpful. This is all the more likely to be so if there is some established perspective from which such introspection can be carried out and the data thus yielded interpreted. One intention of this article has been to introduce the reader to the possibility of attribution theory and other theories of motivation providing just such a perspective.

References

Ames, C. (1981) 'Competitive versus cooperative reward structures: The influence of individual and group performance factors on achievement attributions and affect', *American Educational Research Journal*, 18, pp. 273–287.

Ames, C. (1984) 'Competitive, cooperative and individualistic goal structures: A cognitive–motivational analysis', in Ames, R.E. and Ames C. (Eds) *Research on Motivation in Education: Volume 1. Student Motivation,* London, Academic Press.

Ames, C. (1987) 'The enhancement of student motivation', in Maehr, M.L. and Kleiber, D.A. *Enhancing Motivation*, Connecticut, JAI Press,

Ames, C. and Ames, R.E. (1985) *Research on Motivation in Education, Volume 2: The Classroom Milieu*, London, Academic Press.

Ames, R.E. and Ames, C. (Eds) (1984) *Research on Motivation in Education, Volume 1: Student Motivation*, London, Academic Press.

Atkinson, J. and Raynor, J. (1974) *Motivation and Achievement*, Washington DC, Winston.

Atkinson, J. and Raynor, J. (1978) *Personality, Motivation and Achievement*, Washington DC, Hemisphere.

Bar-Tal, D. (1982) 'The effect of teachers' behaviour on pupils' attributions: A review', in Antaki, C. and Brewin, C. *Attributions and Psychological Change: Application of Attributional Theories to Clinical and Educational Practice*, London, Academic Press.

Brophy, J. (1987) 'Socializing students' motivation to learn', in Maehr, M.L. and Kleiber, D.A. *Enhancing Motivation*, Connecticut, JAI Press.

Child, D. (1986) *Psychology and the Teacher*, Eastbourne, Holt, Rinehart and Winston.

Cooper, H.M. (1985) 'Models of teacher expectation communication', in Dusek, J.B. *Teacher Expectancies*, New Jersey, Lawrence Erlbaum.

Covington, M.V. (1984) 'The motive for self-worth', in Ames, R.E. and Ames, C. (Eds) *Research on Motivation in Education, Volume 1: Student Motivation*, London, Academic Press.

Covington, M.L. and Omelich, C.L. (1979) 'Effort: The double-edged sword in school achievement', *Journal of Educational Psychology*, 71, pp. 169–182.

De Charms, R. (1968) *Personal Causation: The Internal Affective Determinants of Behavior*, New York, Academic Press.

De Charms, R. (1984) 'Motivation Enhancement in Educational Settings', in Ames, R.E. and Ames, C. (Eds) *Research on Motivation in Education, Volume 1: Student Motivation*, London, Academic Press.

Deci, E.L., Schwartz, A.J., Sheinamn, L. and Ryan, R.M. (1981) 'An instrument to assess adults' orientation towards control versus autonomy with children: Reflections on intrinsic motivation and perceived competence', *Journal of Educational Psychology*, 73, pp. 642–650.

Deci, E.L. and Ryan, R.M. (1985) *Intrinsic Motivation and Self-Determination in Human Behavior*, New York, Plenum.

Dweck, C.S. (1975) 'The role of expectations and attributions in the alleviation of learned helplessness', *Journal of Personality and Social Psychology*, 31, pp. 674–685.

Dweck, C.S. (1985) 'Intrinsic motivation, perceived control and self-evaluation maintenance: An achievement goal analysis', in Ames, C. and Ames, R. *Research on Motivation in Education, Volume 2: The Classroom Milieu*, London, Academic Press.

Eccles, J., Midgley, C. and Adler, T. (1984) 'Grade-related changes in the school environment: Effects on achievement motivation', in Nicholls, J. (Ed.) *Advances in Motivation and Achievement, Volume 3: The Development of Achievement Motivation*, London, JAI Press.

Eccles, L. and Wigfield, A. (1985) 'Teacher expectations and student motivation', in Dusek, J.B. *Teacher Expectancies*, New Jersey, Lawrence Erlbaum.

Fyans, L.J. (Ed) (1980) *Achievement Motivation: Recent trends in theory and research*, London, Plenum Press.

Galloway, D., Ball, T., Blomfield, D. and Seyd, R. (1982) *Schools and Disruptive Pupils*, London, Longman.

Hargreaves, D.H. (1977) 'The process of typification in classroom interaction: models and methods, *British Journal of Educational Psychology*, 47, pp. 274–284.

Heider, F. (1958) *The Psychology of Interpersonal Relations*, New York, Wiley.

Jones, E.E., Kanouse, D.E., Kelley, H.H., Nisbett, R.E., Valins, S. and Weiner, B. (1972) *Attribuiton: Perceiving the Causes of Behaviour*, New Jersey, General Learning Press.

Kelley, H.H. (1972) 'Attribution in social interaction', in Jones, E.E. *et al.*, *Attribution: Perceiving the Causes of Behaviour*, New Jersey, General Learning Press.

Little, A.W. (1985) 'The child's understanding of the causes of academic success and failure: A case study of British schoolchildren', *British Journal of Educational Psychology*, 55, pp. 11–23.

Livesley, W.J. and Bromley, D.B. (1973) *Person Perception in Childhood and Adolescence*, London, Wiley.

Maehr, M.L. and Kleiber, D.A. (1987) *Advances in Motivation and Achievement, Volume 5: Enhancing Motivation*, Connecticut, JAI Press.

Mortimore, P., Sammons, P., Stoll, L. Lewis, D. and Ecob, R. (1988) *School Matters: The Junior Years*, Wells, Open Books.

Nicholls, J. (1980) 'A re-examination of boy's and girl's causal attributions for success and failure based on New Zealand data', in Fyans, L.J. (Ed.) *Achievement Motivation: Recent Trends in Theory and Research*, London, Plenum Press.

Nicholls, J.G. (1983) 'Conceptions of ability and achievement motivation: A theory and its implications for education', in Paris, S.G., Olson, G.M. and Stevenson, H.W. *Learning and Motivation in the Classroom*, New Jersey, Lawrence Erlbaum.

Nicholls, J.G. (Ed) (1984) *Advances in Motivation and Achievement, Volume 3: The Development of Achievement Motivation*, London, JAI Press.

Nicholls, J.G. and Miller, A.T. (1984) 'Development and its discontents: The differentiation of the concept of ability', in Nicholls, J.G. (Ed) *Advances in Motivation and Achievement, Volume Three. The development of Achievement Motivation*, London, JAI Press.

Rogers, C.G. (1978) 'The child's perception of other people', in McGurk, H. *Issues in Childhood Social Development*, London, Methuen.

Rogers, C.G. (1982) *A Social Psychology of Schooling*, London, Routledge and Kegan Paul.

Rogers, C.G. (1986) 'Sex roles in education', in Hargreaves, D.J. and Colley, A. (Eds) *The Psychology of Sex Roles* London, Harper and Row.

Rogers, C.G. (1986) 'Attributions for success and failure: The effects of classroom activity', Bristol, BERA Annual Conference.

Rogers, C.G. (1987) 'Attribution theory and motivation in school', in Hastings, N. and Schwieso, J. *New Directions in Educational Psychology, Volume 2: Behaviour and Motivation in the Classroom*, London, Falmer Press.

Rogers, Carl. (1984) *Freedom to Learn in the Eighties*, Ohio, Columbus Merrill.

Rohrkemper, M. and Brophy, J.E. (1983) 'Teachers' thinking about problem students', in Levine, J.M. and Wang, M.C. *Teacher and Student Perceptions: Implications for Learning*, New Jersey, Lawrence Erlbaum.

Seligman, M.P. (1975) *Learned Helplessness: On Depression, Development and Death*, San Francisco, Freeman.

Slavin, R.E. (1983) *Cooperative Learning*, New York, Longman.

Stipek, D.J. (1984) 'Young children's performance expectations: Logical analysis or wishful thinking', in Nicholls J. (Ed.) *Advances in Motivation and Achievement: The Development of Achievement Motivation*, London, JAI Press.

Weiner, B. (1979) 'A theory of motivation for some classroom experiences', *Journal of Educational Psychology*, 71, pp. 3–25.

Weiner, B. (1983) 'Speculations regarding the role of affect in achievement-change programmes guided by attributional principles', in Levine, J.M. and Wang, M.C. *Teacher and Student Perceptions: Implications for Learning*, New Jersey, Lawrence Erlbaum.

Weiner, B. (1984) 'Principles for a theory of student motivation and their application within an attributional framework', in Ames, R.E. and Ames, C. (Eds) *Research on Motivation in Education, Volume 1: Student Motivation*, London, Academic Press.

Whitley, B.E. and Frieze, I.H. (1985) 'Children's causal attributions for success and failure in achievement settings: A meta analysis', *Journal of Educational Psychology*, 77, pp. 608–616.

3
Intervening in Junior Classrooms

Jacquie Coulby and David Coulby

Introduction

This chapter is primarily concerned with modes of intervention in junior class-rooms. In particular, it covers curriculum interventions, management interventions and whole-school policies, and begins with a brief consideration of some of the wider issues which are involved in the notion of alienation in junior schools.

It is rarely helpful, despite the frequency of the practice, to spend too much time at the outset in terminological clarification. Nevertheless, the grammar of analysis in this area is changing so rapidly as to merit some comment. In the three years since 1985, the term for the phenomenon under consideration has changed from disruption, through disaffection to alienation. Although the present writers have played their part in these changes, they cannot be accepted without some reservation (Coulby and Harper, 1985).

The advantage of 'disruption' as a term was that it could be used to describe events in schools and classrooms without necessarily implying the cause or the responsibility for what was enacted. To the extent that it focused attention on disruptive incidents, it was helpful to those concerned to minimize their occurrence. The disadvantage came in shifting from the noun to the adjective: the temptation was to perceive not disruptive incidents or episodes but disruptive children or **the disruptive pupil**. This term confidently offers both cause and responsibility, placing them somewhere in the make-up of young individuals and therefore outside the province of those wishing to reduce disruptive incidents in schools.

To some extent, the shift to the term 'disaffection' can be seen as a corrective to the tendency to place the responsibility for disruption exclusively on pupils. It suggests that there are matters both outside school and within it which are leading young people to be discontented. It is thus possible for analysis to concentrate appropriately on teacher behaviour, school organization or the curriculum. Whilst this is certainly helpful, a slight sleight of hand has taken place. It is surely implied that pupils at least participate in disruptive behaviour because they are disaffected. Although the pupils are not blamed, a notion of causality has reappeared. Pupils engage in disruption because they are — it is implied rightly — dissatisfied with what is going on around them. This is an unwarrantable assumption: do all children who feel disaffected involve themselves in disruption? surely not; do all disruptive incidents stem from wide dissatisfactions rather than from brief and immediate excitements? surely not. Further, although the term disaffection leaves pupils free of blame, it can be used all too readily to blame teachers, with whom, after all, the pupils are so rightly disaffected (Coulby, 1988). Finally, the notion of disaffection allows the analyst to impute motives to pupils. Thus the righteous indignation of pupils who engage in disruptive incidents may be attributed to their resistance to racism, sexism or classism, to the elitist pattern of curriculum and assessment, to the unsatisfactory performance of national football teams or whatever drum is characteristically beaten by a particular commentator. Vitally important extraneous issues can then be causally attached to classroom disruption, making the pupils the little red soldiers of whatever cause is being espoused by the commentator.

The term 'alienation' carries this process one stage further. Whilst the overtones of disaffection are of righteous almost revoluntionary anger, those of alienation connect with the earlier paradigms of individual mental health. Discussion of alienation in the junior school might well concentrate on those aspects of life from which junior pupils — and teachers — are alienated. However, it should seek to avoid the creation of a sub-psychological category, the alienated pupil. Further, it should seek to avoid the dangers inherent in the earlier terminology of disaffection of imputing righteous dissatisfactions onto pupils. Alienation will only remain a helpful term so long as it allows concentration to be focused on, rather than distracted from, those elements in the classroom situation which can be modified in order to ameliorate the experience of teaching and learning.

This is by no means to suggest that alienation does not exist in the junior school. Racist, sexist and classist behaviour is experienced by pupils both from other pupils and from teachers. Curriculum material often presents children with negative stereotypes of their own circumstances. Authoritarian teachers and heads still exist who have no difficulty in generating pupil disaffection and/or alienation. However, it should be emphasized that not all disruptive incidents necessarily have their origins in such dissatisfactions nor that such alienation automatically leads to disruption. Much disruption in schools exists as the product of teachers, pupils, the school organization and the curriculum acting upon each other. It is possible to devise ways in which these interactions can be made more positive and thereby reduce the number and intensity of disruptive events.

Finally, it is important not to overlook the fact that some pupils' alienation from the junior school concerns the disruptive activity of other children. In its mildest form this can refer to those pupils who cannot progress with their work as well or as quickly as they would wish due to the boisterous or interfering activity of other children. At worst it can refer to those children whose school lives are made a misery by the daily experience of teasing and bullying. The reduction of disruptive behaviour is essential if the alienation of these children is also to be treated with due seriousness.

Modes of intervention in the junior classroom

To intervene in a junior classroom need not be to imply that something is wrong. Intervention may occur only in crises, but, as the next section on whole-school policy suggests, there are advantages in the school staff working collaboratively in order to prevent crises occurring. Such collaborative work is not of course restricted to encouraging positive behaviour; it will occur in other aspects of the teachers' work, such as curriculum planning. It is important for teachers to acknowledge that collaboration does include working together to develop positive behaviour and that those having difficulties or those with little experience are not alone in this respect.

Intervention, in this area, can come from within the school or from outside it. Some of the educational agencies maintained by most local education authorities (LEAs) have relevant expertise. These may include the schools psychological service, a local support team or the inspectorate/advisors. Openness to the advice of such agencies is a sign that the staff of a school are looking to ways of dealing with any difficulties and are not inhibited about discussing them openly. Nevertheless, there are limits to the kind of help that can be provided by people outside the school. When the actual disruptive events occur, they are rarely there. Their role tends to be limited to offering support and advice. There is also the danger that outside 'experts' may be seen as the repository of all wisdom, and that people within the school do not value or use the strengths of themselves and their colleagues.

It need not be a conflict between intervention offered from outside the school and that available within. The main resource of the school is the expertise of its own staff. Intervention is the active way in which the staff can make this expertise supportively available to each other. People from outside the school can be called on in a consultative capacity: to provide specific areas of expertise not available within the school, on the basis of providing skills which will subsequently be available in the school; to facilitate discussion within the school or with other outside agencies; to provide assessment and advice on particularly intractable or severe difficulties.

Interventions may be categorized under three broad headings: whole-school policy, curricular intervention and management intervention. A whole-school policy is essential in developing positive behaviour and reducing the frequency and intensity of disruptive incidents. This is discussed in the next section. The influence of the curriculum on patterns of pupil alienation and how this may be ameliorated are then briefly considered. The issue of actual classroom management is then discussed both with regard to the ways in which intervention can lead to improvement and in terms of outlining some of the repetoire of strategies open to the classroom teacher.

Whole-school policy

School policy with regard to dealing with behaviour difficulties is likely to be influential on the modes of intervention which are adopted. In practice this policy will be largely determined by the attitudes and stance of the headteacher. Important aspects of these attitudes include the head's relationship with the school staff, with the agencies and policies of the local education authority and with the parents and wider community. It is the headteacher who can develop particular approaches across the school, erect or erode formality barriers, and involve or exclude parents or external support agencies.

To those headteachers who base their authority on distance, competition and punishment, the idea of providing additional support for pupils and teachers with regard to reducing disruption would be unlikely to be accepted. It would be more acceptable where the head's stance was to lead through involvement and accessibility. The adoption of such a positive stance by the headteacher is often the necessary beginning to the development of a whole-school policy on intervention. Such a decision necessitates an assessment of current school practice, dialogue with colleagues, pupils and parents, dissemination of ideas and a commitment to sharing skills and the generation of common solutions. It involves the head providing a model of openness to communication and to a shared approach. It necessitates the energy to involve staff in structures such as staff meetings and in-service training (INSET) opportunities and to provide them with the information and skills with which to support each other. The staff as a whole can then work co-operatively to draw up a school policy which they will be committed to follow.

The benefits of such an approach include the ability of staff to share skills and the development of an atmosphere in which people can acknowledge the need for support. Again the role of the head is central. Where the head can acknowledge failure and point out ways in which other members of staff would actually have done much better, colleagues will feel more free to behave in a similarly open way. Once the notion of infallibility is eroded, sympathetic discussions about positive solutions can become a matter of course.

The staff as a whole need to consider who has responsibility for behaviour management. If, for example, the deputy-head is formally or informally the discipline person to whom children are sent, this practice is likely to de-skill other members of staff. Class teachers are likely to be perceived by pupils and parents as being unable to cope or incapable of devising solutions. Part of a whole-school policy, then, is likely to be to share this responsibility and to devise structures of support for all staff including helpers and supervisors.

Where prevention has not been sufficient and extensive support is needed, where, for example, a teacher has responsibility for a child who is making excessive demands on her/his time, skill and personal resources, the policy needs to include mechanisms for delivering additional help to that teacher. This could involve other teachers providing cover so that the child and class teacher concerned can have time alone together sometimes; for the child spending some time in another class; for the head covering the class whilst the teacher discusses the child with a support agency or with the parents; for the teacher being confident that colleagues will encourage discussion about progress and setbacks with the child.

It is important that all staff have the opportunity to learn about the range of management styles open to them. Resources need to be made available to facilitate change in the school. The consideration of — often frequent — disruptive incidents in the lunch time period is a good example. Some of the teaching staff might need to be willing to cover the lunchtime period for a week whilst other teachers meet with lunchtime supervisors to discuss the whole-school approach, to encourage their participation and to ensure consistency. Developing a positive approach in the playground might further involve the expense of purchasing equipment to give the children something interesting and purposeful to do during breaks and lunchtimes. But such expense might well save both teachers and supervisors the energy wasted on unnecessary and counterproductive confrontations. Similarly, a special activity can be arranged for Friday lunchtimes, such as a video or a disco, as a reward for all those who have behaved appropriately at lunchtimes during the week. This provides the supervisors with a tangible reward to offer and often leads to the children keeping a check on each other as they do not want their friends to miss the end of week event.

A cooperative and supportive atmosphere among staff is likely to be influential on classroom relationships. A less formal and more open ethos can be established. An important element in a positive approach to behaviour difficulties is the shared evolution of a small number of rules. A shared code can emphasize good, commendable behaviour and outline the inappropriateness of anti-social conduct and the universally administered consequences which it elicits. Consistency of approach to any such behaviour can then be expected from all members of staff. It is important that pupils as well as staff are involved in determining this code and that it is seen as being open to explanation or review. It should not however be lengthy or negative in its tone: its purpose is to encourage a responsible rather than a restrictive atmosphere.

An example might help at this point to illustrate the way in which an actual school involved pupils in creating a shared code of behaviour. The school was relatively large with over four hundred infant and junior pupils, many of whom were bilingual. The staff had been participating in INSET concerned with a positive approach to behaviour management. They wanted to evolve a minimum number of rules that everyone knew about, endorsed, and could consistently implement. They hoped that, by involving the pupils in helping to determine which behaviours to develop or discourage, that pupils would then be more likely to respect the resulting code.

A staff meeting was held to develop a plan and to organize the stages of pupil involvement. The following stages were then implemented:

i.   Each class teacher initiated class discussion on the idea of a set of rules to support a happy safe school environment.

ii.   The idea was formally introduced in assembly. The headteacher spoke about the need for rules and how the pupils were to be involved in their formulation; the pupils were encouraged to think about safety inside and outside the building in both physical and psychological terms; namecalling, fear and racism were contrasted with the things which make children happy at school; and the roles of pupils, staff and parents were stressed.

iii. The assembly was followed up in class with teachers encouraging pupils to make a list of suggestions for a code. The juniors were able to split into pairs or groups and record their ideas.

iv. These lists of suggestions were displayed in each classroom; they were also drawn together in a well-presented whole-school book which was made available around the school.

v. Each class then discussed its list, bringing together similar suggestions with the aim of achieving just three rules.

vi. A staff meeting then brought ideas together, focusing on the pupils' discussion skills as well as their involvement in rule formulation.

vii In an assembly the headteacher used the whole-school book to show the pupils each class's final three choices. With some leading they were able to point out overlaps and similarities. Fourteen rules were then evolved from the original forty suggestions.

viii. In class discussion the pupils were asked to select or vote to prioritize three of the fourteen rules.

ix. Pupils made posters and pictures, and two pupils from each class used these to present their three chosen rules to a school assembly. Following these presentations both staff and pupils joined in a discussion which finalized a list of four rules. The children were thanked for their involvement and arrangements made for the new rules to be disseminated.

x. Classes discussed the dissemination of the rules — posters, letters home etc.

xi. Again this was consolidated by presentations — visual and dramatic etc. — by each class in assembly.

xii. Work was displayed in corridors and the juniors were involved in composing a letter home to parents.

xiii. The rules are still periodically reviewed in the light of behaviour in the school.

The rules developed by the pupils of this school are:

i. We will be friendly and gentle with everyone and play safely together.

ii. We will be nice to each other about all the ways in which we are different.

iii. We will tell someone else as soon as we can if something is worrying us.

iv. We will listen to the adults who look after us and try to do what they ask straight away.

Returning to the issue of a whole-school policy, this itself will need periodic evaluation, revision and restatement. It will need to be considered in the light of the development of other policies such as grouping, resources, classroom organization and curriculum. A whole-school policy necessitates the development of a shared attitude towards the children, an acknowledgement of their equal rights and individuality. The point of the policy is to remove difficulties which might prevent any child reaching her/his highest possible potential. Its aim will be to skill children with alternative productive and appropriate behaviour.

Curricular intervention

There are a number of ways in which an unsatisfactory curriculum is likely to contribute to an increase in pupil alienation. The curriculum may provide some pupils only with the experience of repeated academic failure. For others, it may provide little stimulation or stretching. Alternatively, whilst being able to accommodate the different skills levels of the pupils, it may nevertheless prove uninteresting or routine either in its content or in the way in which it is taught. Finally, the curriculum may prove to be directly offensive to some pupils in presenting negative stereotypes according to gender or race or in offending the views and practices of their family religion.

This is clearly not the place to attempt to recommend curricular perfection for the junior school. Fortunately for the authors, the government itself has now taken on this task. What it is essential to stress at this stage is the link between what is being taught in the classroom and the way in which the pupils in that room behave. A child who is offered only work which is at an inappropriate level — be it too easy or too difficult — will become bored as well as frustrated and will be on the look out for other, more exciting activities in which to engage. In particular, the pupil who experiences undue amounts of failure in the classroom, whose relative weaknesses are regularly exposed both to her/himself and to the peer group may well develop a justifiable set of grievances against the official classroom activities. It is easy to see that such a pupil might look for another unofficial range of activities in which to be a star. It is less easy for those involved to see that such a course could be ameliorated purely by curricular change. Better still, an appropriately planned curriculum could prevent the development of this whole negative cycle.

In some ways this assertion is merely one of insisting on teachers' professionalism. The positive, purposive atmosphere of the classroom should derive from the fact that the pupils are busily engaged in active and stimulating learning tasks appropriate to each individual's skill level. Where such an atmosphere does not exist in the junior classroom, therefore, the first question to be asked either by the teacher or by anyone intervening to offer assistance is whether such a curriculum is indeed in operation and, if not, how it can be rapidly developed. Obviously one important dimension of this process is to withhold placing the blame on any particular pupils.

The development of a positive, purposive curriculum may be easier said than done, but it is possible to offer a few clear principles. Junior teachers need to retain the balance between, on the one hand, detailed planning and, on the other, flexibility with regard to the dynamic of the material or the needs of the pupils. The pupils should be involved in the processes of both long- and short-term curriculum planning. They should know that they have a say in what is taught and how. Pupils need to have equality of access to the resources and materials of the curriculum. There should be no curricular resource privileges based on either gender or perceived ability. Where parents also have an input into the formation of the curriculum, school activities are likely to receive a more firm domestic endorsement than can sometimes be the case. Active involvement with the local community can often provide that cachet of relevance sometimes harder to find in more formal approaches to schoolwork. A whole-school policy helps in the introduction of some element of selectivity in the junior school. Where weekly 'club' activities are offered, the skills and interests of non-teaching staff can often prove an invaluable resource.

Within such a curriculum care needs to be taken to ensure that the backgrounds and beliefs of pupils are not offended. The extent to which racist, classist and sexist material in the school curriculum contributes to the development of disaffection and alienation has recently been stressed (Booth and Coulby, 1986). Offensive and patronising stereotypes of working class or black families and communities are still too often presented in text books. The religious beliefs and practices of non-Christian children are still too often ignored or flouted in assemblies, PE lessons and the day to day life of schools. Girls are all too often presented with occupational stereotyping that does nothing to raise their aspirations or to enhance their feeling of worth in the school. The elimination and explanation of this kind of material is the responsibility of every teacher: it is obviously easier to fulfil in the context of a whole-school policy and mutual support.

Intervening in the curriculum in order to reduce alienation ought to be an approach most attractive to teachers, since it involves a central dimension of their professional activity and one where they can usually be certain that they, rather than some external 'expert', possess the necessary skills and knowledge. The only difficulty may be in believing that curriculum change can have this kind of impact. The answer is to experiment, to test the degree to which curricular change does change the atmosphere and behaviour in the classroom. Ideally the positive behaviour and atmosphere of the classroom can emanate from the activities pursued there.

Management intervention

In practice, classroom management cannot easily be separated from the curriculum. For most primary children management is actually a component of their curriculum in the form of socialization to which teachers legitimately contribute. It is emphasized that this socialization should encourage democratic consultation and cooperation rather than conformity and unquestioning obedience. An inappropriate curriculum can lead to an unnecessary degree of classroom management. However, the most exciting curriculum can lead to disaster if it is taught within a framework of poor management. A relaxed and positive classroom management is essential if a range of different pupils are to achieve success with their curriculum. Acknowledgement of special needs and specific learning programmes can be achieved in an atmosphere of enjoyed diversity. Collaboration, respect and interest can be stressed at the expense of competition and conformity.

Although this approach may appear to be expensive in terms of teacher and pupil time, it is important to remember that a more authoritarian style is wasteful of time in ways which are often neither positive nor appropriate — queueing for adult attention or pursuing and supervising pointless punishments. Many of the procedures suggested below could easily be absorbed into the day-to-day routines of any well-organized classroom. More detailed or elaborate techniques of intervention — such as the use of badges or charts — suitable for use with more extreme behaviour problems are not dealt with below (see Coulby, 1986): the stress here is on the everyday style of the class teacher and the ways in which, through intervention, this can be adapted to reduce disruptive activity.

Teachers' everyday language all too often abounds with labels: 'Zoe, are you last again?' 'Was it you who did this, Douglas?', 'Abdul is so naughty'. These types of comments not only advertise to the addressed child what the teacher's expectations are of her/him, they are also readily available to the peer group to adopt. This can lead to further use and reinforcement of the label. An alternative approach is to use everyday labels more positively: 'Frances, I'm really pleased with the way you've finished this so quickly'; 'How nice of you, Emma, to share those pencils with Jade'.

Part of the effectiveness of the positive advertisement of behaviour is in specifying what exactly the child has done that is appropriate. To know the ways in which she/he behaved will provide the child with the knowledge to be able to repeat the behaviour and thus repeat the reward. It also has the desirable side-effect of reminding other children of which activities are appropriate and praiseworthy. When a child behaves inappropriately this is better discussed with her/him quietly rather than identified aloud across the classroom. Alternative responses can be briefly indicated to provide the child with a choice the next time she/he finds herself in a similar situation. Adopting a positive approach will engage the teacher in acts of encouragement, high expectation, reinforcement and maintenance rather than in blame, failure and punishment.

Praise, as is often stressed, is one of the most convenient and immediate rewards that teachers can use to encourage appropriate activities and a positive atmosphere. It can also be used to defuse and reverse negative situations. Instead of 'Tom, stop talking and messing about', the teacher can substitute 'Tom, I liked the way you were concentrating just now — have you got a bit stuck? Do you need help?' This allows previous good behaviour to be advertized: concentration is the norm and it is uncharacteristic for Tom to be slipping from it. It also focuses on the curriculum and what the business of the class is, rather than being diverted into focus on behaviour and ways in which the class can be distracted from their tasks.

A positive management approach can be integrated with other curricular activities during the daily discussion period. Talking sessions can be the vehicle for dealing with unforeseen events as well as routine activities. Pupils can be called together for short periods to discuss individual or group progress; to participate in planning the arrangements for the day; to share evaluations, solutions, ideas and activities. In this way junior pupils gradually learn social skills and discussion skills alongside each other; listening, taking turns, expressing opinions and so on. Children learn to express themselves with confidence and the teacher has the opportunity to learn about the children's experiences and values and to demonstrate interest and respect for these.

Teachers are often more anxious than children about rewarding and treating some pupils differently from the others. If the class is involved in making suggestions to help one another and their ideas are given appropriate consideration and respect, there is rarely any resentment. Rewarding activities offer a positive alternative to punishment. Instead of punishing a child who is consistently late in the mornings, for instance, she/he may be given responsibility for an interesting and prestigious early-morning task, such as distributing registers or ringing the bell. Alternatively the difficulty could be explored with the other children and perhaps a solution found by them, such as someone who lives nearby calling in on their way to school.

Positive contact with a child's family can be exceedingly rewarding, particularly in those cases where previous approaches have almost always involved complaints. Parents can be kept in touch with endeavours at school via devices such as 'success books'. A specific time can be allocated each week when children assess their achievements in particular areas and comment on these. The teacher can discuss these comments and add to them her/himself. When the books are taken home, parents are thereby provided with the opportunity to discuss success and interests with their children. Parents can then make their own comments in the books before they are returned to school. A page from a success book (see Figure 3.1) demonstrates the involvement of teacher, pupil and parents.

The organization of the layout of the classroom is an important component of a positive management approach. The practices of the classroom are dependent on the layout: is there sufficient space to move about without disturbing people? is there space to display materials? where can children gather informally? For many junior teachers their desks are no more than lockable drawers. Yet those who sit behind them risk children wasting time in queues and a distant, less immediate supervision of the class's work. The removal of the desk can lead to the teacher circulating, the children being more settled and having more space in which to work effectively. The room can be organized to facilitate different types of activities: some children may need to sit alone or facing a wall to aid their concentration on certain tasks; some may like to work on the carpet at times. For children to accept communal ownership of the classroom, it is helpful if they can contribute to its maintenance, its layout, displays and character. If these responsibilities are assessed and shared, the pupils are more likely to treat the fabric of the classroom, as well as the activities that go on there, with respect.

One of the advantages of mixed-ability, collaborative learning is that children develop interdependent relationships as well as the traditional pupil-teacher link. Children can work on a given or selected task with others as a couple or as part of a group according to friendship patterns, interests and skills. The teacher is then able to join individuals or groups assured that the rest of the class know how to ask for and give help to one another. Again the layout of the room and the availability of resources influences the degree of independence which children are able to develop. Children can be taught to gather their materials with the least amount of movement about the classroom. When children are able to organize themselves and make choices appropriate to their activity, the teacher is able to use her/his time to maximum effect.

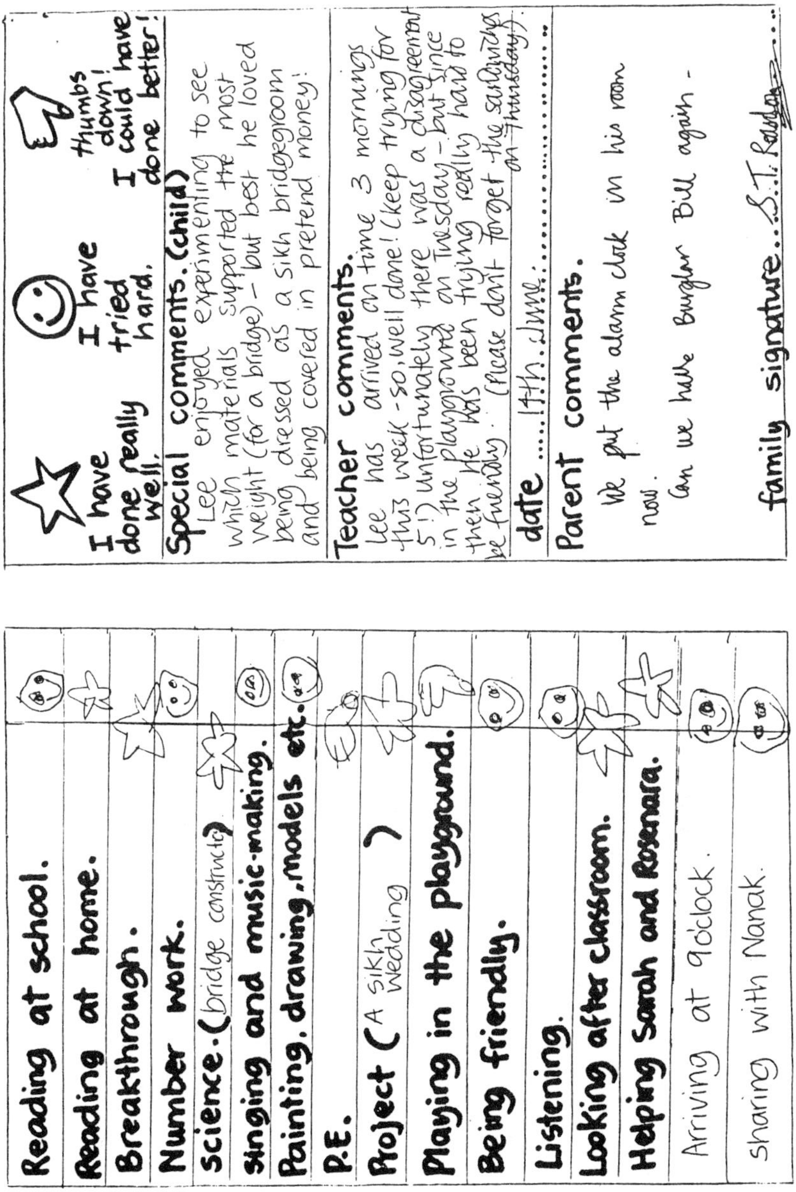

Reading at school.

Reading at home.

Breakthrough.

Number work.

Science. (bridge construction)

Singing and music-making.

Painting, drawing, models etc.

P.E.

Project (A Sikh wedding)

Playing in the playground.

Being friendly.

Listening.

Looking after classroom.

Helping Sarah and Rosemary.

Arriving at 9 o'clock.

Sharing with Nanak.

☆ I have done really well.

☺ I have tried hard.

👎 thumbs down! I could have done better!

Special comments. (child)
Lee enjoyed experimenting to see which materials supported the most weight (for a bridge) – but best he loved being dressed as a Sikh bridegroom and being covered in pretend money!

Teacher comments.
Lee has arrived on time 3 mornings this week – so, well done! (keep trying for 5!) Unfortunately there was a disagreement in the playground on Tuesday – but since then he has been trying really hard to be friendly. (Please don't forget the sandwiches on Thursday.)

date ....17th June......

Parent comments.
We put the alarm clock in his room now.
Can we have Burglar Bill again –

family signature ..S.T. Rashin....

Figure 3.1 A page from a 'Success book'

The tone of the classroom is set by the teacher who can employ a variety of general techniques to maintain a settled atmosphere and avoid major disruptions. Stopping children in their activities and asking them to listen quietly to one person provides an example. Difficulties associated with this can be avoided by having a jointly agreed general signal. Once a signal such as 'Listen please, children' has been agreed, it can be shared with any other adult who works with the class, thereby reducing difficulties for supply teachers and visitors.

Where children have become involved in a disruptive incident, the teacher can employ distraction to avoid confrontation and to re-settle them with the minimum upset. In using distraction, it is essential to avoid righteous indignation. Drawing away the audience is also necessary in order to allow the situation to defuse itself. It is often counterproductive to discuss expectations with a child immediately after the event when both pupil and teacher are probably upset and out of temper. Such discussions are more likely to be helpful and cooperative after the participants have had some time to calm down.

Approaches such as the ones advocated above should minimize the occasions on which it is necessary for teachers to exert their authority. Nevertheless such occasions will arise. Consistency of response is a practical component of the junior teacher's authority. Although, as suggested in the section on whole-school policy above, the number of rules should be kept to a minimum, once these are broken the pupils need to understand that a teacher, however busy, will always respond in the manner that has previously been agreed and publicized. When this is the case then pupils are likely to respect any requests made by the teacher, particularly if they also know from experience that the teacher will follow things up. Using a diary to organize follow-up can be a practical way of ensuring consistency. To ignore an incident which defies the agreed and accepted code can only teach children that with this teacher the code may in the future be ignored. As a consequence that teacher may well have to contend with increased levels of disruptive activity.

Conclusion

Intervention to minimize pupil alienation and reduce disruptive activity is in the interests of both pupils and teachers. For teachers working cooperatively with colleagues in this respect is an important aspect of professional development. It facilitates the development of new skills which will be important throughout a teaching career. It should lead to a more pleasant and relaxed job where the role of the teacher is focused on engendering a positive atmosphere and on curriculum development rather than on the negative aspects of discipline. Teaching remains an equally demanding task but the reward of the friendship and warmth of the pupils is more often and more obviously apparent. Teachers can be confident that the model of normality which they offer to their children is one of cooperation and approval rather than confrontation and condemnation.

For children, access to the national curriculum might be seen as a right. Some pupils need various kinds of special help to enable them to participate in some curricular activities and to make full use of their potential. Those children who have developed alienated attitudes and patterns of behaviour with regard to school, authority, adults or even themselves also need particular kinds of help to enable them to develop higher self-expectations and to contribute to their group. Forms of intervention in junior schools can provide these particular types of help without depriving children of their right to mainstream schooling.

But it is important to stress that it is not only these pupils who benefit. All the pupils in a school benefit when they can pursue their curricular activities without disruptive interruptions. Teachers operating in the context of a positive school and classroom policy are likely to have more time for everyone and more insight into a wider range of individual needs. They are more likely to develop skills of cooperation and participative decision making and positive and caring attitudes towards their peers. A more peaceful and purposive school is in everyone's interest.

References

Booth, T. and Coulby, D. (Eds) (1986) *Producing and Reducing Disaffection*, Milton Keynes, Open University Press.

Coulby, D. (1988) 'Classroom disruption, educational theory and the beleaguered teacher', in Slee, R. (Ed.) *Discipline and Schools: A Curriculum Perspective*, Melbourne, Macmillan.

Coulby, D. and Harper, T. (1985) *Preventing Classroom Disruption: Policy, Practice and Evaluation in Urban Schools*, Beckenham, Croom Helm.

Coulby, J. (1986) 'A practical approach to behaviour in the primary school', *Primary Teaching Studies*, 1, 3, pp. 91–97.

4
Relationships in the Junior School Classroom: Generation, Identification and Approaches to Disruption

Peter Kutnick

Introduction

Before entering the junior school, many experiences — from school, home and media — may have alienated the child from the process of schooling. Additionally, on-going school practices, such as classroom interaction, the structure of learning, and children's social development and expectations, may simultaneously create further alienation between teacher and pupil and between pupils themselves. This chapter will limit discussion to the on-going processes and will adopt a relational approach which focuses on the actions of teachers and pupils in the context of the classroom. It will describe the generation of a number of within-class disruptions, examine the criteria used to analyze the disruptions and question whether their resolution should be left solely in the hands of the teacher. Also discussed will be who disrupts, how disruptions are classified and traditional versus relational approaches to resolving within-class disruptions.

Currently there is a growing awareness that disruption is taking place at all levels of schooling. Classroom disruption may be due to a number of reasons. These include violence (in school, society and the media), social pressures of the classroom, and those increased academic responsibilities of the teacher which may draw her away from traditional pastoral responsibilities. Classroom harmony may also be disrupted with the implementation of the 1981 Education Act if children with special needs are brought into the classroom without the recommended back-up and support. The inclusion of children with special needs is in addition to the already extensive range of ability and background of pupils commonly found in the 'post-Plowden' primary school.

Such constraints imposed on the teacher may force teacher actions into a direction of overt management, control and structuring of the educational experience of pupils; an amount of work must be seen to be done in an orderly classroom.

In this position, teachers are less likely to identify *pupil* problems since they are caught-up in a multitude of *curricular* problems imposed by new and individual-ized curricula and the need for pupils to work in groups (Galton, *et al.*, 1980; Bennett *et al.*, 1984). Yet from the pupils' perspective, school may be the most stable and secure site within which to develop socially, emotionally and intel-lectually. The school thus becomes a testing ground for children's security and affection, taking on an overtly socializing role that has been abdicated in today's society (coinciding with the rise of consumerism, the breakdown of the nuclear family and movement away from established religion). The title of this chapter contains the word disruption, but we are really seeking to understand the pro-motion or abdication of 'prosocial behaviour' applied to academic achievement as well as social behaviour in schools.

Who are disruptive, and why give them attention?

A consideration of disruption in schools today must take into account social and personal factors which exemplify and direct behaviours displayed by pupils. Let us briefly consider the meaning of disruption, the frequency with which it occurs in the junior school, and the forms which disruptive behaviour may take leading to various results for teacher, pupil and class.

There are a number of psychological (pertaining to the individual pupil and family background) and sociological (relating to social class, gender, ability, etc.) factors in the explanation of school behaviour. We should be aware that initial entry into the school represents a movement away from the familiar, ego-enhancing development of the home to an institutional context of bureaucratic and formal rulings, learning with a large number of other children and being taught by an adult to whom the child is not related. Any number of writers have identified the school as an institution based upon and generating norms, rules and guides for appropriate behaviour. Dreeban (1963) has written of the *bureaucratic norms* of schools. Docking (1987) has noted that schooling is fundamentally a problem of 'order'. Alexander (1984) suggests that it would be impossible to imagine a school without *rules*. A closer view of normative schooling places classroom teachers at the chalkface of this institutional concern; they represent school policy and may be said to be the 'purveyors' of norms to pupils. It must be noted that these norms are de-scribed both as social behavioural standards as well as standards of academic achievement and development. A number of studies show that teachers take this representative responsibility seriously. Fontana (1981) states that control of behaviour in the classroom is the biggest cause of teacher anxiety leading to teacher stress.

The teacher's role in the provision of school order may be exemplified in two respects: the pupil's perception of the teacher's role in the classroom and obser-vational studies of classroom action. Studies concerning children's perception of the teacher consistently show responsibilities to include academic/instructional and behavioural control aspects (Morrison and McIntyre, 1971; Kutnick, 1983), although there is a developmental qualification to this recognition. Children's understanding of the classroom and teacher is derived from the actual experience in which they participate, a practical and theoretical point which will be discussed later. Why the teacher is such a focus of responsibility for the child may be explained by past association of adults (from the home) with power and authority, and by studies of classroom action in the junior school in which an 'asymmetry' between the actions of teacher and pupil was identified (Galton, *et al.*, 1980).

Teachers are under traditional pressures and expectations to present knowledge and information to children while being responsible for their social behaviour. Teachers must function within the confines of established school rules and policies which provide normative expectations of academic and social performance of pupil behaviour; they are aware and accountable to, for example, the Head, parents, governors and inspectors. The norms set up a range of acceptable behaviours for the pupil, and any acknowledged deviation from that range will be identified as a 'disruption' (Galloway *et al.*, 1982). In effect, norms and the deviation from them generate an interactional definition of classroom disruption: pupil behaviour which causes the teacher to give an undue amount of attention to any one or group of children while unfairly limiting the amount of positive attention that the teacher may provide for all other members of the classroom group. Deviations from the norm are found in very high and very low academic performers as well as those whose social behaviour causes undue teacher concern. It is a fact of classroom life that, while teachers may hold a normative ideal of the pupil, norms are most clearly identified for pupils by their transgression; hence children learn about norms by breaking them. Thus a main effect of disruption is the identification of children's 'misbehaviour' and a reconfirmation of the teacher's role as purveyor of norms and sanctions.

Moving away from cause of classroom disruption, there are few clear statistics as to how many primary children are disruptive in their school career, what disruptions they present, and the longevity/duration of the disruption. According to the National Child Development Study, as many as 60 per cent of school children have been disruptive during primary schooling (Pringle *et al.*, 1966). But Dawson's (1987) representative survey of Barnseley found that only 6 per cent of the primary and secondary students caused a 'high degree of concern' for their teachers. Merrett and Wheldall's (1987) survey of junior schools found that 62 per cent of the teachers participating were concerned that too much time was spent on disruption. Disruption and violence appear to be increasing in seriousness, but there is little evidence that the actual number of disruptive incidents in the classroom has increased over the last few decades (Galloway *et al.*, 1982). Particular types of disruption do change with time, and teachers will expect that the type of incident causing disruption will change with current media 'fads'.

Disruptions found in the classroom may be explained by a range of theories ranging from personal background to social structure. Disruption may be accounted for by: emotional difficulties, learning difficulties, insecurity, boredom and lack of confidence of pupils (Stoker, 1983). One listing of behaviours that are the cause of disruption includes: school phobia, school absenteeism, giftedness, deviance, varying rates of physical maturity, and learning disabilities (Kutnick, 1988). Not all the particular behaviours in the listing appear within the confines of the classroom, but the amount of attention that a teacher must provide for these children obviously detracts from the amount of attention that is available for the rest of the pupils.

Evidence of disruptions in the classroom cannot focus solely on an isolated individual. Behaviours identified as disruptive are the product of a social comparison between a pupil and other pupils, and between that pupil and the social norms imposed in the classroom. Classroom disruptions are also undertaken with other children, such as bullying in the playground, resulting in enhancement of personal and group reputations (Emler, 1984). Thus, there are a range of behaviours that are potentially disruptive and not all of the behaviours are the same. This range of behaviours has prompted the author to construct a matrix for the identification of disruptions (see Figure 4.1) which questions whether the disruption is short or long-term and whether it may have a personal or social cause. Minimally, the matrix should indicate that each category of disruption be reacted to with a distinct understanding and therapy. Educators are reminded not to make quick, one-off judgements concerning disruption. They must be sensitive to the variations and longevity of disruption before choosing an appropriate action in response.

Figure 4.1   Matrix of characteristics of disruptive behaviour

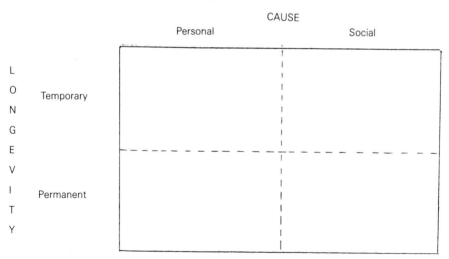

Source: adapted from Kutnick, 1988, p. 205.

Pupil disruption is identified by some conflict between the child and the teacher or the child and other children, but always between the child and an associated norm. Conflicts have to do with the expectations that groups and individuals hold about one another. Teachers, for their part, have certain expectations about the ideal pupil. Teacher expectation has been associated throughout the literature with attitudes and prejudices which may help or hinder the child's educational development (Rogers, 1982). The child who is attentive, helpful, clean and generally conforming to teacher demands will present few signs of disruption, and will often be overlooked in classroom discourse when assertive children make overwhelming demands on teacher attention. This process was found in Pollard's (1985) interviews with junior school teachers who stated a preference for children with a little 'spunk' rather than passive conformers. Variation in classroom conformity is also said to underlie gender and social class differences, which are associated with teacher preference (Worrell, *et al.*, 1988). There is a developmental qualification to expectation by teachers: teachers will accept behaviours, such as talking and movement around the classroom, in younger pupils that are not accepted in older pupils. Pupils also maintain expectations of their teachers. Nash (1973), through the technique of interpersonal construct elicitation, found preference for teachers with the ability to keep order, teach, explain, interest, be fair and friendly. Teachers were expected to maintain social and academic control using strict and passive techniques. Pupils will also give credence to their teacher depending on whether they perceive the teacher as being central to their career development or whether they have had time to develop alternatives to teacher authority.

To exemplify the above discussion let us focus on two aspects of today's classrooms: talk and movement. Merrett and Wheldall (1987) have surveyed troublesome classroom behaviours in junior schools. The most frequently cited problem behaviours were 'talking out of turn' and 'hindering other children'. There behaviours were interpersonal concerns, and involved children potentially disturbing others by their movements around the classroom and untimely verbalizations. Throughout their schooling careers, children have been taught to talk and many classrooms use the integrated day and topic work which necessitates movement. But the same talk and movement may become out of hand, by the teacher's definition, and these actions are labelled disruptive. Benefits and drawbacks of talk and movement in individualized and grouped classes are displayed in Figure 4.2, which is based on several observational research studies of primary school classrooms (Galton, *et al.*, 1980; Bennett *et al.*, 1984).

A great many activities in the classroom are potential points of conflict due to the differing expectations and needs of teacher and child. Reasons for these conflicts include differing perspectives of teacher and pupil, development and social comparisons. Differing perspectives are explained by terms such as discipline and control; teachers expect pupils to show self-discipline and self-control and pupils expect teachers to maintain control and be the focus of discipline. Development will be discussed in a later section of this chapter.

Social comparisons are the inevitable product and confirmation of classroom routine and disruption. As identities of children are established, by their similarity to and dissimilarity from their peers, any point upon which children may compare themselves becomes central to the generation of classroom disruptions. Social

Figure 4.2   An example of the relative benefits (above the diagonal) and drawbacks (below the diagonal) of talk and movement in individual and group oriented classrooms

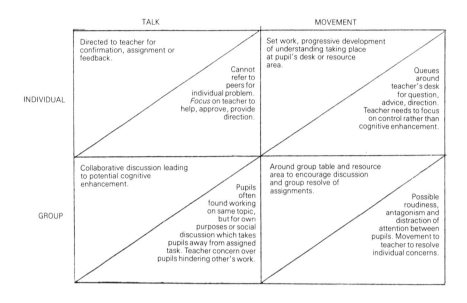

identities are then confirmed between the groups; pupils know one another as being similar to or dissimilar from themselves and preference is expressed for an 'in-group' as opposed to an 'out-group' (Tajfel, 1978). It is both curious and a statement of classroom fact that any form of assessment, whether by number of reading books read, score of a spelling test, or examination result, provides pupils with an insight into the differentials between themselves. The differentials are used to form groupings or 'cliques' of pupils. Sociometric studies by both Nash (1973) and Pollard (1985) have found that children will normally have preferred associates in their classrooms, and these cliques are easily recognizable by ability grouping (the groups tend to be formed on the basis of high, low and middle ability, with a few classroom outcasts who are not invited into any clique). As cliques are generated in association with assessment and evaluation in the classroom, we should also be aware of differentiation between cliques. Initially, teacher sponsored identification of success and failure will lead to an acknowledgement of differences and a ranking in the classroom. This differential information will be used to select cliques based on similarity (of ability). Children will also choose to stay away from others who are not the same as themselves. An academic explanation for this process is supplied by Pollard (1985) who labelled teacher identification of ability as 'primary differentiation', and clique formation, undertaken by the pupils themselves as 'secondary differentiation'. Children are vitally aware of ongoing classroom processes and this is confirmed in their clique formation and preference for traditional teacher authority; identities generated are necessarily a product of classroom action.

Classroom action related to disruption

This section considers selective areas of educational research on classroom action and interactions which exemplify and explain norms and the generation of disruptions within the classroom. The literature reflects actual experiences in the classroom, and teacher and pupil ability to conceptualize the process. Concurrently, it should be noted that changes in society over the last twenty years (including the down-grading of the extended family, increase in nuclear and one-parent families, decline in traditional role of the church, increase in consumerism, for example) has placed increased pressure on the school to assert a purposeful and forceful normative influence on its charges. Also, perceived increases in classroom disruption have been associated with the child-centred, progressive primary school movement. Given the weight of charges against 'progressivism' and the importance of the school in the socializing process, the role of classroom action and behaviour is central to the understanding of disruption. Studies of classroom action do not show evidence of the 'progressive revolution'; classrooms are found to have a strong basis in traditional authority and necessitate particular patterns of organization to avoid occurrence of disruption.

A normative picture of the junior school is presented in a large-scale, representative series of studies undertaken by the ORACLE team at University of Leicester (Galton *et al.*, 1980; Simon and Willcocks, 1981). Teachers and pupils in their classrooms were observed through an academic year. Some of the main findings were as follows:

i. While both teacher and pupil interacted, there was an asymmetry in the interactions. Teachers often worked with individual children, but class numbers rarely allowed an individual child to have quality contact with teachers.

ii. Pupils spent most of their time engaged in classroom tasks, and most of their interactions took place with peers. Their work was undertaken in pupil groups, but these rarely showed evidence of cooperation; rather children co-acted as individuals, doing the same thing at the same time as others, but not 'with' the others.

iii. The layout of classrooms appeared to promote progressive movement and practice, but classes were firmly under the control and direction of the teacher, who used many low order directions, such as citing a certain page of text, calling the class to order, allowing visits to the toilet, in their interactions with pupils.

iv. Talk between teacher and pupil had limited educational function. Talk between peers was not directed to the promotion of learning.

v. Classroom organization appeared informal, teachers grouped children and individualized learning was evident. But pressures of class size, reliance on the teacher to correct and support learning and an inability by children to cooperate showed these junior classrooms to be 'traditional' in the way that they functioned; the progressive revolution was not in existence. Reliance on the teacher for control, direction and confirmation of classroom learning reinforced the identification of school as a normative institution, with pressure placed upon the teacher to represent values and norms.

Another classroom study (Bennett *et al.*, 1984) focused on individualized learning in infant schools. This study has important classroom implications:

i. Teachers used individualized curricula needed to 'match' pupil ability to curricula demands. Children were assigned to the level and aspect of the curriculum which was suited to the teacher's perception of that child. As children worked on their individual assignments, any questions or misunderstanding meant that the pupil had to confer with teacher; peers could not be asked as they would be working on something different or at a different level.

ii. Children formed long queues by the teacher's desk to ask questions, seek corrections, confirm completion of the task, or request new tasks. Often in this situation, talk between child and teacher had little to do with the 'cognitive enhancement' that was to underlie the individualized curriculum. Teachers had to work their way through the growing queue, and were forced into a didactic, managerial role through curriculum and dependency needs.

The studies of classroom action show that the teacher is in a particular directorial role and that class size, curriculum and personal action limit the quality of contact between teacher and pupil. The asymmetry forces the teacher to act in a ritualized manner. This quality of contact has two implications. The first is that teachers can rarely carry out a lengthy, educational conversation with a child. Interaction between child and teacher is often 'functional' in that the teacher demands information from the child and the child responds as he/she expects the teacher requires. Children spend most of their intensive conversational time with peers, and most of that conversation does not relate to school learning. The second implication is that, under pressure to cope with their classes, teacher interaction tends to work in a stereotypical fashion. The amount of information that teachers must take into account about each pupil is immense. They are forced to condense the amount of information that they can process, look to ideal images, and question whether the child confirms or opposes that image (Rogers, 1982). While it may be functional for teachers to create and confirm images of pupils, this process does have the effect of 'typing' pupils, and creating the conditions of 'primary differentiation' as identified by Pollard (1985).

The actions and interactions between teacher and pupil provide a frame for learning and comparison of intellectual and social behaviour to norms. Children are aware of the actions around them, and these actions affect their performance. In a junior school study over the course of an academic year, Worrell *et al.* (1988) found that children acknowledged teacher preferences and differentiation between gender and level of pupil achievement. They responded to preferences and differentiations in actual friendship choices (cliques) and quality of interaction with teacher over the year (girls and high ability boys interacted more with teacher than low ability boys). Complementary 'reciprocity' of action (of teacher behaviour to child adaptation) provides a spiraling explanation similar to the 'self-fulfilling prophesy', and has obvious implications for children's self-esteem and image. A behavioural example of the spiral is found in Fry's (1987) observations of children who misbehaved in the classroom, were punished or ignored by teacher and lost the ability to achieve any positive reinforcement in the classroom.

In terms of activity in the classroom, children show an awareness of differentials from the norm and between themselves as identified by the teacher. But, before fully accepting this 'differentiation' view, a few cautions should be mentioned. First, we do know that children are very aware of the activities of the classroom and make use of any substantial information that they gain about themselves and others. As primary differentiation generates polarization/disruption, non-differentiation may generate a collaborative classroom by the same process. Second, there is a strong developmental phenomenon at work in the classroom; teachers show certain expectations based on children's perceived age and needs expressed over the academic year, and children's ability to adapt to information will also develop over time. Third, and with reference back to Figure 4.1, Topping (1983) has noted that approximately 60 per cent of the children who have been disruptive in school will show 'spontaneous remission' — they improve by remaining in the classroom, not being given undue attention for the disruptive incident, nor being labelled prematurely as disruptive.

Some social developmental and relational qualifications

Virtually all researchers in the area of children's cognitive development have concluded that children adapt to the experiences offered in their environment. An example of the adaptation of young primary school-aged children is that of pre-operations. Children repeat experiences over and over again before coming to the realization that it is the same amount of water and sand, no matter what shape container it is poured into. Similarly, if classroom activities and rituals are repeated throughout the year, children will act in their assigned roles, as pupils, and eventually come to expect the didactic nature of the teacher's role. A similar sequence of conservation is followed in children's adaptation to authority and rules. Most young children do not challenge this state of authority: they feel secure in it because it has been generated in a relationship of love and trust at home and transferred to early primary school. For most children conservation of authority is initiated in the secure atmosphere of the home and adapted to their early teachers, upon whom they can rely and trust, and an explanation for early conformity is established. But dependency on the teacher may not apply to all children. Some may not have had an initial tie established in the home and are suspicious of new relations. The school may become an experimental ground for these children to play-out behaviours — to establish and affirm a secure relationship which they have lacked. Simultaneously, these children may be seen to be antagonistic to the rest of the class, receive reprimands from the teacher, which causes anxiety, and be tempted to withdraw from class activities thus limiting opportunity to establish security and positive classroom relations (Glidewell, 1978).

Another developmental phenomenon of the classroom is seen in the child who enters school with more social experience than the other children in the class. Social experience for primary school children may be identified in their ability to communicate with one another. Because children's main pre-school experience is the home, they will have developed an ability to talk to and focus on adults. Pre-school children with advanced peer experience will have the ability to communicate with both adults and peers, and will talk to either with equal ease. For the teacher, it will be easier to maintain the attention of the adult-focused child. Teachers must compete for the attention of the other child. It is easy for the teacher to make an example of this child, for by citing his or her peer-oriented communication skills the teacher tells the rest of the class which behaviours to avoid.

Social development in the classroom is, perhaps, the key to understanding the generation of disruption and ways to resolve disruption. We are aware that the child's movement from an egocentric, authority-oriented being to a socialized one will depend on the quality and quantity of experience offered. Children who have few peer-oriented experiences before entering school will be prone to teacher dependency. Children with peer-oriented experiences may find themselves in conflict with teachers. But it has recently been found that children with preschool peer experience (mother and toddler groups, nurseries, etc.) perform at higher cognitive and social levels by age 11 than similar children without the social experience (Osborn and Millbank, 1986). Also, current research into cognitive development has found that children working in cooperative pairings tend to perform at higher stages than those that they are capable of individually (Doise, 1978), but they need to communicate effectively for this development to occur. Thus, the cognitively effective classroom is one in which a lot of talking occurs, with its contradictory consequences as displayed in Figure 4.2; and in which this talk involves peers as well as teachers.

On another social level, teachers should be aware that the development of children's social identity is dependent on the quality and security of their early relationships, which affects self image. Apart from experiences which may lead to a secure relationship between child and teacher, teachers are also responsible for organizing experiences which lead to the formation of cliques and subgroups. Formation of friendships depends on similarity and approachability. Similarity is initially and immediately recognizable by the child's sex and race (referred to as 'ascribed' characteristics). Additionally, interaction in classrooms provides ability and social behaviour bases for social identification ('achieved' characteristics). In classrooms where differentiation occurs, these stereotypical bases become criteria to associate with particular others and to avoid association with others. In contrast, classrooms based on cooperative groups have been found to be much less antagonistic and more interactional (Slavin, 1983). The traditional classroom is closely associated with the differentiation process, which will exacerbate tensions and disruption in the classroom. The cooperative classroom encourages the ability to work with a wide range of other children and the adoption of pro-school norms.

Well-organized teachers who plan for academic and social outcomes of their classes should be aware of the critiques of classroom practice found in observational studies, the potential of social relationships and how they may be structured in the classroom, and the normative system by which they compare pupils. The social, developmental and relational issues raised point to a necessity of 'practising what you preach'.

What can a teacher do?

The literature on classroom disruption indicates two distinct directions or approaches which the teacher may undertake when dealing with disruption, while still maintaining a well-organized and caring classroom. The first of the approaches may be labelled 'traditional' and seeks to maintain classroom order and discipline — but in a caring, consensual and considerate way. The alternative approach seeks to extend responsibility for learning and control beyond the realm of the teacher to pupils (and groups of pupils) themselves; one example is cooperative learning. Differences between the extremes of traditional and alternative approaches focus on the teacher's relationship with individual pupils and learning groups respectively. The traditional approach seeks to humanize a differentiated system. The alternative approach moves away from competitive comparison to shared knowledge and experience.

The traditional approach

Classroom order and discipline may be handled in many ways by the teacher. Pupils themselves have distinct preferences for particular methods by which teachers handle incidents of disruption. Pollard and Tann (1987) have discussed classroom control in terms of unilateral and consensual acts undertaken by teacher and pupil. Unilateral acts exclude others from decision making and forces them to comply. Tensions resulting from these acts may be eased if pupils are informed of the need for the act and allowed to participate in some discussion of its application. Greater opportunity for consensual acts leads to fewer instances of disruption as there will be less cause for misinterpretation and rejection. Consensual acts still draw upon the realization of elements of teacher control but in a concerned and caring context.

There are a range of strategies that a teacher may adopt to promote the consensual elements of the classroom. One study, a classic in the American educational literature, observed effective teaching and learning (Kounin, 1970). This study found that classroom atmosphere promoting learning and good behaviour was evident if the teacher showed a 'withitness' — not substantially differentiating herself from pupils, and responding to pupil ideas and initiatives. In Britain, Leach and Raybould (1977) identified aspects of a concerned and consensual approach as including: communication of trust and faith in all pupils; ensuring that words and actions correspond; modelling of desirable behaviour; taking responsibility for maximizing everyone's achievement; and establishment of good classroom practices. Leach and Raybould wish that classroom rhetoric and reality would coincide. More specialized behaviours to ensure classroom order and control suggested by Fontana (1981) include: interest the class; be fair and humorous; avoid mannerisms; avoid unnecessary threats and humiliating pupils; be alert and positive; show that you like children; avoid overfamiliarity; offer opportunities for responsibility; and (above all) be well-organized. Children will respond positively to this caring and positive relationship with the teacher. Burns' (1982) review of self-concept literature relating to education found that clear guidelines, standards for conduct, avoidance of censure and establishment of realistic goals for achievement results in improved 'on-task' time, decreased misbehaviour and enhanced self esteem for pupils.

These traditional strategies call for a planned and caring but controlled classroom environment. The extreme forms of the traditional approach were a critical impetus for the progressive movement in education. But positive outcomes of the controlled environment have been found to be the effective in dealing with disruptive pupils (Topping, 1983). One form of control is behaviour modification, the application of psychological techniques of reinforcement to establish new and sociable forms of behaviour. Behaviour modification is not a simple enterprise — it requires an agreement between teacher and child that certain behaviours must be improved, what the new behaviours should be, a programme of positive reinforcement to gradually shape new behaviour and an agreement on what can be used for reinforcement. In a paternalistic mode, Roberts (1983) suggests that 'one of the soundest arguments for setting up conditions for controlled behaviour in a primary school is that they make it easier for teaching and learning to take place'. But teachers must also consider whether the dependence engendered in a controlled and paternalistic regime will allow development of pupil autonomy. Certainly many children respond well to the controlled environment. Their response is indicated in the preference for a teacher who 'keeps order', is 'firm but fair', 'non-punitive' and 'not too friendly'. These preferences, of course, are based on the actuality of their didactic classroom experiences (as few genuinely 'progressive' classrooms have been found according to the ORACLE critiques).

There are further traditional strategies which can be drawn upon to cope with disruption in the classroom. Once a child displays some disruption in the traditional classroom a cascade system is usually brought into effect. Topping (1983) displays the cascade as an inverted triangle; the broad top contains all pupils of the class and the narrow bottom contains children requiring specialized attention in specialized situations. Disruptions handled within the class keep the child in a 'normal' environment, but detract from the amount of attention that the teacher is able to give to the rest of the class. Pupils requiring further attention may be partially withdrawn from class. Some children may be taken to special centres or be placed in a special unit. Movement away from the class allows for specialized attention and curriculum. As soon as behaviour improves, the child is expected to move back to the 'normal' class. Herein lies a fundamental problem with the cascade: as the child moves toward specialized attention, teaching and curriculum become focused on immediate need, thus limiting a general education. There is a likelihood that the child will become labelled as disorderly by teacher, classmates and self. Labelling may in turn lead to 'stigmatization', which will limit the child's opportunity to act normally in class. Even if re-entry were possible, the disruptive child's learning would be behind the advancing movement of the rest of the class.

A number of schools and teachers have recommended that children be screened for difficulties upon entry to school. Screening is an effective diagnostic measure for identifying physical, social and intellectual problems. Teachers should be aware, though, that some disruptions are the result of temporary traumas which the child may grow out of physically, mentally and socially. Too early and too firm an identification may initiate a labelling/expectational process. Certainly screening is important and necessary in physical problems such as hearing and sight, which, if not diagnosed, will slow the child's educational development.

Traditional approaches to disruption place great stress on the teacher and leave her in a contradictory position. Stress results from the need to work with children who are potentially disruptive while maintaining close attention to the rest of the class. In a pastoral sense, the teacher must be aware of problems, be a counsellor and a professional educator. Additionally, the didactic, traditional classroom focuses children's attention and dependency solely on the teacher. In the worst of circumstances, dependency forces the teacher away from creative and cognitive enhancing attention toward controlling and behavioural measures — which serves to generate more disruption and limits personal development towards autonomy. Necessarily, any sound traditional approach requires much organization by the teacher and a caring, consensual individual.

Non-traditional alternatives

The identification and recommendation of alternative approaches to disruption rest on concerns of responsibility and control in the classroom and the need to shift these ideal images from the teacher to the pupil. In traditional and didactically run classrooms, children are 'socialized' into the perception that adult authority is the decision-making, confirming, and comparison-setting basis to the classroom. But children can take responsibility and be fair within their own actions if allowed the opportunity. Examples of such actions come from as far afield as Russia, Italy and the United States. Damon (1977), in a small scale exercise of children aged 7 to 9 years sharing out sweets, purposely gave slightly more sweets than children in the group. He found that everyone was given one sweet and the group discussed how to share the extras. Without adult intervention, they managed to divide the extra sweets into parts and shared the parts equally. This type of experiment is reminiscent of Piaget's (1932) 'morality of cooperation', where children became sensitive to needs of others and acted accordingly. This cooperation took place without the directive presence of adults or leaders. The artificial imposition of an adult authority often hinders the discussion and decision making power of peers. The hinderance is exemplified in an Italian experiment on conservation (Girotto, 1987). After children were pre-tested for their ability to conserve, children were asked to complete another conservation task, either in peer-pairs or working with an adult. While all children showed some improvement in performance, the peer-paired groups showed improved performance and were able to explain why they had come to their decisions. The adult-paired children mainly rationalized their performance as an imitation of the adult performance, without the underlying reasoning. Bronfenbrenner (1974) has provided several examples from Russian schooling. He noted that cooperative activity and responsibility was stressed throughout. Instances of misbehaviour in the classroom were judged by a panel of peers, who attempted to understand why the disruption had taken place and helped the child resolve the problem rather than punish the offender.

The practices cited above come from a range of cooperative alternatives for teaching and schooling. Cooperation, as a planned and meaningful activity, shifts responsibility for learning and behaviour onto the pupil. It involves children working with one another on projects while developing a trust and tie to peers, in the way that children generate ties to their teachers, thus avoiding co-action. With this peer-oriented tie, children are capable of teaching each other any number of 'pro-social' behaviours. They are also capable of helping one another reduce anti-social behaviour. They can teach each other interpersonal thinking skills and how to spell words (peer teaching). These activities are at the root of thinking and development and lead to educational and social benefits (see reviews of cooperative learning by Slavin, 1983; Kutnick, 1988).

A cooperative alternative should not be taken lightly, however. It requires much planning by the teacher: structuring of heterogeneous groups, ensuring that activities involve everyone, allowing children to actually help one another, using group assessments so that work undertaken in groups is meaningful to the group, and allowing peers to develop a sense of trust and reliance in each other. A number of studies have found that cooperative groups enhance academic and social performance. According to a review of classroom based cooperation studies undertaken by Slavin (1983), as much, if not more, cognitive and practical learning takes place in cooperative groups, children's self esteem is enhanced, groups generally adopt pro-school norms, and children spend more time 'on task' in the classroom and express greater liking for their class and classmates.

Cooperation can only be achieved if a number of characteristics are adhered to. According to 'contact theory' (Allport, 1954) children must see themselves as working towards a mutual goal, they must be allowed the opportunity to get to know one another, avoiding superficial and arbitrarily imposed contacts, and they must interact as equals, avoiding the assignment of a leader within the group. Deutsch (1949) also noted that cooperation can develop if the group realizes that individual goals can only be achieved if all other members of the group reach their own goals. In effect, cooperation both grows out of and leads to further trust amongst members of the group; much the same sort of trust that children will show for and expect of their teachers in the primary school.

Conclusion

The previous section identified that teachers are responsible for normal and non-disruptive classrooms no matter which approach they adopt. Teachers are under pressure to raise children's standards of learning through responding to pressures such as the National Curriculum, testing, accountability and provision for children with special needs. They are aware that undue attention given to a child, or groups of children, will lead to unequal attention for the rest of the class. Disruptions are acknowledged as some deviation from the norm of the classroom, whether generated by the school hierarchy or individual teacher. Classroom norms cover both academic and social behaviour. A fine line exists between care, labelling, and stigmatization, especially as teachers must make quick and categorical judgements concerning their charges. They should be aware that many disruptions may simply 'remit' without specific attention being directed at them; the temporary/permanent, social/individual matrix can help locate and avoid premature categorizing of disruption. Outside agencies, especially medical and social services, should be consulted in the proper screening and identification of disruption. Teachers should be aware that there are a number of alternative approaches to cope with the generation of disruption. Teacher concern and commitment to progressive education will not preclude disruption in the classroom. Teachers are responsible for the structure of relationships between pupil and teacher and pupils themselves, as well as the content and portrayal of the curriculum. If traditional methods are applied, pleas for self-control and self-discipline are not enough for a class — the dynamics of individualization and differentiation in the classroom will accentuate deviations from the norm. On the other hand, a naïve faith in classroom groups and cooperation will not help unless groupings, activities and assessments within the class are carefully planned.

References

Alexander, R. (1984) *Primary Teaching*, Eastbourne, Holt Rinehart and Winston.
Allport, G. (1954) *The Nature of Prejudice*, Cambridge, Massachusetts, Cambridge University Press.
Bennett, N., Desforges, C., Cockburn, A. and Wilkinson, B. (1984) *The Quality of Pupil Learning Experiences*, London, LEA.
Bronfenbrenner, U. (1974) *Two Worlds of Childhood: USA and USSR*, London, Penguin.
Burns, R.B. (1982) *Self-concept Development and Education*, Eastbourne, Holt Rinehart and Winston.
Damon, W. (1977) *The Social World of the Child*, San Francisco, Jossey-Bass.

Dawson, R. (1987) 'What concerns teachers about their pupils?, in Hastings, N. and Schweiso, J. (Eds) *New Directions in Educational Psychology, Volume 2: Behaviour and Motivation in the Classroom*, Basingstoke, Falmer Press.

Deutsch, M. (1949) 'A theory of competition and cooperation', *Human Relations*, 2, pp. 129–51.

Docking, J. (1987) *Control and Discipline in Schools: Perspectives and Approaches*, London, Harper and Row.

Doise, W. (1978) *Groups and Individuals: Explanations in Social Psychology*, London, Cambridge University Press.

Dreeban, R. (1967) 'The contribution of schooling to the learning of norms', *Harvard Education Review*, 37, pp. 211–37.

Emler, N. (1984) 'Differential involvement in delinquency: toward an interpretation in terms of reputation management', *Progress in Experimental Personality Research*, 13, pp. 173–239.

Fontana, D. (1981) *Psychology for Teachers*, London, Macmillan.

Fry, P.S. (1987) 'Classroom environments and their effects on problem and non-problem children's classroom behaviours and motivations', in Hastings, N. and Schweiso, J. (Eds) *New Directions in Educational Psychology, Volume 2: Behaviour and Motivation in the Classroom*, Basingstoke, Falmer Press.

Galloway, D., Ball, T., Blomfield, D. and Seyd, R. (1982) *Schools and Disruptive Pupils*, London, Longman.

Galton, M., Simon, B. and Croll, P. (1980) *Inside the Primary School Classroom*, London, Routledge and Kegan Paul.

Girotto, V. (1987) 'Social marking, socio-cognitive conflict and cognitive development', *European Journal of Social Psychology*, 17, pp. 171–86.

Glidewell, J.C. (1978) 'The psychosocial context of distress at school', in Bar-Tal, D. and Saxe, L. (Eds) *Social Psychology of Education*, New York, Wiley.

Kounin, J. (1970) *Discipline and Group Management in Classrooms*, London, Holt Rinehart and Winston.

Kutnick, P. (1983) *Relating to Learning*, London, Allen and Unwin.

Kutnick, P. (1988) *Relationships in the Primary School Classroom*, London, Paul Chapman Publishing.

Leach, D. and Raybould, E.C. (1977) *Learning and Behaviour Difficulties in School*, London, Open Books.

Merrett, F. and Wheldall, K. (1987) 'Troublesome classroom behaviours,' in Hastings, N. and Schweiso, J. (Eds) *New Directions in Educational Psychology, Volume 2: Behaviour and Motivation in the Classroom*, Basingstoke, Falmer Press.

Morrison, A. and McIntyre, D. (1971) *Schools and Socialization*, London, Penguin.

Nash, R. (1973) *Classrooms Observed*, London, Routledge and Kegan Paul.

Osborn, A.F. and Millbank, J.E. (1986) 'Long term effects of preschool education', Paper presented at Preschool Education Conference, University of London, Institute of Education.

Piaget, J. (1932) *Moral Judgement of the Child*, New York, The Free Press.

Pollard, A. (1985) *The Social World of the Primary School*, Eastbourne, Holt Rinehart and Winston.

Pollard, A. and Tann, S. (1987) *Reflective Teaching in the Primary School*, Eastbourne, Cassell.

Pringle, M.L.K., Butler, N. and Davie, R. (1986) *11,000 Seven Year Olds*, London, Longman.

Roberts, T. (1983) *Child Management in the Primary School*, London, Allen and Unwin.

Rogers, C. (1982) *A Social Psychology of Schooling*, London, Routledge and Kegan Paul.

Simon, B. and Willcocks, J. (1981) *Research and Practice in the Primary School*, London, Routledge and Kegan Paul.

Slavin, R. (1983) *Cooperative Learning*, New York, Longman.

Stoker, R. (1983) 'Disruptive behaviour', *Junior Education*, 7, p. 15.

Tajfel, H. (1978) *Differentiation Between Social Groups*, London, Academic Press.

Topping, K. (1983) *Educational Systems for Disruptive Adolescents*, Beckenham, Croom Helm.

Worrell, N., Worrell, C. and Meldrum, C. (1988) 'Children's reciprocation of teacher evaluations', *British Journal of Educational Psychology*, 58, pp. 78–88.

5
The Management of Children's Emotional Needs in the Primary School

David Winkley

Introduction

There is increasing evidence not only that children's emotional and social needs are important to their learning (Pringle, 1974), but that a growing number of children have problems which, if not responded to, will become persistent and severe. These children are often alienated from home, sometimes from their school, from their friends and not infrequently from their own better judgement. Research in recent years has indicated, although conservatively, that there are likely to be around approximately 7 per cent of pupils who will present serious emotional behavioural problems in school, and this is a figure that will rise much higher in areas of urban deprivation (Robin, 1966; Rutter, 1973). In a study I carried out at a Borstal institution there was substantial evidence that a very high proportion of those attending the institution had severe problems in their primary schooling. Many of these young people would take their problems into adulthood. Apart from being unhappy as children their problems were accompanied by academic failure and a diminishing personal esteem. Once pupils have moved beyond the primary school age their social and emotional difficulties are very difficult to handle (Urwin, 1977).

Not all schools, of course, face the experience of the inner cities: but no teacher is absolved from the general responsibility of considering the emotional and behavioural needs of their pupils, or from the fact that they can expect that a significant number of pupils will need support and attention.

Normality and alienation

It is important not to confuse general disciplinary issues with the needs and problems of pupils with more persistent social and emotional difficulties. Naughty children are for the most part emotionally secure and well adjusted, testing the rules and constraints of home and school life as a natural part of growing up. Such testing is normal and healthy when kept within bounds and managed with balance and good humour. Most children learn to accept and understand the need for limits and discipline, just as football players test but observe the rules and accept the penalties involved in playing the game (Winkley, 1987). Pupils with persistent emotional difficulties often lack such balance. They neither internalize nor easily accept constraints. They demand and require special consideration, and the problem for the school is how to manage their behaviour in a way that seems both fair to all the other children and also constructive for the child presenting the problems.

Who then are these pupils, whose moods are not just passing, but whose behaviour is beyond acceptability, or who find it difficult to make relationships like other children? Rutter (1975) suggested that it might be useful to group children into (a) those children with conduct disorders who persistently misbehave, are disruptive, characteristically attention-seeking and slow to adapt to behaviour, and a proportion of whom may be delinquent, and (b) those pupils who find relationships difficult, who are unhappy, moody, easily distressed, often under-achieving, sometimes isolated and even bullied or bullying. Some of the children in the second group find school itself a problem especially if they are unable to manage separating out school relationships from family relationships. Within these two basic groups of children there are numerous individual differences with overlaps and interconnections.

I have, over the years, come to the conclusion that there are four major criteria worth considering in measuring the degree of difficulty a school is likely to have with children:

i. Is the child delinquent outside the school, does he steal, and has he been in trouble with the police?
ii. Is the child cared for and controlled at home, or is he neglected and out of reasonable parental control?
iii. Is the child's behaviour seriously disruptive or disturbed at school to a degree which presents management problems or general anxiety for teachers?
iv. Is the school's management of the child likely to be supported by the parents, and will the parents visit, take an interest, listen and support the teachers, including helping in managing the child at home?

In general, any child who negatively fulfils all four of these criteria will present serious problems, possibly to an extent where intervention from outside and work with the family may be needed. In my experience the fewer the negative criteria, no matter how serious the criteria that do apply, the more positive is the likely outcome.

These indicators are crude indeed, although they can of course be refined by supplementary data in all kinds of ways, but they do provide a starting point. They give some idea of the kind of difficulties the school and child have to face, and some guidance to overcoming these difficulties. From then on, the analysis must be carefully and subtly descriptive, examining how the child actually behaves, avoiding prescriptions and prejudices, giving due weight to intuitions about how children are feeling, and appreciating how individuals are not convincingly 'boxed' into a category where they remain ever quiescent. The borderline between those pupils who are naughty and those who are emotionally and socially disaffected is not a Berlin wall, and there is no substitute for the experience and judgement of the perceptive analytical teacher who is able to see one pupil's behaviour in relation to another's, and a child's behaviour one day in relation to his/her behaviour on another, looking for patterns, changes and above all signs that the child is improving.

A sense of success

It is important, both for the school and the pupil, to have the ambition of success. There seem to be three principal objectives:

i. that the school and parent, working together in the child's best interest, create an environment in which the pupil feels secure and valued;
ii. that children gain insight into their own difficulties and learn how to decide for themselves how best to fulfil their talents and aspirations;
iii. that the contentment and stability which arises from the first point leads to fulfilment and positive achievement in the pupil's academic and social life.

These are general principles but we cannot just take them at face value. We need gradually to build up evidence of success in the daily management of the pupil. This means taking the pupil really seriously, and being determined to do whatever is necessary to set the child on the road to success. It means keeping records of progress. It means monitoring the pupil by clearly observing his behaviour and showing sensitive and insightful understanding of development. Success will often be slow and uneven, partial and unpredictable, but we must be sure that it is happening if we are not to suffer self-doubt of 'sitting on a problem' for years, with a child growing older and less adaptable all the time. On the other hand we mustn't panic and there is a danger of expecting success too soon. Also we must be careful not to be overly disappointed when the child seems after a period of improvement to temporarily regress, thus giving the feeling that nothing has been achieved.

I can well remember a teacher despairing at a particularly upsetting incident where the behaviour of the pupil made the teacher feel that 'he'd gone right back'. This is where good records can act as a reassurance. In this case there was evidence that this was the first incident of this kind for six months and previously there had been an incident once a week or more. What was important was the long term diminishing of incidents. This particular pupil's progress continued and he is currently doing equally well in secondary school.

There are clearly different ways of monitoring this progress. It is useful, for example, to write brief impressionistic reports on a regular basis. The perceptive teacher builds up insights and checks and balances in her own mind, giving herself a 'sense' that the pupil is generally making progress. There are those who tend to spurn impressionistic evaluation, but in my experience the intuitive teacher can give a very useful commentary of the pupil's general progress. Such impressions, however, need amplifying with more formal evidence. Checklists can be useful here, particularly those which describe a particular behaviour over a period of time. 'Incident counting' is legitimate and useful in noting whether or not a particular behaviour is diminishing, bearing in mind how easy it is to forget a pupil's history.

Records of all kind can be difficult to keep, however straightforward they seem in practice. The demands of the day make precise record-keeping for a single pupil difficult, and there may be more than one person in a school dealing with incidents with the pupil. It may help to keep the records simple. It is useful to distinguish between each of the following:

i. Behaviour that is dangerous, violent, aggressive or thoughtless (such as stone throwing) all falls into a particular serious category. Such behaviour needs eliminating for the obvious reason that dangerous behaviour is wholly unacceptable in the normal school community.

ii. Physical aggression that is not inherently dangerous. Some children will lose their temper, make much noise and fury, but are not really dangerous. They will often be holding themselves back to a degree, not being deliberately vindictive or completely out of control. With these pupils fighting would normally come into this category. The vast majority of fights between pupils in fact seem to be bound by unspoken rules and pupils rarely hurt each other seriously.

iii. Verbal aggression or abuse, which has the effect of stirring up trouble but does not involve physical violence.

iv. Classroom disruption, including such irritations as wandering about, shouting out, throwing pencils around and bothering and distracting other pupils.

v. An inability or disinclination to work, or to concentrate on work.

These categories can be useful indicators of progress. They help the teachers to observe incidents more closely, and to focus on 'levels' of difficulty. At my own school the major first-line objective when admitting a difficult pupil to the school, often a pupil suspended from a previous school, is to overcome behaviour problems in the early, more serious categories. A pupil whose difficulties are largely focused on the latter levels is manifestly more manageable, however irritating the behaviour may be.

Analyzing incidents

It is a useful exercise to categorize an incident. James was a boy who came to us with a record of physical violence in his previous schools, having taken a knife to a teacher on one occasion. One day a teacher brought him to me, very angry, for violent behaviour. Looking at the incident closely it turned out that the boy had taken someone else's pencil, the other child reacted, the teacher intervened demonstratively, the child exploded (at the other child) abusively, the teacher put her hand on the boy's shoulder, the boy shrugged the hand off, the teacher then lost her temper, convinced that the boy had hit her. A careful reconstruction of the incident, which had many witnesses, finally convinced the teacher that this was an escalating incident which began in category (v) and regressed to category (iii) and almost to (ii). But this was not clearly in itself a very serious category incident. The child was not deliberately and uncontrollably physically violent or dangerous: he didn't go completely over the top. There was arguably an important element of self-control, in fact a possible sign he was making progress.

My response, as a mediator and, psychologically, as the father-figure dealing with the situation, was to reassure the teacher that the incident was not as serious as she first assumed. She realized herself that she would have managed the incident better by being calmer in handling it. The pupil recognized that this behaviour was unacceptable, and deserved punishment. Children often scare themselves by such incidents, and mild punishment and controlled reprimands are actually often helpful, reassuring the child that the incident was controllable and accepted and dealt with as normal naughtiness. This confirms for the child his own sense of normality, being part of the school and dealt with like other children.

The aim is to help the pupil to think: the key development is the pupil accepting himself that he deserves punishment. After that the actual punishment is almost an irrelevance, and should be little more than an inconvenience or a reminder. This is a true sign of insight — the pupil beginning to understand and developing confidence in managing his own behaviour, with help. The interview should then end, either immediately or at a later point in the day, with a definite re-assurance to the child that he's making progress. It could be pointed out that though the affair was clearly unacceptable there were positive features. He was not wholly out of self-control; the child had showed some insight. These were important signs of progress to be marked up by both the teacher and child.

It is worth adding here that incidents can sometimes be seen to have *patterns* — and recording is useful in identifying these. Children may behave in particular ways at particular times of the day or the week. Children are, for example, often un-settled on Monday, find Fridays (especially Friday afternoons) difficult to manage, and are particularly difficult at the ends of terms (endings of all kinds are often difficult to manage for disaffected children). Misbehaviours are often commoner at midday breaks or when supervision is relatively lax. Knowing this, the school can try to anticipate incidents. It is unfair to put a child in a situation when you know that there is a good chance of him not managing. If a child simply cannot manage, say, for example, playground behaviour then he needs removing from the play-gound and re-introducing on a progressive programme a bit at a time, until he can manage successfully, with each successful moment monitored. For although the focus, at this stage, is in a sense negative, with a view to eliminating or avoiding un-desirable behaviour, the aim is positive — to lay the ground for good things to happen.

It is by such careful reconstruction of evidence that a picture of a child's progress can be carefully put together. The teacher may finally find it useful, say once a week, to write a short review of the child's progress which might be seen by child and parents, particularly in the early stages of overcoming a child's obvious problems in school — with the emphasis here always on what the child has positively achieved.

Progress needs rewards, and a more formal record of achievement follows logically. The more settled and contented a child becomes, the more he is able to do, the more he will be liked, the more the positive features of the person become evident, like a sun shining after a gloomy, tempestuous day. It becomes easier, as progress is being made, to start to like and appreciate the child much more. It is important that such achievement, however small — in work, behaviour or attitude, games or art — is continuously pointed out to the child and constantly referred to until eventually progress is made on a multiple front.

On the other hand too much mustn't be expected at once. Children often have the cards stacked heavily against them. Small steps forward must be noticed and greatly valued. Gradually, then, the child will feel more sure of himself — and be very well aware that you as a teacher, and you as a school, are truly bothered about him.

A sense of success, then, is essential and acts as a reassurance to teacher, child and parents. It needs to be focused on with great determination — and underpinning it should be a conviction that the teacher is determined that the child will do well. Half-heartedness and ambivalence generate lack of conviction and insecurity. Disaffected children always seem to manage better with warm, positive, determined teachers who don't allow setbacks to get on top of them. Such teachers will allow some give and take, but will from time to time be as tough as old boots. They will also be clear-headed, patiently monitoring, trying to understand and give insight to the child. They will also be accepting, and be prepared to put themselves out a bit to have such children in their class. They will scrutinize their own management strategies and ask themselves the key question: am I the problem?

Managing success: the role of the teacher

There is an extreme version of behaviourist theory which implies that disaffection has a kind of causal purity which can largely be identified in the school environment. This seems to argue that it is useful to begin with the proposition that it is the teacher who might be the problem not the child. It is assumed, moreover, that disaffection, having environmental causes, can be largely overcome through manipulation of external environmental factors. This view, whilst having some merits, leaves me uneasy. The proposition in this pure form suffers from the indeterminancy and selectiveness of the view of 'the environment', which it tends to see as the process of measureable and determinable events. No account, in this version, is taken of feelings, intuitions, attitudes, and the gamut of subtle interactions enlivening the relationships between teacher and child or between the child and other children. There is in such accounts no attention to the world of feelings, the world which might be best described as 'internal consciousness'.

The behaviourist perspective has, however, value in encouraging a precise use of record keeping — linked with systematic rewarding and a descriptively accurate sense of progress; and whilst it can become narrowly and sometimes unrealistically deterministic in designing the pattern of progress for the child — neglecting his sense of himself as a person — none the less it works from the sensile premise that schools and teachers make a difference. Some teachers manage quite difficult children with remarkable aplomb. Others allow normally well-behaved children to regress. There are class management skills which make the management of all kinds of children easier.

Basic requirements

All children require a secure and calming environment in which adults treat them positively, firmly and with considerable respect. The underlying principles are those of good parenting. Rewarding is essential; consistency, fairness and firmness equally so. Beyond that, good humour, common-sense and an ability to relate to, and listen to, children is important. Some of these principles are commonly seen in practice in classrooms, and some are surprisingly rare. There seems to be a spectrum of difficulties in developing and implementing effective management strategies. It is for example, relatively easy:

> to like most children;
> to manage small groups with activities that children enjoy;
> to set simple classroom rules;
> to send children to someone else (e.g. the head, or parents) for punishment or reprimand;
> to apply very mild sanctions to individuals;
> to get angry at particularly unpleasant behaviour;
> to be nice to children generally;
> to be generally fair;
> to moralize.

It is much more difficult:

> to manage large groups of lively youngsters for long periods of time;
> to like individuals who seriously or persistently misbehave;
> to deal with serious misbehaviour yourself, calmly;
> to cope with children's anger without becoming angry yourself;
> to listen closely to criticism from children;
> to be sympathetic with individuals across a whole class;
> to reward all children equally;
> to be self-critical in managing behaviour;
> to pick up and attend to individual children's feelings deliberately and thoughtfully;
> to hold the individual needs of the child in mind in the whirl of the day;

to be firm with children, without fear or favour, but to encourage freedom and self-responsibility in situations where there's a risk of things going wrong;

to constantly adjust your teaching style to suit the needs of individuals who need (say) a more structured regime, or can manage a more open one;

to cope personally with day-to-day stress of dealing with lively, sometimes difficult, youngsters, retaining a sense of personal balance and self worth;

to admit you haven't got all the answers yourself, and may need help from others.

It seems to me important to promote the second group of skills and attitudes. Teachers with success in a broad range of the second-level skills tend to be able to manage a variety of behavioural problems much more effectively than those who broadly accomplish the first list, but have problems with crucial items in the second.

There are undoubtedly children who appear disaffected and difficult under one regime, whose difficulties substantially disappear under a different regime — so dramatically in some cases that it is easy to fall into the trap of thinking that all problems are indeed of the teacher's (or the institution's) making. And those truly distressed children who bring problems to school which are not easily resolved are invariably managed better and set on a positive forward course by teachers with the more sophisticated skills of the second group. They set about their professional task of trying to understand and then manage the child, admitting difficulties, but not externalizing, not blaming the child, or covertly implying, as sometimes happens, that the child is there, in some way, to serve their own convenience. The teachers who succeed are above all determined to succeed, and are not unduly impeded by occasional failures.

Some of these skills, of course, reflect the teacher's personality, and are very hard to learn and transfer. But there are some procedures and skills which can be more easily picked up. A student might begin by looking at basic management techniques, the use of rewards and sanctions and the role of feelings and insight in the teaching experience. Here we have bundles of issues worthy of long discussion in themselves.

Learning begins, however, through focus on the school as a whole. All teachers work most effectively in a school context which is rational, encourages mature skills and practice, communality, group-support and common attitudes.

The whole-school context

Success with disaffected children must be seen in the context of the management of all the children in the school. Rules and policies need to be agreed amongst staff, discussed with children and explained to parents. The aim is consistency. The school will benefit from identifying procedures which seem fair and which everyone understands, answering questions such as 'What do I do if . . . ?'. The staff need to understand the philosophy underlying procedures, and to be committed, fairly rigorously, to working as a team to implement them. The philosophy underpinning the management of the children needs to be based on the principles of good-enough parenting. I like Winnicott's (1972) phrase 'good enough' and find it usefully transfers to teaching (see also Bettleheim, 1987). At heart we are concerned with attitudes of teachers (and other adults in the school) towards children, creating, as a good home does, a consistent, warm, good humoured and co-operative environment, in which problems not unduly destabilize the familiar world. Even quite large institutions can think of themselves as families and learn a lot from the best texts on parenting. We might remind ourselves of the importance for the child of good experiences in schools, especially where experiences at the home are less than satisfactory. The aim is to create a culture in school in which children are listened to, respected and given some conjoint involvement in the school world. The school, after all, is *for them*. A sense of such caring is created through the accumulation of small signs: friendly contacts, commending, noticing, asking opinions, always speaking politely and thoughtfully, smiling. These build into a powerful set of clues and impressions. It is easy to assume caring is happening. In fact there is a great deal more most schools can do to strengthen the child's impression that we feel he or she matters.

It is important, however, that this sense of caring is not overly sentimental or romantic. The school must balance a hint of utopianism with down-to-earth realism. Not to be as firm and as demanding as it is reasonable to expect is to be patronizing. Beneath the effort to create stability and calm, there needs to be a certain toughness. It is the same in the home: 'My father was actually too kind with me, so I never had the experience of someone being really tough or angry with me, and when it happened later on it rather scared me' (Skynner and Cleese, 1983). This is a sobering observation from Robin Skynner, distinguished commentator on parenting. Of course such a remark needs to be taken in context: there is no limit to demonstrative affection, but there are times when limits need to be set and adhered to, and the adult is the boss, commanding and controlling the immature parts of the child. It might be added that for the teacher, unlike the parent, it is a professional job in which one needs to be highly conscious of one's own behaviour. Losing your temper, as a teacher, for example, is, in my view, invariably a mistake: 'OK, let me see if I get the gist of all this. Children need clear boundaries' (Skynner and Cleese 1983). So they do — but let's not pretend that any of this is easy. Success requires an odd mixture of tolerance and firmness that can only come with experience of managing a great many children of different kinds.

It is quite possible, however, to create this balanced, success-orientated atmosphere with warmth, good humour and through encouraging children to think for themselves. Most important of all, perhaps, is not 'speaking down' to children: you try to treat them as you would adults, whilst facing up to the immature side of their personalities. You need to listen carefully, to try and 'read' what the child is trying to say, taking complaints and observations seriously, as you might a friend or a child of your own. Such good listening — whilst it sounds easy — is actually extremely difficult in the maelstrom of the school day, and calls for an ability to hold the child in mind, to focus closely on his thoughts, to disentangle what is actually being said when he does not necessarily have the actual *words* to explain properly, and to use observations intelligently as a focus for discussion and communication.

The staff working together towards common approaches and attitudes provide the groundbase for managing even the most difficult children. The difficult child, after all, simply has needs which highlight in increased force the needs of all children: the difficult or unhappy child seems to need *more* of everything, affection, attention, containment.

Management and parents

Whilst it is not essential to ascribe 'causes' to children's behaviour, it is important to try to understand why children might feel the way they do: and the teacher, in understanding the management of the child, needs to see why parenting experiences might have been less than helpful. Parents are of overwhelming importance, of course. In many cases the unhappy child is deprived of good parenting experiences (not the same, it should be noted, as being financially deprived). Any school response which fails to understand this and fails to engage the parents in the subsequent management and support of the child is forgetting a critical element in the jigsaw of the child's needs. It is presumptuous to suppose that the school can resolve issues of disaffection on its own. A first step in helping to make the child happier and more settled will be to enlist the support of parents, and to bring the family as far as possible into the business of managing the child in school. This may be seen as a two-way process: the school may also be helpful in supporting the management of children at home. A recent survey identified 60 per cent of parents in our own school who felt the school had a key role — and could do more — in helping manage the child at home (Carrol, 1986).

The developing triangular relationship between child/school/parent is an interesting one that requires careful handling. Important questions arise:

The child

What is the status of the child when it comes to keeping confidences? What, for example, do you do if the child confides something personal about home to the teacher? What if a child behaves very badly and yet the school knows that if the parent finds out the child will be severely or inappropriately punished or that the information will put a strain on the child-parent relationship? What if the child protects the parents? How does the child feel about teacher-parent contact?

The parent

How does the school deal with situations in which the parent will not support the school — may even consort against the school in its efforts to manage the child? I can recall, for example, a parent who brought her enormous 11 year old son to school (a boy who reminded me of Kennedy Toole's extraordinary character,

Ignatius Reilly [Toole, 1980] holding him by the hand — and resisting any attempt to help the child break away to a sense of independence. When the child rebelled, she blamed the school. A curious folie à deux had developed that was extremely difficult to deal with. Neither the child nor the mother seemed capable of insight.

Another school I know had an entire family consorting deliberately against them, with preposterous expectations for their daughter, even demanding a cushion for her to sit on in class. Steadily her behaviour deteriorated, largely through her inability to make social relationships with other children. The parents blamed the school. Efforts by the school to control her temper tantrums led to accusations of victimization. The child's wrist was held during one of her performances leading to accusations of assault. All this in a well-off middle-class home, in a settled residential area.

Such cases seem beyond the scope of the school to manage in the end, and some kind of external intervention is obviously needed.

The school

Many parents would benefit from insight and support: how can the school best manage this, given the limits of time, and of teacher expertise? Is there a danger of the school taking on the role of the 'containing father', alienating the child from school as well as home? What is the school's role in dealing with delinquency *outside* school? I once had a case, for example, of two children who behaved well enough in school but climbed out of the bedroom window at night, breaking into shops or disorientating home life — and turning up back at school next day as though nothing had happened.

It has to be said that there are no precise rules and regulations to be laid down in any of these cases: responses to such questions are matters of judgement, and the constraints may be such as to make teachers' efforts little more than adequate. There are principles, however, which we can usefully consider:

i. Teachers have a responsibility to both child and parent, and need to take the fundamentals of good-enough parenting as their guide.
ii. The teacher needs to act in a supporting role and should not try to take over from the parent. The integrity of the child must be respected and there is great judgement in knowing how to act professionally in 'managing' children's confidences.
iii. Sometimes things children say will call for action which goes beyond the confines of the teacher's responsibility and professional skill. Teachers may need to contact social workers, doctors, educational psychologists, child psychiatrists and others for second opinions, or to engage specialist skills in the management of particularly difficult problems. The teacher must know the boundaries of her own skill and professional involvement, and remember that the younger the child is, the more can be done. Time must not be wasted. The decision to involve others is of particular importance where disaffection is found to be linked to some kind of child abuse.

iv. Teachers have a responsibility for managing the child/parent/school triangle, and while the school needs a planned policy to monitor the time commitment required, teachers ought to realize the value of giving up some of their time to developing links.

v. There are times when the school's good judgement in managing the triangle will have great benefits leading to improved understanding and mutual support. Schools can, for instance, help parents a good deal in managing their own children, both by discussion of the practice of good parenting but also by temporarily helping to manage particularly difficult (and sometimes straightforwardly naughty) children. In some cases we have had great success with a report card system, whereby the parent records some specific behaviour which the teacher and parent are jointly going to tackle with the child (e.g. not kicking Mum, or going to bed at a reasonable time, or coming in at night at a sensible time, and so on). The head sees the record card each morning at school, monitors the child's behaviour, and helps the parent handle things more systematically, and gives specific targets for the child combined with appropriate sanctions and rewards. The child gets to know where he stands, feels safer, is often less tired and irritable, and feels, underneath, that the school and parent together are really bothered about him.

Special attention and personal needs

Normalizing the environment

It is important to see the personal needs of every child, however difficult, in the context of the whole school and not as separate from other children. At my own school, we have tried wherever possible to include even the most difficult children in normal life and activities, to deal with them in similar ways, and to integrate them in mainstream education.

There are dangers in thinking of the disaffected or difficult child as 'someone different'. The mythology of reputation can gather round a child like a forest fire. Even experienced staff can become anxious about a child in a way that begins to set in motion a self-fulfilling reputation, when actually with difficult children it is particularly important to try to maintain a sense of containing calm and balance. Children who are unhappy or difficult don't thank you for creating a hysterical or overprotective mystique around them.

The paradox is that though the child demands your attention and help, it is generally not in his best interests to be obviously noticed, pillorized, categorized or marked up as a 'special case'.

We recently had a boy who behaved just like a Chinese emperor — peremptorily demanding his own way with everything, and genuinely appalled when he did not get what he wanted. At home he was actually waited on by mother and grandmother, whom he ordered about like servants. The key to progress was to ignore his selfish behaviour as much as possible, being very strict when it went too far into violence and tantrums. His 'performance' was a persona: there was a less narcissistic boy underneath who was shy, sensitive and weak. It was important to help this more loveable side of his character grow — and bit by bit, as he realized what we were trying to do, he himself tried to co-operate to overcome the preposterously vain part of himself. Here was a boy, then, who benefited greatly from the impression he was being ignored (even though, of course, his teacher thought a lot about him).

The child's feelings here are all important, and staff must think carefully all the time about what they say to and about the child, moderating their own feelings and their language, and trying to maintain a calm, supportive environment. Nothing is worse than the teacher exploiting her feelings of anxiety or distress through drawing in other colleagues in a dramatization of the behaviour or problems of a child: the outcome is often destructive, mirroring the child's behaviour. It does nothing for the rational process of the child's path to success.

Anticipating withdrawal

This is not, however, the end of the story. Even when the school has worked through its attitudes towards handling the children, and even in cases where the class teacher seems to be engaging in sensitive management of the child, there will be times when the teacher will be unable to manage, and where there is insufficient progress being made. There will be occasions when the child will benefit from withdrawal into smaller groups or even from individual attention from another member of staff. Anticipation is of enormous importance here. Questions arise such as, can this teacher manage this child in this situation? Is this child coping adequately in this class? Will the child manage (say) the last day of term, the school trip, the class party, the PE lessons? Does the child need more individual attention in a way that the teacher is unable to offer? Is the teacher under unreasonable stress? Do the other children in the class need a break? And all this, of course, is apart from the academic needs of the child which may accompany the child's emotional difficulties and require attention all of their own. The head's role is of course crucial here, and requires a mixture of being tough, perceptive, bothered, and gently diplomatic. The toughness lies in the preparedness to face evidence of failure, or the perception that in another situation the child might do better — without falling into the easy, the fearsomely natural personal trap of thinking that 'someone out there' might necessarily manage the child better than you — when you are really saying that you are too frightened, or lacking in confidence, or unprepared to put up with the inconvenience of the child to want him any longer in the school. Before rejecting, or admitting failure with a child, you need to ask yourself: have I really tried everything, have I made use of all the opportunities I have at my disposal?

Anticipation here means *planning*. It is no good simply responding to the child at moments of crisis. The head may take responsibility for handling behaviour that has got out of control, even punishing occasionally, but only in the context of a planned and developing relationship. Nothing is worse than the head becoming a kind of last-ditch prison warder, a time-out supervisor, with the child spending much of his time standing in gloomy isolation outside the head's room. The child's regime, even at times of failure, needs planning and preparing as carefully as possible.

Help beyond the classroom

Only up to a point can a class teacher give the distressed or difficult child extra attention. Once the teacher has convinced herself (and others) that she is doing what she can for the child, then she has a responsibility to find help outside the classroom. Too many children are referred on to psychologists and psychiatrists too late to be given maximum effective support. The rule should be — if in doubt, ask.

There are two indicators: the first is evidence that the teacher cannot satisfactorily manage the child. Maybe the child is continually acting out, playing up, disrupting the class at particular times of the day, and so on. This evidence is not always clearcut. This is because the underlying concepts are always open to interpretation. Teachers are not perfect: some are simply unable or not ready to adjust in the time needed for a particularly difficult individual. Some children are irritatingly predictable, combining periods of relative calm with periods in which they effectively demand the whole of the teacher's attention.

Other children have problems which are easily overlooked but which the perceptive teacher becomes anxious about. A second indicator comes from the child itself, and it is important here for teachers to recognize that some children have problems which are easily overlooked. The language of feelings — opaque, subtle, indeterminate — needs picking up. It sounds unnecessary to describe children as people with feelings, but it is surprisingly easy for adults to think of children as another planetary species in behavioural matters — as though they do not experience feelings in the way that adults have them. This was brought home to me strongly by an instance of a school trying to manage the outlandish behaviour of an 8 year old boy (unsuccessfully) by star-reward systems to keep him on task for five minutes or more, whilst at home his mother was dying with cancer. The way through with this particular child proved to be discussing his fears and anger and distress carefully and thoughtfully with him over a period of time, getting him to come to terms with his own feelings, and giving him support over a difficult period. The star-rewards proved unnecessary as well as ineffective. Children feel sadness, depression, anger, concern, vulnerability and failure like adults, and can respond as adults would to sensitive support and discussion. Children, like adults, are capable of insight, just as adults, like children, can regress into immaturity. Gerda Hanko (1985) is surely right in noting how important it is for a teacher 'to see beyond the behaviour displayed to gauge a child's needs which the behaviour may mask'.

We are concerned, therefore, to offer help to children who in one way or another signal that they would like it. They will ask for it by demanding attention. They may be depressed. Their behaviour may change, their relationship with teachers or friends may deteriorate. They may begin to steal. They may become edgy or silent, and the current concern with child abuse may itself indicate that the child needs counselling, consoling or listening to. It may be that the child has something particular to say. Or it may be that this is a mood, an unhappiness with a long history, which it will take time to understand. Or there may be *no* reason — just the child is as he is, and indeed we should not become over-obsessed with reasons. It may be that the child simply has a difficult personality, and wants time to understand himself.

There is, of course, no tradition or provision in most schools to offer much to children over and above 'extra attention' given by a sensitive and committed class teacher. The head and senior management and experienced staff can help by giving time, listening to and talking *with* (*with* not just *to*) such children. And in some cases parents may also be drawn in to help. In some schools everything will have been tried and the end of the road will finally be reached and the child will, rightly, need to be suspended. Thoughtful and caring schools that actively demonstrate the subtlety, order, flexibility and sensitivity of their handling of children should be under no pressure not to suspend such children at the end of the day. Suspension, however, ought not to come out of the blue. Schools should prepare the ground well ahead and act on the advice of external consultants — particularly educational psychologists, who at best act as acute analysts of the child's relation to the school environment, offering advice and judgements on management, determining whether progress is being made, how handling may be improved and so on. The educational psychologist will often be in the best position to recommend another school, or another kind of approach for a child. He can offer a contextual diagnosis as well as an informed personal view, based on the evidence. Suddenly announcing to a psychologist that a child has become unmanageable and 'nothing more can be done' is not the way to proceed. The school needs to make full use of the insights and practical advice a good consultant can offer. On occasion, too, the child may benefit from psychiatric assessment — remembering that a good child psychiatrist will be able to not only assess the state of the child's feelings, but also discuss the child's full story and difficulties with the parents, and at best engage in a sustained support and counselling service for the child. This may involve psychotherapy (often of considerable help in moving the child towards personal insight) and social work support for parents. This does not mean that the child is 'mentally ill', nor does it necessarily mean removal from the school. Patient working together of professionals in a sustained way can be of enormous long term benefit for the child and family.

There are many children who gain enormously from regular counselling from a sympathetic and trained listener based within the school. My own prediction is that eventually every school, primary and secondary, will have its own trained teacher-counsellor. The importance of the management of emotional needs, combined with increasing pressures on schools to offer a front-line listening and assessment service for children in need, including abused and unhappy children, will lead to radical reassessment of the need to offer a properly attuned response. For the moment, the priority has to be those schools, often located in the inner cities, with a high proportion of children from disordered, unhappy or unsupporting families. At my own school we have the advantage of a trained teacher who has built up a service within the school to support children with emotional or behavioural difficulties. The teacher offers support, through groups and individual counselling, to children who benefit from planned time out of class. She helps anticipate the best arrangements for the child, working with the class teacher on trying to get the right balance between small-group teaching, class teaching and personal discussion sessions. She also helps direct and manage the whole-school disciplinary context. Some children come from other schools (suspended, usually for very good reasons). Others are children identified by the teachers as seeming to need further assessment and possibly out-of-class support. Some teachers find feed-back on management useful, and having someone else to support you helps relieve anxiety and the burden of managing a child 'on your own'. The special needs coordinator also takes responsibility in serious cases for maintaining relationships with parents and keeping records of progress from everyone concerned with management of the child. She has her own base in the school, and is trained to use a variety of ways of 'talking with' the child, using play, conversation, and group discussions as well as supporting teachers in helping manage the child in class. None of this obviates the responsibility of the head or other senior staff for overviewing and handling the behaviour of the child in the school context. The children are continually monitored and expected to learn to cope with the normal school rules and environment.

Conclusion

The logical outcome of a growing sense of success is the ability of the school and the teaching staff to help a *range* of children with difficulties of one sort or another. Any school prepared to engage in the understanding and handling of disaffected children is likely to learn a good deal about itself as an institution. Equally the individual teacher will learn a good deal about herself. Vulnerabilities are exposed: the difficult child above all disturbs calm, threatens the thin plaster of the ego, undermines order and disorientates convenience. I have described elsewhere (Winkley, 1986) my own experience of getting violently angry with children and I am very well aware of the raw nerves children can touch. Some schools can avoid the distress of children by pretending it is not there, by rejecting problems — or by being lucky enough to have an intake of children who seem for the most part well-parented and good-humoured. In such schools disaffection may even seem not to matter or to exist. It is, however, rare in my experience for schools not to have at least one or two distressed children — and most children may potentially have unhappy moods that a school should take into account. There are, of course, schools in deprived areas that have little choice other than to face the world they are living in. In these cases discipline, attitudes, caring and understanding also become major issues profoundly linked to the success of the school as a whole.

But at the end of the day, a good deal of what the developing professional teacher learns through facing such difficulties seems worth learning in itself. It takes us into deeper levels of understanding, helps us handle relationships with children better, and gives greater insight into the nature of learning (for all learning is linked with qualities of listening, emotional security, openness, sensitivity of discourse, and feelings). Quite apart from our human obligations to assuage and face distressed children, there is a professional consideration: if as teachers we learn — easy to say but so hard to achieve — something more of how 'to act as if all children were equal and then respect as well as cater for their differences' (Pringle, 1974, p. 153) then understanding the disaffected child is truly worthwhile.

References

Bettelheim, B. (1987) *A Good Enough Parent*, London, Thames and Hudson.

Carroll, C. (1986) 'An analysis of views on discipline', Birmingham University Institute of Local Government Studies.

Hanko, G. (1985) *Special Needs in Ordinary Classrooms*, Oxford, Blackwell.

Irwin, E.M. (1977) *Growing Pains*, London, MacDonald Evans.

Pringle, M. (1974) *The Needs of Children*, London, Hutchinson.

Robin, L.N. (1966) *Deviant Children Grown Up*, New York, Williams and Wilkins.

Rutter, M. (1973) 'Why are London children so disturbed?', *Proceedings of the Royal Society of Medicine*, 66, pp. 1221–5.

Rutter, M. (1975) *Helping Troubled Children*, Harmondsworth, Penguin.

Rutter, M., Tizard, J. and Whitmore, K. (1970) *Education, Health and Behaviour*, London, Longman.

Skynner, R. and Cleese, J. (1983) *Families and How to Survive Them*, London, Methuen.

Toole, K.J. (1980) *A Confederacy of Dunces*, Harmondsworth, Penguin.

Winnicott, D.W. (1972) 'The capacity for concern', in Sutherland, J.D. (Ed.) *The Maturational Processes and Facilitating Environment*, London, Hogarth Press.

Winkley, D.R. (1986) 'The angry child in the ordinary school', *Maladjustment and Therapeutic Education*, 4, 3.

Winkley, D.R. (1987) 'The paradox of discipline', *Education 3-13*, 15, 3.

6
Responding to Disaffection:
Talking about pastoral care in the primary school

Peter Lang

Introduction

The ethos or climate of the school as a whole is central to establishing and maintaining high standards of behaviour. Where clear priorities are co-operatively agreed and pursued, the communal sense of purpose engendered is a source of great strength . . . . The school's ethos is based on the quality of relationships — both the professional relationships between teachers and the ways in which pupils and teachers treat each other. Where teachers treat pupils courteously, respect their ideas, value their individuality, and listen carefully to what they have to say, pupils learn by example, and are much more likely to respect teachers and behave considerately and sensibly themselves. (DES, 1987, paras 51–2)

This statement, based on HM Inspectors' observation in schools, highlights what in my view are some of the major potential outcomes of effective pastoral care. If this view is correct, and pastoral care does make a significant contribution to the effectiveness of pupil learning and the quality of their behaviour, then we might expect that it would be, if not regularly discussed in the primary school, at least an issue that arises from time to time.

In many primary schools the term 'pastoral care' is rarely used in discussion, and there are many primary teachers who have little or no idea what pastoral care means or what its central concepts imply. This is somewhat surprising as the term has been used in the English education system for at least fifteen years. Its origins can be traced back to the great Public schools of the early nineteenth century (Lang, 1983) and organization and related practices described as pastoral have existed in many secondary schools since the early seventies. It must also be noted, however, that in spite of this, and despite the commitment of many secondary teachers to the notion, statements about its precise nature have until recently tended to be pitched at a general, warm and supportive level rather than at the level of precise objectives. This in part explains the lack of understanding by some primary teachers.

In 1974, Marland stated:

> One can say that the phrase 'pastoral care' covers all aspects of work within a school other than pure teaching . . . in this book pastoral care means looking after the total welfare of the pupil. (pp. 8–9)

This is certainly a reassuring definition, but tells the reader very little of what pastoral care is about. Six years later the definition suggested by David and Cowley (1980), though more developed, is still expressed in broad and general terms:

> Pastoral care is an expression of the school's continuing concern for the individual's integrity and welfare, its involvement in the development of his personality and talents and its readiness to support him at all times and especially when his work is adversely affected by personal and domestic circumstances. (p. 26)

If the nature of care is as described here, it would appear to have considerable relevance to primary schools. The reasons why pastoral care, at least as a term, has not been generally favoured by primary schools will be returned to later in this chapter.

During the 1980s there has been considerable progress in our understanding of pastoral care. The concept was considerably sharpened when Marland (1980) proposed the idea of the pastoral curriculum. This idea formalized the need for planning in relation to pupils' affective development, both personal and social, and the need for some pastoral care to be provided through group processes. Previously, pastoral care had been perceived as being provided mainly through a one-to-one case work mode. In the pastoral curriculum model, content is developed in response to identified needs, the stress is on proaction rather than reaction, and pastoral care is concerned with the development of all pupils rather than just those with problems. As the concept developed it was recognized that a fully developed pastoral curriculum has implications for whole-school policies, ethos and climate, and in particular the hidden curriculum (Lang, 1988; Bulman and Jenkins, 1988).

Typical of the way the pastoral curriculum is now construed at secondary level is the following view:

> Conceived more broadly, the pastoral curriculum is an altogether more significant development than the advent of structured tutorial programmes, encompassing all those parts of the curriculum more often seen as health, social, careers or moral education. More recently the development of programmes of life and social skills and personal and social education may be seen as an important move towards a holistically conceived pastoral or welfare curriculum. (Bell and Best, 1986, p. 89)

Again, such a concept has such obvious relevance to the primary school that it is surprising to find it almost totally ignored. These increasingly developed conceptions of the pastoral curriculum have incorporated the idea that, through such provision and the resulting promotion of positive school climate and ethos, not only will the healthy personal development of all pupils be encouraged but problems of pupil disaffection and disruption ameliorated. This, it is suggested, will happen partly as a result of the more positive feelings that pupils will develop about themselves and partly as a result of the schools' organization and ethos being less likely to aggravate problems. In short, strategies for addressing problems such as disaffection and disruption can only work effectively within a broad positive framework. This is why the concerns of this book and those of pastoral care merge, and why I am suggesting that pastoral care has much to offer the primary school.

From this standpoint I shall argue that talking about pastoral care in the primary school should involve all staff and should be systematic and explicit. I take this view not because I seek to suggest that pastoral care is necessarily the right term to describe what ought to happen in this area in the primary school, but because the concerns which it represents and the areas it covers provide the most comprehensive and challenging initial focus. For it is only through consciously addressing the questions raised by the term and its relationship to other closely related usages that a number of key issues will be brought into the open. These issues of care and the promotion of personal, social and moral development, concern not only what we are doing and shouldn't be, but also what we are not doing and should be. Indeed, it may be that some of our implicit practices actually promote some of the problems with which we are concerned. It is only when the issues are recognized that effective responses can be developed and a basis provided for the sort of planned and structured class and school approaches that I believe are central to the promotion of this aspect of the education of all pupils, particularly those encountering and creating difficulties of an emotional, attitudinal and behavioural nature.

The pressures and constraints imposed by the national curriculum make it especially vital that such processes take place. The view which has often been quoted to me by primary teachers, 'surely all this is caught not taught?', is not, in my view, acceptable, and 'but this happens automatically and doesn't need to be planned and understood' is even less so.

In this chapter I propose to provide a blueprint for action which I hope will both stimulate thinking about pastoral care and lead to a discussion on the elements of an agenda for action. Of course, it is for individual schools to construct their actual agenda and to act upon it, and if they choose to describe their thoughts and actions under an alternative name this is of no particular significance.

The meaning of pastoral care

So far, I have made some claims for the value of pastoral care but have only provided fairly general statements about what it means. Before considering the contribution of pastoral care to the handling of disaffection and disruptive behaviour, a fuller understanding of its nature and potential relationship to the primary school will be helpful. I wish, therefore, to consider some further material to clarify this. I will then present my own view of its key elements in relation to the primary school and raise some specific issues before moving to a consideration of the ways a pastoral approach can underpin the effective handling of disaffection and disruption in the primary school. As a starting point I shall use an example drawn from an official publication issued by the Ministry of Education in Ontario, Canada:

Encouraging affective development

The suggestions that follow are designed to assist the teacher to develop and maintain a positive classroom environment and to manage specific behavioural difficulties that may arise. These suggestions are all based on the premise that positive behaviour is more likely to occur when students are given the opportunity to develop a sense of belonging and an identity within the school environment. The teacher who assists a student to internalise feelings of competence and self-reliance may significantly affect that student's participation in, commitment to, and ability to benefit from the learning experience. The self-confidence that ultimately results from ongoing successful experience can provide the foundation for the student to effectively direct his or her own behaviour to meet future demands of an academic or social nature. (Ministry of Education, Ontario, 1986)

The above extract spells out the link between pastoral care, positive behaviour and effective learning. Though the central concern is a response to the problems of disruption, it is suggested that any response to inappropriate behaviour and disaffection should not only involve strategies for handling it, when it arises, but also an overall policy for promoting the affective development of all pupils. Among other things, this will serve to decrease the number of cases where specific problems arise with particular individuals, problems which may ultimately manifest themselves as attitudinal and behaviour difficulties. Such a stress on the relation between the promotion of positive climate, effective learning and the reduction of pupils' problems is exactly the relation on which current thinking about pastoral care and the pastoral curriculum would lay considerable stress. Equally both the Ontario statement and the pastoral perspective suggest that responses to problems of disaffection and disruption, when taken in isolation without concern for their broader context, are at best likely to be ineffective and at worst counterproductive. The above extract illustrates how the concerns of pastoral care are found in other places under different names, for the term 'pastoral care' does not feature at all.

To pursue this line further the following extract, also from Canada, illustrates the point specifically with respect to the concerns of the primary school:

Self-esteem is cumulative. The concept of the self grows out of the child's early interactions with significant others and continues throughout the early school years. The family has a powerful impact on the formulation of the self-concept and self-esteem but so do teachers, friends, and other powerful socializing agents such as the media. Therefore the learning environment in school can have a marked effect on helping to build self-esteem or in undermining it. Teachers and counsellors carry responsibility for establishing a positive learning environment that focuses on strengths and successes, not on what a child cannot do, and to value children for what they are rather than what they can achieve. The focus on self-esteem needs to be all encompassing, development beginning in kindergarten and continuing throughout the school years and permeating all aspects of the school programme and curriculum through an integrated app-roach . . . . Involving students in decision making is critical if we wish to reinforce beliefs of personal adequacy. Children who engage in decision-making learn to experience control over their own existence and gain confidence in their ability to think and judge. They also develop the courage to take risks and to learn from mistakes. When teachers alone establish expectations, children rarely question them. Instead they are likely to question their personal adequacy in meeting them. The child may conclude that his/her failure to meet expectations or to understand is a reflection of himself/herself and may feel deficient in some way. (Magee, 1987, pp. 35–36)

This quotation comes from a paper in a Canadian journal read by both counsellors and teachers in that country. It is noteworthy that this issue was devoted to papers concerned with guidance in elementary schools, the parallel of primary schools in the UK. Here again some of the central concerns of pastoral care are reflected: the importance of self-concept and its relationship to the approaches used by teachers and schools; the importance of providing pupils with decision making experiences; and the insistence that these experiences should be provided through a planned, integrated and curriculum-based approach which continues throughout the whole process of schooling. Indeed, it is precisely points of this kind that should be included in the discussion when the staff of primary schools talk about pastoral care. My own experience suggests that where schools decide to discuss seriously issues such as the development of the self-esteem, the staff come to recognize that these are areas for which hitherto they had no real policy: at best things were left to chance, and at worst aspects of pupils' school experience were producing negative results. In seeking to promote awareness and good practice in English primary schools within the perspective provided by pastoral care, valuable lessons can be learned from examining the practice of some other countries. It is my view, for example, that the level of awareness and effective practice in terms of structured and planned approaches found in some Canadian elementary schools is in advance of what is found in the majority of primary schools in this country. What then are the key ingredients of pastoral care in the context of a primary school? As has already been indicated there are alternative terms for the concerns of pastoral care. In Canada for example they are covered by the concept of 'guidance', a term also used in Scotland. Though the terms are different the concerns are very much the same: the critical importance of the pupils' self-esteem to their social and academic success is as central to 'pastoral care' in this country as it is 'guidance' in Canada. More specifically the value of the involvement of students in decision-making, stressed in the quotation from Canada, is equally recognized in those English primary schools where pastoral care has been taken on board. One example of this recognition can be found in a booklet provided by Coventry LEA, *Decision Making: Approaches to Personal and Social Education in the Primary School*. Using case studies, this booklet illustrates the way pupils in infant, junior and primary schools can be given the opportunity to be involved in decision-making, and it brings out the benefits this has on their personal development.

I believe that in the case of primary schools we are talking of those aspects of pastoral care concerned with the welfare, care and social development of all pupils. In going beyond the more prevalent notion that only individuals with particular difficulties deserve support, such a perspective is as important during the primary phase as any other. Developing this idea, Watkins (1985) draws out the special features of pastoral care which are to be distinguished from other related areas:

i. pastoral casework, where the main focus is on individual pupils, their achievement and development;

ii. pastoral curriculum, where the focus is on pupils and the social/personal skills and knowledge they need at school and elsewhere, for study, in later life; and

iii. pastoral management, where the focus is on the school organization, its staff, curriculum and relation to others outside the school.

Though these categories were probably formulated with secondary schools in mind they have considerable relevance to primary schools. Pastoral care if taken seriously will include not only specific work with individuals (currently not nearly as frequent as is imagined) but also planned work with groups and classes. In some instances this work would be informed by the notion of a pastoral curriculum, and it also raises issues in terms of the management of primary schools. So far as the focus of this book is concerned, pastoral care includes positive approaches to discipline and disaffection, particularly in relation to its stress on proaction rather than reaction, prevention rather than cure.

Developing pastoral care in the primary school involves an insistence on *planning* coupled with *review*. Such planning requires a full understanding of where we are before we plan where we are going, shared discussion, and some ownership by all, including pupils. Plans should cover management, school organization and climate, curriculum and teaching style, classroom management and organization. I shall return to some aspects of its development below.

Though I advocate the use of the term pastoral care, I have already indicated that there are a number of alternative and in some instances competing usages. David and Charlton (1987) provide further detail in relation to this point plus a definition particularly produced with primary schools in mind. It is interesting to note that their book, which is concerned with caring in the primary school, includes the term pastoral care in its sub-title. They state:

Many titles are used in describing the work to which we refer. We hear of: personal and social education; social and moral education; affective education; life skills teaching; personal education; pastoral care;

guidance and care; and welfare and counselling. While subtle differences sometimes exist between them they generally share two common themes:

The knowledge, skills, understanding, attitudes and values which children need to become happy members of, and valued contributors to, society. These may permeate, or be additional to traditional primary class work.

The guidance, welfare, counselling and support which enable children to cope with their personal situations at home, in school, or elsewhere. (David and Charlton, 1987, pp. 3–4)

For many primary teachers, pastoral care is something they associate with secondary schools. They assume that it is of no concern to them or even that it is inappropriate for the primary stage. In some cases primary teachers have unfavourable views of the secondary stage, and where this is the case pastoral care is likely to be seen in the same unfavourable light. Where the importance of pastoral care is recognized, primary teachers often assume that the special nature of their schools and classrooms automatically takes care of this area. Elsewhere, I have discussed this issue in connection with the closely related area of personal and social education:

Though it is seen as 'self-evident' among primary teachers that personal and social education should be at the centre of what is done in the primary school, this does not mean that personal and social education is regularly discussed in primary schools or much reflected in the documents produced relating to school policy. What it is more likely to mean, in most instances, is that when primary teachers are actually questioned about the importance of personal and social education, they will respond that it is central to all they do, both in their classrooms and in the school as a whole. They will probably add that in their view the personal and social education of their pupils is already well catered for through their current practice. Thus even the 'taken for grantedness' of PSE is usually at an implicit rather than explicit level. (Lang, 1988, pp. 2–3)

Though PSE is a term more widely used than pastoral care in primary schools, the situation I describe in this quotation would apply equally to either term. Indeed, of all the parallel terms PSE is the most interchangeable with pastoral care and already used in a number of primary schools. However, as I have suggested, the broader focus of the latter provides a more adequate basis for developing a response to the issues with which this book is concerned.

The issues connected with the 'taken for grantedness' of pastoral care are touched on along with some other issues in the following personal reflection from a primary teacher working in Coventry:

Barriers to Pastoral Care in Primary Schools

There are several areas of concern in considering pastoral care in the primary school and each one throws up several major problems. Two of these are the most difficult to overcome in any attempt to improve the situation: they are 'Time' and 'Oh-I-already-do-all-that'. The time factor is simply a physical and organizational one. How does a teacher with a class of 32 children ensure adequate time for each child's pastoral needs? Some children you seem to be dealing with constantly; others you rarely speak to: a few who are 'difficult' are also drawing time to themselves without necessarily that time spent being positive in its result. Even assessing the social abilities of children through active participation in groups is a problem since time must be spent preparing situations and also considering the method of assessment. The demands on the teacher's time are already high and on the horizon we have a mountain of further work, with the implication that a specific allocation of teaching time will be forced upon us, which will increase the problems.

The 'Oh-I-already-do-that' syndrome is unfortunately very common and we all fall prey to it at times. The needs of the developing child are outlined for us — social ability, confident communication, group skills, moral foundations, sense of identity, respect for self and others — and each one can be tossed aside with 'oh RE takes care of morals' or 'we do group work in science' or 'she's confident enough — you should hear her in the playground', none of which are valid or worthwhile assessments of individual children, however experienced the observer is in 'observing children'. It occurs to me that there is not merely a need for a close look at the pastoral process in primary schools, there is also a need for a look at what primary teachers actually acknowledge as their means of assessing that process, if they indeed actually acknowledge its existence. Many primary teachers have very limited skills in developmental drama which can be a major tool in both the process and its assessment. Also there is still a suspicion that the outgoing individual, the imaginative and creative child, is positively discouraged within the classroom, because the conformist, quiet child who takes the teacher's line is easier to deal with. It may be therefore that there is a guilty conscience lurking behind the teacher who claims to be 'already doing' pastoral care, a nagging doubt which points the finger at their own classroom practice. I would include myself in that statement, although I hope only to some extent.

This is a more explicit and conscious critique than some primary teachers would be capable of making. However, in spite of the unusual level of self-awareness, this teacher does confirm at a very personal level some of the issues which have been identified in relation to primary teachers' attitudes to pastoral care. These comments also act as a salutary reminder of the real tensions, pressures and stresses, to which even the most committed and hardworking teachers find themselves subjected. Plans for the development of pastoral care need to take this into account.

So far I have dealt with the sort of issue which could form the basis for 'talking about pastoral care': I shall now turn to some thoughts on what might form part of the agenda for action and what form some of that action might take.

Managing pastoral care in the primary school

In their book on the management of primary schools Paisey and Paisey (1987) include the following comment in a chapter entitled 'Caring for Children':

> Competence by the head in achieving the best organization possible to give each child the richest and most varied experiences and a full share of the total resources available is the most sophisticated form of caring. This is caring through the professional process of organizing the school. The child's cumulative experience of pupil grouping in the school is itself a substantial element in his or her education. (Paisey and Paisey, 1987, pp. 92–3)

This is a top-down model of organization and all education, particularly that concerned with pupils' affective development, requires a balance between top-down and bottom-up management. If staff are not involved in decisions and feel no ownership of what goes on, things are unlikely to be very effective. Pastoral care in particular requires real commitment from staff of a kind that cannot be achieved when even the most concerned heads take it upon themselves to make all the plans and give all the instructions. Clearly, given the lack of understanding, the ambivalent feelings and the 'taken for grantedness' mentioned above, a critical management task will be to introduce the topic in a way both sensitive and positive enough to gain the interest and concern of the staff. Teachers have to feel this is something worth discussing, and when the discussions take place they have to feel that they have gained something, had a part to play and a contribution to make.

In what ways might a headteacher gain the commitment of staff? At one local primary school the head regularly takes all the infant pupils for the last half hour of the school day on one day a week, and all the junior pupils on another. Staff are thus freed for regular on-going discussion without the constraint of the head's presence. This practice significantly changed staff involvement in what went on in the school. Initially much of the agenda for these sessions emanated from the head, but over a period of about three years the balance changed to a situation where most of the agenda is set by the staff themselves. The message here is that if you want to promote free and productive discussion between pupils you need to promote it amongst staff first.

The head of a large infant school argues for taking things a stage further in what she describes as a holistic approach to pastoral care and personal and social education. She feels that staff must not just be provided with the opportunity for discussion but also with the opportunity to take real responsibilities and to make decisions themselves. She believes that it is only by providing the staff with such opportunities that they in turn will provide them for their pupils. The process of managing pastoral care in the primary school does not only mean involving teachers but *all* those working in school, as well as parents and to some extent pupils. Views and ideas should be sought and information disseminated so that all will understand not only what is happening but why it is happening. Management on these lines can contribute significantly to creating a positive school climate and encouraging the creation of a pleasant environment. It allows the deployment of resources in terms of space and time so that the opportunity for individual pupil-teacher contact in privacy is a reality rather than an unsubstantiated ideal. The aim should be to provide *all* pupils with ready and unthreatening access to individual and extended interaction with their teachers.

Most importantly the effective management of pastoral care demands a regular review of current practice, which will then be understood as it is, rather than as it is assumed to be. What is valuable can be developed, and what is not, modified or abandoned. Not only does the head's management role play an important part in promoting shared views and consensus on appropriate action, it is also crucial in the development of inservice training for the support and development of pastoral care within the school. It is possible for individual schools to handle their own training and development and a number have been quite successful with such 'go it alone' policies. However, there is no denying that in small schools this is quite a difficult task. There are a number of ways of overcoming this. For example, the use of consultants has been shown to work well where the fit between the school's needs and the consultant's expertise is close (Hanko, 1985; Wagner, 1988). A further valuable approach is where schools with similar concerns are able to work together sharing in ideas, training and the development of strategies. Further examples of the way pastoral care can be managed will emerge from the two case studies that conclude this chapter.

Pastoral care through the curriculum

With the advent of the National Curriculum the development of pastoral care within a curriculum framework becomes even more important. There is no doubt that much pastoral care can take place through the regular curriculum. The opportunity to make decisions provides a clear example. This is a process that could well be developed in a number of different subjects. However, some co-ordinating principle is needed to provide a structure and focus to the pastoral care element. It is here that the concept of a pastoral or guidance curriculum is appropriate. The starting point for this should be the identification of the needs to be met through this curriculum — a complex process which should involve considerable consultation and discussion.

Fairly typical of the kind of list of affective needs that a school might use as the starting point for discussion of what should underpin its pastoral curriculum at the following:

    i.   Self-esteem: self-acceptance and a healthy self-image
    ii.   Self-confidence
    iii. Personal and social skills
    iv. Responsibility
    v.   Initiative: the ability to undertake and sustain independent effort
    vi. Honesty/trust: the ability to express feelings honestly and openly to others

vii. Empathy
viii. Judgement: the ability to make appropriate decisions independently and to adapt behaviour to the demands of the situation
ix. Flexibility
x. Patience
xi. Humour

It must be emphasized that this is not presented as a definitive list but simply as a basis for discussion. Different schools with different pupils may want to add, omit and amend.

However, once a list has been agreed, these needs will have to be translated into aims and objectives which will form the basis of the school's pastoral curriculum, which will then inform the work undertaken in the school. So far as the formal curriculum is concerned, teachers should consider whether it is planned and offered in such a way as to help children gradually acquire those understandings, attitudes, values, beliefs, feelings, skills and behaviours which contribute to the achievement of the above list of affective needs. This will involve an examination of what is taught and how it is taught. It is partly through the teaching process that children learn about their own values and the values of others. Some approaches to teaching are likely to give greater scope than others for children to take responsibility for their own learning and to engage in experiences which will promote the quality of the pastoral care they experience. Some examples of the way the aims of the pastoral curriculum can be translated into practice will be found in the case studies at the end of this chapter.

Classroom strategies to promote pastoral care

The basic principle that underpins a response to disaffection and disruption through pastoral care is the idea that we are more likely to find positive behaviour when students are given the opportunity to develop a sense of belonging and an identity within their primary schools. Translated into a prescription for classroom management, this means that a teacher who helps a pupil to internalize feelings of competence and self-reliance may significantly affect the pupil's participation in, commitment to, and ability to benefit from the learning experience. Such help should also decrease the likelihood of a pupil's drifting toward apathy, disaffection and poor behaviour, for the self-confidence that can result from ongoing successful experience can equip the pupil to meet more effectively future demands of an academic or social nature. In relation to this, a pastoral approach in the classroom would involve encouraging pupils both individually and in groups to think about and examine various aspects of their own development in order to gain a better understanding of themselves and others. Some significant aspects of this development might be found in the list of needs presented above.

What then should teachers do to implement a pastoral approach through their actual classroom practice? Below are some practical suggestions which experience has shown to be effective. Again it must be stressed that this is not presented as a definitive list but simply as a resource. It is also important to recognize that pastoral care does not have a monopoly on the strategies listed; they could well appear individually as elements of other approaches. However, the essential qualities of pastoral care are reflected through a range of strategies such as the following.

In order to create a positive climate in their classroom teachers should:

- clearly define specific and realistic expectations with the minimum number of rules simply stated in positive terms, and do so as early as possible in the school year, before difficulties arise in the classroom;

- involve pupils, whatever their stage and age, in formulating or modifying these rules;

- make sure they communicate in advance to pupils any change in behavioural routines or expectations;

- notice and encourage appropriate classroom behaviour;

- emphasize strengths rather than weaknesses, rewards rather than punishments, encouragement rather than correction;

- provide opportunities for ongoing successful experiences that will enhance the self-esteem of each pupil in the classroom;

- promote and encourage the development of social skills within the curriculum.

As well as this, in order to gain an understanding and to communicate acceptance of individual students, teachers should:

- become familiar with typical behaviours for children at various developmental stages (cognitive, physical and affective);

- listen actively to pupils to gain an appreciation of their perception of situations;

- capitalize on pupils' strengths and interests to encourage the growth of confidence and self-esteem;

- respond to each pupil's behaviour and performance in terms of individual differences and needs;

- encourage pupils to develop self-awareness in and about their relationships with peers and adults;

- make efforts to demonstrate the kind of openness that signals to pupils that the teacher is available to discuss a pupil's feelings and concerns in private;

- exemplify through their own behaviour and attitudes a respect for the pupils and themselves.

In order to foster and maintain positive pupil-teacher interaction, teachers should:

approach pupils in a consistent, encouraging, supportive, fair, flexible, and honest manner;

encourage pupils to participate in formulating positive behavioural goals and methods of attaining those goals;

provide security through the consistent application of fair, realistic, and age appropriate consequences;

act to avoid power struggles with pupils;

if either teacher or pupil is upset or angry, delay discussion and / or decisions until emotional stability is restored;

discuss inappropriate behaviour in private unless the problem involves the class as a whole;

accept that both teacher and pupil can make human errors.

Pastoral care and problems

In this chapter I have spent most of my time discussing the role of pastoral care for pupils in general. This is not because I do not recognize the important role it has in helping provide support for individual pupils with problems. Clearly schools need adequate referral systems and also to be part of an adequate welfare network. In particular, provision needs to be made to ensure that it is the person who knows the pupil best who attends case conferences; this will usually be the class teacher. Schools need to develop expertise in the handling of issues such as child abuse in its various forms, and equally there is a great need for the development of counselling skills amongst those working at the primary stage. These areas could well form the basis of a further chapter. My point, though, is that where a school has already promoted the kind of positive and pervasive pastoral ethos with which I have been concerned, the likelihood of individual problems being detected and effectively handled is far greater.

Case studies

Finally, two case studies are presented as examples of aspects of the type of approach which I have been concerned to promote in this chapter. The pastoral care practices of both the schools have been written up in chapters in a book I have edited (Lang, 1988).

The first example (Brier, 1988) is from Wybourn First and Middle School in Sheffield, where the response to disruption is set within a broad positive framework. It is described through the following notes:

(1) *Basic philosophy of the school*: Good of the child
(2) *Focus*: Proactive before reactive

— A ton of prevention is cheaper than an ounce of cure
— Preventive education through the school's problem-solving framework
— An organization which avoids potential for conflict
— A whole-school ethos based on mutual support, i.e.:
    child — child
    adult — child
    individual — groups
    school — community
— Responsibility
    for self and actions
    to others, especially those less able/fortunate than self
    to reason and discuss any problem.

(3) *Disruptive children*

— Early identification of exact problem
    learning } probably
    behaviour } linked
— Early physical checks for possible physical origins of behaviour problem (especially hearing)
— Early consultation with parents (emphasis on cooperative approach):

    i.   to aid understanding of any psychological and/or cultural origins;

    ii.   to share school's and parents' understanding of each other's approach, and to attempt to gain some degree of consensus in handling and expectations of the child;

    iii.   to attempt to develop good mutual support links for the child (eliminates the 'play off' strategy);

    iv.   to explain how various strategies work, and the parent's role.

— Use of contracts (even with quite small children)
— Daily report:

    i.   helps child to monitor own behaviour:
    up to 1 week, report on each work and play session;
    if OK, then for 1 week, report at end of each day for whole day;
    if OK, then one end-of-week report for whole week (usually OK for a time, but may need to be repeated).

     ii.   helps to put relationships on positive side again:
child has to take responsibility for own behaviour;
report has to be shown to headteacher/year leader at end of
each day, and taken home for parents to read and sign;
opportunity is taken to discuss problems and to help child
to apply problem-solving strategies where appropriate;

— 'Time out':
gives time for all concerned to cool off, but:

    i.   not easy to give adequate supervision of child while
ignoring him/her;

    ii.   tempting to over-use both in frequency and length of time
spent out of group;

    iii.   use must be closely monitored, and under strictest guide-
lines.

(4) *Affirmation assemblies for younger children (5 to 7 years)*

— Self-adhesive badges, each written by a teacher and specifying
behaviour, e.g.:
'I helped Peter finish his model'
'I cleared away the sand myself'
'I was kind to Jane'
'I worked hard in reading'.

(5) *Personal achievement awards for older children (8 to 12 years)*

— Four categories:
working well
caring for others
improving the environment
helping the community.

    i.   children and teachers nominate members of their own
class/year group;

    ii.   each nominee receives a badge;

    iii.   one child is selected for each category each week and
receives a certificate;

    iv.   teachers spend time with class discussing nominations
before they are entered each week.

(6) *Educational visits*

— First hand experience is an important part of the basic philosophy of the school:

    i.   children are taken out of the immediate environment of the
school in both large and small groups from the earliest
stages;

    ii.   first focus is on how to behave in a considerate manner, i.e.,
social development and good behaviour habits are the first

lesson to be learned, before exploration, investigation, etc;

iii. preparation and carefully drawn lines of behaviour expect-ation are paramount.

(7) *Residential visits*
Aid the formation of close relationships with peers and teachers:

i arranged as early as possible, starting with one or two nights at 7 or 8 years;

ii. children prepare food and keep residence clean, as well as taking part in challenging activities appropriate to age group;

iii. focus is on special development and personal achievement, with mutual support in the group;

iv. as children get older the length of the residential stay is extended and more challenging activities are intoduced, e.g. potholing, climbing.

v. preparation:
emphasis on importance of being a good guest/ambassador for the school;
behaviour expected clearly specified, especially for situationally appropriate behaviour, e.g. talking to VIP/adult/stranger compared with a friend in the playgound;
full information on what is to be encountered on the visit.

The second case study (Richardson, 1988) comes from Green Lanes Infant and Junior school in Solihull. The school prefers to use the term 'personal and social education'; however, the approach illustrated is precisely that with which we are concerned.

Practical strategies for developing PSE

1. *Individual personal and social development charts (4 to 11 years)*
These are provided for all the school. One set of four skills is selected for the infant aged children (4 to 7 years) and a different set of four skills for the juniors. The skills are made explicit to the children by being expressed as 'I can do' statements, e.g. 'I can tidy away sensibly', 'I can hang my coat on my peg'. Each child has the four skill statements listed on the left of a sheet, to the right of which is space for stars, ticks and crosses as a reward for achieving the task. Rewards are given either as the teacher sees the child achieving the task or during class review sessions when each child is awarded stars for effort.

2. *Rewarding special effort as part of an assembly (4 to 11 years)*
One child is selected from each class every week by the teacher. The child's name is

entered in a special book and the child is presented with a certificate in a special assembly. This is a means of valuing all childrens' social achievement, such as helpfulness, politeness and enthusiasm, as well as academic achievement.

3. *Presentation of badges (stickers) (4 to 11 years)*
This is used in special effort assemblies, the stickers being presented with the certificates. Children are given stickers at other times by the head teacher for being helpful, behaving sensibly, or for making any sort of special effort. Children may be sent to special assemblies by their class teacher at any time.

4. *Developing attitudes through the curriculum (4 to 11 years)*
Teachers jointly choose six attitudes to develop each term. These include such attitudes as co-operation, tolerance of others, self respect and consideration for others. The attitudes are selected from a list of eighteen which are repeated each year, thus providing opportunity for the child to develop these attitudes as he grows and matures.

5. *Involving children in monitoring their own progress (4 to 11 years)*
One piece of work is selected each half term by the teacher and the child. This is dated and placed in a portfolio of the child's work. The portfolio is stored in a filing cabinet to which the child has access. At the end of the junior school the portfolio is taken to the secondary school.

6. *Developing a PSE skill alongside other skills in topic work (4 to 11 years)*
A PSE skill is selected to be developed along with other skills such as map reading, observation and classification and problem-solving. The skill is one of six chosen collaboratively each term by staff to be developed during topic work. Skills include such activities as 'I can take turns to speak in a group' or 'I can share equipment'. All the skills are made explicit to the children, and at the end of the topic a comment about the child's achievement in each skill is negotiated and then recorded on the child's individual topic record sheet.

7. *Class counselling and discussion (9 to 11 years)*
The children sit in a circle. They are invited to comment on the behaviour they have observed in other children during the week. This may be a negative comment provided it is proceeded by a positive remark about the pupil concerned.

8. *Class discussion and implementation of Behaviour Modification Strategies (9 to 11 years)*
The purpose is to improve behaviour when a teacher other than the class teacher is taking the class. Children discuss in pairs and then groups what constitutes appropriate and inappropriate behaviour in class. The final agreed list is displayed on the classroom wall. Stars are awarded on a regular basis when all members of the group have behaved well. A large chart is displayed on the wall and parents are invited to view this at any time. Red stars are given for disruptive behaviour and cancel out

other colours. A certification is presented after ten stars have been won, and after twenty stars a reward of the children's choice is granted, e.g. extra playtime, cooking, computer time.

Conclusion

The title of this chapter stated that we should talk about pastoral care in the primary school and the chapter itself went on to argue that there were at least two important reasons for doing this. The first was a general one, that pastoral care was a positive and valuable concept that had much to offer primary schools and their pupils. The second was more specific, that pastoral care had a valuable contribuiton to make in terms of an effective response to problems of disaffection and disruption in the primary school. I also set out to stress from the outset the problems likely to be created by lack of understanding of, and lack of sympathy with, the notion of pastoral care to be found amongst many primary school teachers.

The form this chapter has taken is a direct response to these factors. I have tried to present a whole range of ideas from the fairly theoretical to the very practical. I have not pulled my punches where I feel thought is lacking or practice inadequate. My aim has been first to provide a jolt to the perceptions of those involved in primary schools, and then to provide them with plenty to reflect and build upon. One aspect of this has been my insistence of the use of the term 'pastoral care' which, through its unfamiliarity in the primary context, may provide a greater stimulus to thought. This chapter has sought to illustrate both the meaning of pastoral care in a primary context and what is has to offer the primary school.

In terms of action and what it can offer the primary school, I have sought to provide three kinds of illustration: through some general principles such as the notion of a pastoral curriculum; through specific prescriptions for action; and lastly through actual examples of practice in schools. My message has been that this is something that should be on the agenda for discussion in all primary schools. The ideas in this chapter would provide an adequate basis for such discussions, but where these discussions lead in terms of actions and outcomes must be the responsibility of the schools and their staff.

References

Bell, P. and Best, R. (1986) *Supportive Education*, Oxford, Basil Blackwell.

Brier, J. (1988) 'Developing a structural social development programme in an inner city school', in Lang, P. *Thinking about . . . Personal and Social Education in the Primary School*, Oxford, Basil Blackwell.

Bulman, L. and Jenkins, D. (1988) *The Pastoral Curriculum*, Oxford, Basil Blackwell.

David, K. and Charlton, T. (1987) 'The Caring Role of the Primary School' in *Pastoral Care and Personal and Social, Education in Primary Schools*, London, Macmillan.

David, K. and Cowley, J. (1980) *Pastoral Care in School and Colleges*, London, Edward Arnold.

Department of Education and Science (1987) *Education Observed 5: Good Behaviour and Discipline in Schools*, HMI Report, London, HMSO.

Hanko, G. (1985) *Special Needs in Ordinary Classrooms*, Oxford, Basil Blackwell.

Lang, P. (1983) 'Pastoral Care: some reflections on possible influences', *Pastoral Care in Education*, 21, 2, pp. 136–146.

Lang, P. (Ed.) (1988) *Thinking About . . . Personal and Social Education in the Primary School,* Oxford, Basil Blackwell.

Magee, D. (1987) 'Nurturing self-esteem', *Guidance and Counselling*, 2, 5, pp. 35–39, University of Toronto.

Marland, M. (1974) *Pastoral Care*, London, Heinemann.

Marland, M. (1980) 'The pastoral curriculum', in Best, R., Jarvis, C. and Ribbins, R. (Eds) *Perspectives on Pastoral Care*, London, Heinemann.

Ministry of Education, Ontario (1986) *Resource Guide: Behaviour*, Ontario, Ministry of Education.

Paisey, A. and Paisey, A. (1987) *Effective Management in the Primary School*, Oxford, Basil Blackwell.

Richardson, T. (1988) 'Education for personal development: a whole school approach', in Lang, P. (Ed.) *Thinking About . . . Personal and Social Education in the Primary School*, Oxford, Basil Blackwell.

Wagner, P. (1988) 'Developing co-operative learning in the primary school' in Lang, P. (Ed.) *Thinking About . . . Personal and Social Education in the Primary School*, Oxford, Basil Blackwell.

Watkins, C. (1985) 'Does pastoral care = pastoral and social education?', *Pastoral Care in Education*, 3, 3, pp. 179–183.

7
Pupil Achievement and Pupil Alienation
in the Junior School

Pamela Sammons and Peter Mortimore

Introduction

As part of a recent longitudinal study of school effectiveness (the London Junior School Project described by Mortimore *et al*. 1986, 1988a and b) a wealth of information about the attainment, progress and adjustment of junior-age pupils was collected by the ILEA's Research and Statistics Branch. Because of the size of the sample (comprising a total of fifty schools and nearly 2000 children) and the scope of the research, the study provides a detailed and, in many ways, unique account of the factors which influence pupil achievement and adjustment during the junior years of schooling. In particular, as the research was designed to explore the influence both of home background and of school upon a broad range of pupils' educational outcomes, it was possible to identify and separate the contribution of home background factors to achievement and adjustment from that of school attended. The measures related to pupil intakes and their educational outcomes are of special relevance to the study of achievement and alienation.

Aims

The Project had four major aims:

    i. to produce a detailed description of pupils and teachers, and of the organization and curriculum of schools in an inner city area;

   ii. to document the progress and development, over three and a half years of schooling, of an age group of nearly 2000 pupils;

iii. to establish whether some schools were more effective than others in promoting pupils' learning and development, when account was taken of variations in the characteristics of pupils in the intakes to schools;
iv. to investigate average differences in the educational outcomes of different groups of pupils. Following the Equal Opportunities initiative within the ILEA, special attention was paid to variations in achievement related to the race, sex and the social class background of pupils. In addition, the effect of differences of age on children's achievement was investigated.

In order to pursue the research aims it was necessary to obtain a wide variety of information about the individual pupils in the sample, and about their schools, teachers and classroom experiences. The research data can be divided into broad categories which reflect the questions addressed by the study and, in turn, influence the nature of the results. These are measures of the pupil intakes to schools and classes; measures of pupils' educational outcomes; and measures of the classroom learning environment and school processes.

Measures of the pupil intakes to schools and classes

So that the effectiveness of schooling for different groups of children (classified according to age, social class, sex or race) could be explored, and the impact of background factors upon their educational outcomes could be examined, detailed information about pupils' characteristics was required.

The measures of intake used in the Junior School Project cover two areas: the social, ethnic, language and family background characteristics of the children, and their initial attainments at entry to junior school. The selection of background measures was made with reference to the results of previous research which has investigated disadvantage in education (see reviews by Majoribanks, 1979, or Rutter and Madge, 1976). All information was obtained at the level of the individual child and, because of the longitudinal nature of the study, it was possible to explore the cumulative effects of background factors upon school achievement and adjustment over several years.

Data about each child's cognitive attainments in assessments of reading, mathematics and visio-spatial skills, and a class teacher's rating of behaviour were also collected at entry to junior school. This information enabled account to be taken of differences in the *past* achievements of pupils (which may be related to their previous membership of particular infant classes and schools). It also provided the necessary baseline against which to assess the later progress and development of individual children during the junior school years.

The major focus of the Junior School Project research was the analysis of school effectiveness. Even within an inner city area there are often considerable differences between schools in the characteristics of their intakes, as educational priority research has demonstrated (see, for example, Sammons *et al.*, 1983). Given this, it was important for the Project to collect comprehensive background data about the pupil intakes to the fifty sample schools. Without such data, research into schools' effects on their pupils would be misleading, because of the failure adequately to compare 'like' with 'like' (see Gray, 1983; Gray and Jones, 1983). Because detailed background information was collected at the level of the individual pupil, however, the research design chosen for the JSP ensured that it was possible to identify the separate and combined influences of different background characteristics upon pupil achievement and adjustment, and, in addition, to examine the impact of school attended once the influence of background was taken into account.

Measures of educational outcomes

The results of studies of school effectiveness are dependent, to a certain extent, on the choice of measures of educational outcomes chosen for the research. Most studies of secondary school effects have been criticised for concentrating on too few measures of educational outcomes (usually examination success and attendance), and studies of the junior age group have, in general, also focused only on children's attainments in the basic skills.

The aims of primary education are diverse, as is the curriculum in many primary schools. Basic skills are considered important by the vast majority of teachers, but other areas — including aspects of non-cognitive development such as attitudes, behaviour or attendance — are also a focus of attention. Studies which use only one or two measures of educational outcomes, therefore, may give an unbalanced and simplistic view of class and school effects.

In the Junior School Project, therefore, a wide variety of cognitive and non-cognitive outcomes were investigated:

Cognitive outcomes

The standardized tests (of reading, mathematics and visio-spatial skills) have been shown to be reliable instruments with adequate content validity and to be good predictors of later academic success.[1] Because of the considerable variations in children's attainments in these skill areas at entry to junior school, pupils were assessed regularly to enable the investigation of progress over the first three junior years. Only by studying pupils' *progress* could proper account be taken of the very different levels of skills possessed by children at the start of junior education.

An individually based assessment of practical mathematics, based on the ILEA Checkpoints procedure, was conducted in each school year (incorporating items of increased difficulty in later years). To take account of the importance of writing in the junior curriculum, an assessment of creative writing was also made on an annual basis. This included measures of language complexity and the quality of ideas, as well as of structure and technical skills.

Finally, because of the strong emphasis placed by some teachers on the development of pupils' oral skills, and to broaden the assessment of language development, the oral skills of a sample of children were assessed in the fourth year, using exercises developed specifically for the study by the Language Survey Team of the Assessment of Performance Unit of the Department of Education and Science (see Gorman and Hargreaves, 1985).

In addition to these data, the children's scores in the London Reading Test and in the Authority's Verbal Reasoning test were collected in their fourth year.

Non-cognitive outcomes

Studies of school differences have tended to neglect the 'social' outputs of education (such as pupils' self-perception, attendance, and attitudes). Yet these areas are of importance, and it has been argued that schools may have greater effects on non-cognitive than cognitive outcomes (Reynolds, 1982). In order to do justice to the diverse aims and breadth of the curriculum of junior schools, a wide range of non-cognitive measures were also included in the research. These are described in the technical appendices of the Project's main report (Mortimore *et al.*, 1986).

Information about the children's behaviour in school (as assessed by their class teachers) was collected, using an instrument specially developed for use with the junior age group (for full details see Kysel *et al.*, 1983). This information was collected for each child in the autumn and summer terms of each school year. In this way it was possible to examine changes in behaviour during the three years, and to obtain an overall measure of behaviour.

A self-report measure of pupils' attitudes towards different types of school activities, curriculum areas and other aspects of school was administered in each school year. In addition, measures of each child's perception of how they thought they were seen by the teacher and by their peer group, as well as their views of themselves in the context of the school environment, were obtained at the end of the third year. Full attendance data were also collected for each child in the three terms of each school year.

Methods of analysis

Analysis of the JSP data was necessarily complex and employed a variety of statistical techniques. Every effort was made to learn from the methodological criticisms of earlier research into school and teacher differences in effectiveness (see Tizard *et al.*, 1980; Goldstein, 1980; Radical Statistics in Education Group, 1982). To overcome some of the problems arising in previous research related to the use of aggregate data, the analyses of pupils' educational outcomes (in reading, mathematics and writing progress, attainment in oracy, and in attendance, attitudes, behaviour, and self-concept), which were designed to establish whether schools differed in their effects, were all conducted at the level of the individual pupil. The impacts of background factors and initial attainment were explored in depth in the analyses of progress (for details see Mortimore *et al.*, 1988b). Only when full account was taken of these relationships was the question of school effects on pupils' achievement and adjustment addressed.

In addition to analyses of school and class effects, the attainments, progress and non-cognitive development of children were examined for all individuals and separately for different groups. When investigating differences in outcomes due to age, social class, sex or race, the analyses controlled simultaneously for all other background factors. This means that, in reporting the significant differences, the figures represent the *separate* effects of a given factor, when the impact of all other background characteristics have been taken into account. Thus, the effect of sex on attainment, for example, was identified *net* of the effects of age, social class, race and other background factors.

As well as examining the *overall* relationships between progress and achievement in different cognitive and non-cognitive areas for all pupils, it was possible to examine the relationships for children with different characteristics (according to age, social class, sex and race). The relationships between attainment and progress and teachers' ratings of pupils' abilities were also investigated. Again, the analyses were conducted for all pupils and, separately, for children of different groups.

The impact of background

Children included in the Junior School Project sample were drawn from a wide variety of backgrounds (see Appendix for details). Some lived in families which were advantaged in material terms, while others were living in very difficult circumstances. Such differences in circumstances can have a considerable impact upon pupils' educational outcomes (see Essen and Wedge, 1982 or Sammons *et al.*, 1983, for example). Within the area covered by the ILEA there is growing evidence that the incidence of disadvantage is increasing amongst inner city pupils (see Hunter *et al.*, 1985).

Educational research has frequently demonstrated that social background and income are good predictors of cognitive attainments among primary pupils (see reviews by Rutter and Madge, 1976, or Mortimore and Blackstone, 1982). Family variables — such as size and birth order — also appear to be related to educational outcomes (see Marjoribanks, 1979).

The strength of differences due to race has been debated extensively in recent years, and evidence of under-achievement by children of some ethnic minority backgrounds is a cause for serious concern (see Essen and Ghodsian, 1980; Rampton, 1981; Swann, 1985; Eggleston *et al.*, 1985; Mabey, 1985). Differences in achievement amongst pupils of primary age have also been found to be associated with sex, differences usually being found in favour of girls at this stage (see MacCoby and Jacklin, 1980; APU, 1981, 1982).

It should be stressed that, although differences in achievement have been identified for children of different social class, sex or ethnic groups, the *causes* of such differences are seldom clear (see Mortimore, 1983). Moreover, although there is evidence that such factors are related to cognitive attainment, their relationship to *progress* has rarely been studied. In addition, little attention has been paid to variations in the non-cognitive outcomes of education for different groups of pupils.

The aims of the analyses of these factors in the JSP was to establish their impact on the educational prospects of junior age children from different backgrounds. Particular care was paid to measuring the relative progress made by children from different groups when account was taken of attainment at entry into junior education.

The existence and size of differences in pupils' educational outcomes related to social class, sex and race were explored as part of the research. It was found that such differences were already marked even at the age of 7 when children first entered junior school. Furthermore, background factors were related both to measures of achievement in the cognitive outcomes and to measures of adjustment to school (the non-cognitive or social outcomes).[2]

Differences according to age

Although it is well known that attainment in cognitive assessments is related to age (such that the majority of tests take into account a pupil's age in the standardization of results), rather less attention has been given to the long-term prospects of children within the same year group who are the youngest members of the class. The studies which have investigated age effects have tended to look at achievement and have not examined non-cognitive outcomes. Most were also conducted over twenty years ago (see, for example, Freyman, 1965; Thompson, 1971; Williams, 1964). For a recent study of older age groups, see Russell and Startup, 1986.

The majority of educational studies have controlled for the effects of age when comparing children's attainments in cognitive areas. Although correct, this procedure obscures the size of differences in actual attainment within a year group which may have an impact upon teachers' assessments of children's ability and performance in class work. It is not always easy for a teacher to take into account pupils' ages when comparing work, especially in year-based classes. For this reason, variations in junior pupils' attainment and progress due to age were investigated in detail. (Full account was taken of other background factors — including mother's and father's occupations; eligibility for free meals; family size and position; nursery experience; fluency in English; sex and race — when estimating the effects of age in individual level analyses).

Cognitive outcomes

As noted earlier in this chapter, the JSP research involved the collection of information about pupils' performance in a wide range of cognitive areas (described in detail below) at different stages during their junior school careers. Because of this, analyses of the links between achievement in different cognitive areas could be undertaken, and the progress made by individual pupils in particular areas over time was investigated. Poor achievement in school is one factor which can affect pupil's adjustment to and feelings of alienation from school. Because data were collected at the level of the individual child, it was possible to explore the extent to which measures of pupils' attainment and progress related to those of their adjustment.

Reading

Marked differences in the reading skills of pupils were identified even at the start of their junior education. Thus, in terms of the reading assessment taken in the autumn term of their first year (where the maximum score possible was 91), the average score was 46 points. However, a quarter of the sample obtained scores of 24 points or lower, and a quarter scores 68 or more. This represents a very marked variation in reading ages.

Table 7.1 *Mean raw reading scores at each assessment by term of birth*

Term of Birth Birth	Reading Assessment							
	Year 1 Autumn	N	Year 2 Autumn	N	Year 3 Autumn	N	Year 3 Summer	N
Autumn	51.4	(577)	66.3	(548)	43.1	(489)	54.9	(473)
Spring	46.5	(616)	64.7	(602)	41.1	(514)	53.0	(492)
Summer	40.8	(574)	59.1	(522)	36.8	(477)	47.9	(458)
Overall Mean	46.2	(1767)	63.4	(1702)	40.4	(1480)	52.0	(1423)

Highly significant differences between the mean scores of sample children born in the autum, spring and summer terms were identified at each assessment of reading (see Table 7.1). In each year, the youngest children (summer born) performed less well in reading than those born in the autumn. Thus, at entry to junior education nearly 33 per cent of pupils born in the summer, compared with only 19 per cent of those born in the autumn term, obtained scores in the bottom quarter of the distribution. These proportions remained remarkably consistent over time, such that, at the end of the third year, 32 per cent of the summer born group, but only 21 per cent of the autumn group, obtained reading scores in the bottom quarter of the distribution.

Analysis of London Reading Test (LRT) results for the fourth year revealed a similar pattern; 32 per cent of the summer born group, but only 21 per cent of their autumn born counterparts, scored less than 35 points in the LRT. This score was the 'cut-off' recommended for individual special needs screening at transfer to secondary school.

Taking into account all other background characteristics, the month of birth made a highly significant difference to the statistical explanation of variation in reading attainment. This represented a difference of 13 raw points compared with an overall mean of 46 in terms of the first year assessment between the oldest children (born in September 1972) and the youngest (born in August 1973).

In analysing progress, account was taken of pupils' attainments in reading at entry to junior school. The first assessment acted as a baseline for the measurement of *progress* over the next three years. In contrast to attainment, reading progress was not related to pupil age. Thus, the 'gap' in performance between older and younger pupils neither increased nor decreased during the junior years.

Mathematics

As with reading there was a marked range in children's written mathematics skills at entry to junior school. In this case, the maximum score possible was 40 points. A quarter of the sample scored more than 29, and a quarter obtained 19 or fewer points. The average score was 24.

Table 7.2 Mean raw mathematics scores at each assessment by term of birth

Term of Birth	Mathematics Assessment							
	Year 1 Autumn	N	Year 2 Autumn	N	Year 3 Autumn	N	Year 3 Summer	N
Autumn	25.9	(577)	25.6	(549)	30.3	(525)	28.2	(507)
Spring	24.7	(616)	24.6	(610)	29.6	(552)	27.3	(538)
Summer	22.3	(579)	22.5	(558)	28.0	(521)	24.5	(497)
Overall Mean	24.3	(1772)	24.3	(1717)	29.3	(1598)	26.7	(1542)

At each assessment, age was highly significantly related to mathematics attainment (Table 7.2). As with reading, a much higher percentage of summer than of autumn born pupils obtained scores in the lowest quarter of the distribution (34 per cent compared with 19 per cent respectively) in the first year. These figures remained very similar in later years (the equivalent figures for the summer of the third year were 31 per cent and 18 per cent for the two groups).

Taking into account all other background factors, the difference in attainment between the oldest and youngest pupils in the sample (those born in September 1972 and in August 1973, respectively) reached five raw points in the first year compared with a mean of 24 for the whole sample. This difference remained highly statistically significant throughout the junior years. Once account was taken of initial mathematics attainment, age did not make a significant contribution to the statistical explanation of variations in pupils' progress during the junior years.[3]

Visio-spatial skills

As with other cognitive areas, attainment in visio-spatial skills was highly related to age. Thus, in the first year, the mean raw score of summer born children was 22.5 compared with 25 for the autumn born group. The overall mean was 24 points. A similar gap in average achievement was in evidence at the second assessment.

Controlling for background characteristics confirmed the clear pattern of differences, according to month of birth, in favour of older pupils.

Because visio-spatial skills were assessed on two occasions only, the progress measure for this area covers a one year period. Analyses indicated that age at test was not related to progress, when account was taken of other factors.

Writing

As was noted for the other cognitive assessments, there were marked differences between children in terms of writing skills in the first year. Experienced junior teachers assessed the children's creative writing in terms of quality of language and ideas, and more technical aspects such as legibility, use of punctuation and length. Differences were identified between children's performance in both qualitative and technical aspects (and the two were quite closely related at this stage).

Some children's work (around 18 per cent) read very well, showing a sophisticated use of language, a sense of audience and use of adjectives, adverbs, similes or metaphors. Nearly half the sample's work showed some sense of audience and read fairly well, though pupils generally used 'pedestrian' language. (For details of the writing assessment see Strachan and Sammons, 1986; Bunch, 1984.) A third of the children, however, showed little or no sense of audience in their work, used little variety in their language and produced stories which were difficult to read. In all, 16 per cent of pupils produced written work with a clear storyline — well expressed and clearly developed ideas which were well connected. At this age, however, in 31 per cent of pupils' written work the storyline was unclear or absent, ideas were sketchy and not well connected.

A measure of 'maturity' (a sense of other people) showed that 44 per cent of first year children showed little or no sense of other people in their writing (in terms of thoughts, motivations or characterization). There were marked changes in this measure of maturity as the children progressed through the junior years.

The vast majority of children (86 per cent) produced very legible work in their first year and, at this stage, the majority continued to use a clear, well-formed print script. There were differences, however, in the use of punctuation. Over 57 per cent made minimal or no use of punctuation, whereas a fifth generally used capitals and full stops correctly. Only a minority made use of more sophisticated punctuation in the first year.

There were marked differences in the length of stories produced. Over a quarter of children wrote 115 words or more, but a quarter wrote less than 52 words. Three children wrote nothing. The average length for first year writing was 88 words.

Children in the sample completed an exercise involving creative writing in the summer term of the first, second and third years. The two assessments of quality of language and of ideas were found to be closely related ($r = 0.80$) and were combined, therefore, to give an overall measure of the quality of writing for each child at each assessment. Variations in the length of writing were also investigated.

Analyses provided strong evidence that, within a year group, month of birth was related significantly to writing performance. In the first year writing assessment, there was an average of a half-point difference between summer and autumn born pupils in the quality of writing (the assessment being based on a ten point scale). This difference — which favoured the older group — remained fairly constant in later assessments. The percentage of pupils whose writing was assessed as below average in quality also differed according to term of birth, though the differences were less marked in the third than in the first year assessment (see Figure 7.1).

Variations in the length of children's writing were also related to age. This

Figure 7.1: Quality of writing by term of birth (years 1 and 3)

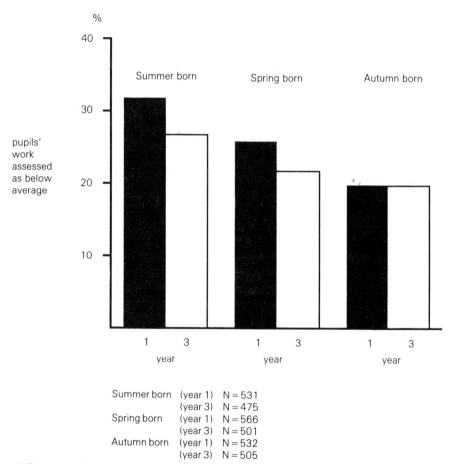

Summer born (year 1) N = 531
(year 3) N = 475
Spring born (year 1) N = 566
(year 3) N = 501
Autumn born (year 1) N = 532
(year 3) N = 505

difference, when account was taken of other factors, remained highly significant in all years, On average, summer born children produced stories 70 words long in the first year while autumn born children produced stories of average 90 words. In the third year, the equivalent figures were 224 compared with 256 words. There was also a difference in more technical skills, such as use of punctuation, in favour of the older members of the group.

There was no evidence that age affected progress in the quality or the length of writing between the first and the third year. Thus, although the gap in attainment remained highly significant, it did not increase or decrease over time.[4]

Practical mathematics

For a sample of the children (around 12 per cent) performance in practical mathematics tasks was examined in each year. The assessment covered five different skill areas — number, weight, volume, length and sets.

In line with performance of the written mathematical assessments, there was evidence that age was related to performance in practical mathematics. The practical assessments were conducted with a sub-sample of pupils (due to the need for 'one-to-one' administration of the test). Age was related to overall performance in practical mathematics in the first year but, when the five skill areas assessed were considered separately, some differences emerged. It appeared that performance in number work was significantly affected by age. Younger children attained less highly than older children. However, there were no significant differences in volume, length, weight or sets. A similar set of results were identified for the second year assessment.

In contrast to the first and second year assessments, age was related to performance in weighing activities in the third year, but no longer to number work. (Differences which were identified were in favour of the older children but these were small and not statistically significant.) Thus, in contrast to the results in written assessments, age did not have a significant impact on all practical mathematics performance tasks. In practical tasks, age differences related mainly to number work in the first and second years, but in the third year assessment, number work performance was no longer affected.

Oracy

An oracy (speaking skills) assessment was used to broaden the measures of language achievement included in the study. Five scales were used — a holistic impression mark, a task-specific impression mark, measures of verbal and non-verbal performance features, and one scale for the structural (lexico-grammatical) features of speech. The assessments were designed to judge communicative effectiveness. (The oracy assessments were described in detail by Gorman and Hargreaves, 1985. Further results of the analysis of the oracy data were provided by Ecob and Sammons, 1985). Oracy was assessed on only one occasion. It was not possible, therefore, to examine the relationships between oracy performance in different years. However, because assessments of several different aspects of children's oral skills were included, it was possible to analyse relationships between these different aspects.[5]

The results show that there was a strong relationship ($r = 0.82$) between general oral performance and the child's ability to fulfil the requirements of the different tasks (the specific assessment). The quality of the children's performance in terms of the language and ideas used was also closely related to general verbal performance ($r = 0.73$). However, there was a much weaker association between the non-verbal performance features (such as the use of eye-contact, gesturing and orientation to the listener) and the general assessment. A similarly weak relationship was identified between the lexico-grammatical features of speech and the general assessment ($r = 0.48$). Thus, a child's ability to communicate effectively with others — measured by the general assessment — was not strongly related to the structural aspects of her or his speech. Children can be good communicators even if they do not speak 'correctly'.

In marked contrast to findings for other cognitive areas, age was not found to be related to performance in any of the five oral assessments (there were some trends in favour of older pupils but all were small and none reached statistical significance). It appears that the ability to communicate effectively was not related to variations in age of less than one year (the age range within the Junior School Project sample).[6]

Teachers' assessment of pupils' ability

Teachers were asked, on four occasions, to assess each child's ability in terms of a five point scale ranging from 'well above average' to 'well below average'. There were significant differences between summer and autumn born children in the proportions rated as below and above average ability. These differences were in favour of the oldest children. Summer born children were consistently more likely to be

Table 7.3 *Percentages of children assessed as above and as below average ability by their class teachers, by term of birth*

Term of birth	% rated above average	% rated below average
Autumn year 2 assessment		
Autumn born (N = 546)	35.4	21.8
Spring born (N = 604)	31.3	28.6
Summer born (N = 532)	25.4	32.7
All pupils (N = 1682)	27.7	26.3
Autumn year 3 assessment		
Autumn born (N = 479)	33.6	21.7
Spring born (N = 515)	28.6	25.6
Summer born (N = 474)	25.5	30.6
All pupils (N = 1468)	29.2	25.9

judged as of below average ability than were their autumn born counterparts (see Table 7.3).

Further analyses of teachers' assessments of ability suggest that teachers were influenced in their assessments primarily by children's reading, writing and mathematics attainment. The significant gap in attainment in these areas due to age thus seems to influence class teachers' judgements of ability. It appears that teachers did not take full account of the effect of age differences on attainment when judging children's ability. This finding indicates that even within year-based classes, teachers may need to pay particular attention to age when assessing children's work and ability.

Non-cognitive outcomes

In order to measure the non-cognitive outcomes of junior education, both teacher-based and pupil self-report assessments were used. The various measures of pupils' non-cognitive outcomes included in the JSP provide a series of useful indicators of junior-age pupils' adjustment to and alienation from school. The set of measures covered pupil attendance, attitudes, behaviour in school, and self-concept. Poor adjustment to school may contribute towards pupil alienation. However, signs of poor adjustment, in part, also may be a reflection or response to existing feelings of alienation.

Behaviour

Information was collected about children's behaviour in school using the 'Child at School' schedule. (For a fuller description of this measure, see Kysel *et al.*, 1983.) This was completed on an individual basis for each child by her or his own class teacher. The behaviour schedule measured three aspects of difficulty — aggression, anxiety and learning problems. It is, of course, possible for a child to be assessed as having more than one type of behaviour difficulty.

Teachers assessed the pupils' behaviour at the beginning and end of each school year. Overall, the percentage of pupils assessed as having disturbed behaviour remained fairly stable, at around 17 per cent. In order to be assessed as having disturbed behaviour, a child had to be rated highly on one or more of three aspects. The percentages of pupils assessed as having difficulties on the three behaviour subscales in the autumn and summer of each year are shown in Table 7.4.

On each occasion that assessments were made, learning difficulties were identified most frequently. Aggression was usually the least often noted area of difficulty amongst this age range of pupils. On the learning difficulties subscale, in the first two years more pupils were assessed as disturbed at the beginning of the year than at the end. The reverse was true for aggression in all three years. The proportion of 'anxious' pupils remained fairly stable over the three years, whereas there were

Table 7.4 *The percentage of pupils assessed as disturbed on each behaviour subscale at different points in time*

	% Disturbed					
	Learning	N	Anxiety	N	Aggression	N
Year 1 (autumn)	13.3	1762	5.1	1765	3.9	1763
Year 1 (summer)	11.6	1742	5.1	1740	4.1	1738
Year 2 (autumn)	11.9	1765	5.6	1762	5.6	1761
Year 2 (summer)	11.0	1530	5.8	1529	6.1	1524
Year 3 (autumn)	11.4	1596	5.8	1594	4.6	1591
Year 3 (summer)	12.5	1409	5.5	1410	5.2	1402

more fluctuations in the number of pupils assessed as showing learning problems and aggression.

In general, behaviour was more stable in the second year (as measured by the correlation between autumn and summer ratings) and least stable in the first year. Of the three subscales, anxiety was generally less stable (the average correlation over the year between autumn and summer ratings was 0.69) than either aggression (average $r = 0.74$) or learning difficulties (average $r = 0.75$).

Changes in behaviour over time were explored. Over 70 per cent of the sample were never assessed as disturbed by their teachers, but nearly 30 per cent showed some kind of behaviour problems in school during the first three years of junior education. One in ten were identified as showing behaviour disturbance in two of the three years. Analyses of the relationship between age and pupils' behaviour indicated that, at each assessment, a higher percentage of summer born than of autumn born pupils were assessed by their class teacher as having some kind of behaviour difficulty (see Figure 7.2).

In all, 23 per cent of summer born pupils, compared with only 13 per cent of their autumn born classmates, were assessed as having some kind of difficulty in behaviour by their first year class teachers. Thus, age had a significant impact upon behaviour in school. Age was found to be related to the overall behaviour measure and to the learning difficulties sub-scale. Again, the youngest members of the year group were at a disadvantage. It is likely that this relationship may be due, at least in part, to an association between behaviour difficulties and low cognitive achievement. It has already been shown that summer born children performed less well than autumn born children in nearly all of the cognitive assessments. Poor attainment may lead to behaviour problems or reinforce them, but it is also likely that poor behaviour has an impact upon attainment in school. (The links between behaviour and cognitive achievements are discussed more fully later in this chapter).

Comparisons of pupils who were assessed as having some kind of behaviour disturbance in two or more years demonstrated that 16 per cent of summer born pupils, in contrast to only 10 per cent of autumn born pupils, were seen to have difficulties by their teachers. Overall, behaviour difficulties were more common and more persistent for younger members of the age group.

Figure 7.2: *Percentages of pupils assessed as having behaviour difficulties by term of birth (years 1, 2 and 3)*

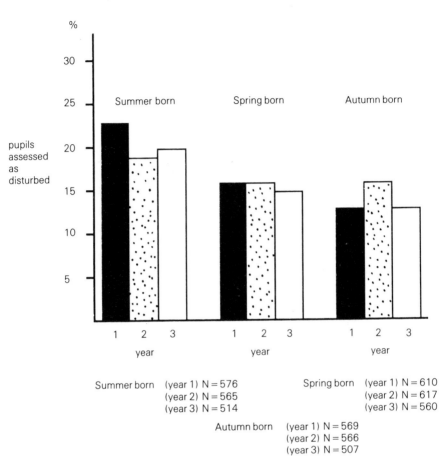

Taking a combined measure of behaviour over three years and controlling for sex and all other background factors, it was found that the month of birth still made a highly significant contribution to the statistical explanation of behaviour difficulties in school during the junior period.[7]

Attitudes

The pupils' attitudes to school and various school activities were measured using the 'Smiley' form, a five-point scale ranging from very positive to very negative. This used happy and sad faces to represent each point on the scale. This self-report instrument was verbally administered to reduce the likelihood of problems in completion for children with low attainment in reading and writing.

In each year, attitudes to 'basic skills' curriculum areas (mathematics and language activities) were less favourable than those to other curriculum areas (such as art and craft, music, PE and games). Children's attitudes to school, and to relationships with the teacher, varied. Items such as 'breaking school rules' and 'the whole class being told off', which have a disciplinary connotation, elicited more negative attitudes. There was a tendency for children's attitudes to specific curriculum areas and school activities to be more positive than their general attitude to school.

Overall, children's attitudes become slightly less positive in the later years of junior schooling. This was especially marked in attitude to school. The only area to show a slight but consistent improvement over the years was attitude to project work.

A comparison was made of attitudes to the three curriculum areas in which marked age differences in attainment had been identified. Age was found to be unrelated to attitudes to either reading or writing. However, for attitude to mathematics, age differences were identified. These occurred in the second and third year assessments and were particularly marked in the third year. At this stage, 31 per cent of the youngest (summer born) group compared with only 19 per cent of the oldest (autumn born) group had an unfavourable view of mathematics. It is possible that this poorer view of mathematics was related to the lower attainment of younger pupils in this area. However, there was also a 'gap' in both reading and writing attainment due to age, but no age-related variations in attitudes to these curriculum areas were identified. Individual analyses, taking into account sex and background factors indicated that month of birth was highly significantly related to attitude to mathematics in the third year.

Differences related to age were also identified in pupils' general attitudes to school. These differences were most marked in the third year. At this stage, 37 per cent of summer born, compared with only 28 per cent of autumn born pupils, had a negative view of school. Again, individual-level analyses indicated that age made a highly statistically significant contribution to the statistical explanation of variation in pupils' attitudes to school.

Self-concept in school

The children's self-concept was assessed at the end of the third year. It was not studied earlier because previous research has suggested that young children have difficulty in completing self-report questionnaires on this topic (see Piers and Harris, 1964). The instrument (the 'Me at School' schedule) consisted of a series of questions based on the 'Child at School' schedule used for obtaining class teachers' assessments of children's behaviour in school. These questions were concerned with the child's perception of her or himself in terms of four areas — anxiety, aggression, learning and behaviour.

Only a small percentage of pupils (3 per cent) indicated that they perceived themselves as always or usually anxious. The percentage who rated themselves as aggressive was only a little higher (4 per cent). However, slightly more children indicated that they usually or always had some problems concerned with learning (6 per cent). Eight per cent of children thought that they were usually or always naughty in their behaviour in school. These results suggest that the majority of children had fairly positive self-concepts.

Amongst the items on the self-concept scale, a strong relationship ($r = 0.62$) was found between the child's assessment of their own behaviour and their perception of their teacher's assessment. This is higher than the correlation ($r = 0.31$) between children's perceptions of their teacher's assessment and the teacher's assessment itself.

Analyses of the children's responses to the 'Me at School' indicated that age was not related to this measure of self-concept. Younger children were not more likely than older members of the year group to have an unfavourable view of themselves in school.

Attendance

Full attendance data were collected for every child in the sample for each term of their first three years at junior school. The attendance measure was based on the number of half days the pupils could have been present. From this information, the overall average percentage of time children were present was calculated.

Average attendance was very high in all three years: 91.8 per cent in the first year; 91.2 per cent in the second year; and 91.7 per cent in the third year. This represents an average absence of 15 school days in the first and third years and 16 days in the second year. In all years, attendance was slightly poorer in the spring term than in other terms. The variation between children in their attendance was greater in the third year than in other years.

Age was not found to be significantly related to children's attendance at school in any year. In all years, average attendance was very good (exceeding 90 per cent) irrespective of term of birth. Thus, in contrast to most of the cognitive and other non-cognitive outcomes, age did not influence school attendance during the junior years.

Length of infant school experience

As might be expected there was a close and highly statistically significant relationship between a pupil's age and the length of time she or he had spent in infant school. For example, prior to transfer, summer born pupils had an average of only 26 months infant school experience. Spring born pupils, in contrast, had an average of 31 months, while autumn born pupils had an average of nearly 35 months experience of infant education. Expressed as a correlation, this relationship between month of birth and months in infant school was also found to be very marked ($r = 0.83$, p.< 0.001).

The link between age and length of infant experience reflects policies on the age at which children are encouraged to enter infant school (usually the term of their fifth birthday in the ILEA). As a result, summer born children, in general, spend far less time in infant departments or schools prior to transfer into junior education than do the older members of their year group. It appears that summer born pupils tend to suffer the double disadvantage of being the youngest members of a class and of having substantially fewer months of infant education, in comparison with their autumn born peers.[8]

Analyses indicated that length of infant school experience was weakly, but significantly, associated with reading and mathematics attainment at entry to junior school ($r = 0.25$ for both cognitive assessments). The relationships were stronger in the first than in later assessments, suggesting that length of infant school experience is a more important influence upon attainment for pupils at transfer into junior education than is the case in the second and third years.

The relationships between infant school experience and cognitive attainments were, in part, a function of age (because age largely determines the length of infant schooling). Nonetheless, infant experience remained significantly, though weakly, related to reading and mathematics performance, even when account was taken of pupils' age at test (partial $r = 0.11$ between months in infant school and first year mathematics attainment; partial $r = 0.11$ between months in infant and first year reading attainment).

When account was taken of the impact of age, sex and other background factors upon reading and mathematics attainment, length of infant school experience was found to have a significant but small impact upon attainment in the first year reading assessment, but the relationships were not significant in later assessments. For mathematics, length of infant experience had an impact in both the first and second year assessments, but no effect in the two third year assessments. The length of infant school experience was not, however, related to pupils' *progress* over three years in either reading or mathematics. This finding is in line with those reported earlier on the impact of age, which indicated that age did not affect junior pupils' progress in these two cognitive areas.

In summary, therefore, the research revealed differences in attitudes to school, a greater incidence of behavioural difficulties and a marked 'gap' in reading, writing and mathematics attainment between the younger and older members of the sample. These differences indicate that younger children are at risk of experiencing greater difficulties in adjustment to junior school. The results of the analyses suggest that it is important to promote teachers' awareness of the impact of age differences within year-based classes of pupils.

In particular, it appears that, amongst any year group, younger children have had significantly less infant school experience than other groups, and that this helps to account for age differences in attainment at entry to junior school. Length of infant schooling thus plays an important part in determining children's attainment and adjustment in junior school. These results are of especial significance because recent work indicates that age-related differences in achievement can continue throughout formal schooling and into higher education (see Russell and Startup, 1986).

Differences according to social class

Cognitive outcomes

In assessing the impact of social class upon attainment, it must be emphasized that the broad scale developed by the Registrar General neglects many important aspects about the child's home, relationships with parents and lifestyle (see the discussion by Mortimore, 1983). Nonetheless, the strength of relationship between this characteristic and attainment throughout a child's school career has been tested in numerous studies, and work on the Junior School sample confirms the importance of this factor, even when account is taken of aspects of parents' activities with their children, housing and income (see Sammons *et al.*, 1985).

To assess the impact of social class upon children's attainment and progress in the junior years, information about both mother's and father's occupations was collected for the sample of pupils. (For details see Appendix). Overall, the majority of children were from working class homes, a reflection of the social class composition of the inner London population.

Reading

Both mother's and father's occupation were highly related to reading performance at entry to junior school. The average score for the non-manual group was 55.5; for the skilled manual group 46; for the semi- and unskilled manual group 41.1; for the unemployed 39.6, and for those where fathers were absent 43.7 raw points.[9]

In assessing the impact of social class upon attainment and progress in cognitive areas, numerous analyses were conducted. Full account was taken of other factors, including ethnic family background, fluency in English, family size and birth order, eligibility for free school meals, experience of nursery education, sex and age. This set of variables was chosen from analyses of the full range of background data to cover all the major factors which previous research has suggested may be influential. Therefore, differences between the social classes can be seen as 'net' of the impact of other factors.

Even having taken full account of other influences, a difference of 14 raw score points — which represents a gap of nearly ten months in reading age — was found between children with fathers in professional or intermediate non-manual work, and those with fathers in unskilled manual work. A similar effect was in evidence for the mother's occupation. Long term unemployment of either parent was also associated with poorer reading attainment.

The relationships between social class and reading attainment remained marked throughout the period of junior education, on all four occasions that reading was assessed. By the summer of the third year, the differences due to father's occupation had become even greater than at entry to junior school. At entry to the juniors, 20 per cent of those with fathers in semi- and unskilled work, compared with 41 per cent of their non-manual counterparts, obtained reading scores in the top quarter of the distribution. By the end of the third year, 19 per cent of the semi- and unskilled manual group obtained scores in the top quarter of the distribution, compared with 46 per cent of the non-manual group.

In the London Reading Test (taken in the fourth year), differences were again identified. In all, only 16 per cent of the non-manual group scored fewer than 35 points in this assessment (the 'cut-off' recommended for special needs screening). The equivalent figure for the semi- and unskilled manual group was 28 per cent. The results of analyses of individual reading performance over time identified marked and increasing differences between the social class groups during the junior years, even when important relationships with other factors have been taken into account. These findings support the conclusions of the longitudinal study by the National Children's Bureau (see Essen and Wedge, 1982).

Analysis of the impact of social class upon individual pupils' progress in reading during the junior years was possible because of the longitudinal nature of the study. Each pupil's first year reading score was used as the basis for assessing her or his progress over the next three years. [10] The results indicate that, although some individuals change considerably, reading attainment at entry accounts for much of the variation in performance three years later (62 per cent). The social class of father's occupation continued, however, to have a statistically significant relationship with progress. Mother's occupation did not, however, make a significant contribution to the statistical explanation of differences in pupils' reading progress (this is likely to reflect the high proportion of mothers who were not in paid employment and for whom no occupational data were therefore available). Overall, children whose fathers were in non-manual work made significantly greater progress than other groups. The difference was four raw score points, compared with a mean of 54 and a possible maximum of 100 points for the whole sample in the summer of third year. In contrast, children from manual backgrounds tended to make less progress in reading when account was taken of other factors and initial attainment at entry to junior school.

Mathematics

The relationships between children's social class background and attainment in mathematics were investigated in the same manner as reading. Again, substantial differences between children of different social class backgrounds were identified at entry to junior school. For example, the mean raw score for the non-manual group was 27 points; for the skilled manual 24.5; for the semi- and unskilled manual group 23.1, for the economically inactive/long term unemployed group 22.8, and for those whose father was absent 23.4. This compares with a maximum possible score of 40 in the mathematics assessment, and an overall mean of 24.3 raw points.

The results of the analyses of the relationships between attainment and mother's and father's social class, taking into account other background factors, indicate that both were significant. Children whose fathers were in non-manual occupations had significantly higher attainment than those whose fathers were in unskilled manual work. For mother's occupation, children whose mothers were in professional or intermediate non-manual work had the highest attainment and those whose mothers were absent, unemployed or not working, the lowest. The difference in mathematics attainment between the professional and intermediate non-manual groups represented around nine months in terms of age — a very similar gap to that identified in reading.

This pattern of differences remained at each of the four assessments of mathematics. For example, in the summer of the third year, children whose fathers were in professional or intermediate non-manual work obtained scores more than 7.5 raw points higher than those with fathers in unskilled manual work (compared with a mean of 27 points), when other background factors were taken into account. However, the differences in mathematics attainment between the social groups did not appear to increase over time. In the first year, 43 per cent of the non-manual and 23 per cent of the semi- and unskilled group obtained scores in the top quarter of the distribution. By the end of the third year the figures were little changed, at 42 and 22 per cent respectively.

In contrast to reading, progress in mathematics was not statistically significantly related to social class when the effects of initial attainment and other background factors were controlled.[11] Thus, although the gap in achievement in mathematics between the social classes remained large throughout the junior years, it did not increase — in contrast to the results for reading. This finding suggests that home factors are less important influences upon mathematics progress and attainment than upon reading. It seems likely that mathematics progress may be more affected than reading progress by school work because parents are likely to provide greater help at home with reading than with mathematics.

Visio-spatial skills

Attainment in the visio-spatial assessment was less closely related to background than attainment in reading or maths. In contrast to findings for reading and mathematics in the first year of junior school, the results of the analyses did not favour those of non-manual backgrounds over those from families with manual origins. By the second year, however, the relationship between father's occupation and visio-spatial skills followed the pattern identified for both reading and mathematics . At this stage, children of non-manual backgrounds had higher attainment than those of unskilled manual origins or those whose fathers were absent or unemployed. Mother's occupation, however, was not related to children's attainments in either year.

When initial attainment in the Raven's test of visio-spatial ability was controlled, father's occupation continued to make a statistically significant contribution in explaining progress in this area. As in other cognitive areas, children whose fathers were in non-manual work made greater progress than other groups.

Writing

Marked differences in writing performance (in terms of both quality and length) according to social class were identified in each year. Thus, 28 per cent of the semi-

and unskilled manual group produced writing which was assessed as below average in quality in the first year, compared with only 18 per cent of the non-manual group.

Results of analyses of the relationships between background factors and the quality and length of writing produced by pupils in their first year clearly indicated a significant relationship with father's social class. For quality (assessed on a ten point scale), the difference between the writing of children whose fathers were in non-manual work and those in unskilled manual work exceeded one point (compared with a mean of 6.2 and a maximum possible score of 10). In terms of writing length, children with fathers in non-manual work produced stories 22 words longer than the sample average (of 88 words), whereas the writing of those whose fathers were in unskilled manual work was 15 words shorter than the average.

Mother's social class was less strongly related to quality of writing than father's social class, and did not have a significant impact upon length. The pattern of relationships between social class and the quality and length of children's writing remained highly significant at each assessment. Father's social class was highly significantly related to progress in both the quality and length of writing, even when first year attainment was taken into account. Mother's social class did not make a statistically significant contribution to progress in this area. Again, children whose fathers were in non-manual work made greater progress than those with fathers in unskilled manual work (a difference of nearly half a point in terms of the ten point quality assessment). However, those whose fathers were not working, or were absent, also made rather greater progress than predicted by their first year attainment. [12] The non-manual children produced stories 32 words longer than expected (compared with a mean of 246 words), given their first year attainment.

It is clear, therefore, that in the formal language-based areas of the curriculum (reading and writing) children from non-manual backgrounds make greater progress than others over the junior years, in addition to their superior attainment at entry.

Practical mathematics

The practical mathematics assessment covered five areas — number, length, weight, volume and sets. Analysis of attainment in these different areas indicates that children with fathers in non-manual employment tended to perform more highly than other groups in particular activities. These differences were statistically significant in two areas — volume and length — in the first year. In the second and third year assessments, however, significant differences in attainment were identified in volume, length and sets work. In the second year, differences were also identified in number work and, in the third year, in weighing activities.

Therefore, in addition to differences in attainment in the written mathematics assessment, differences in practical mathematical skills were also related to social class background.

Oracy

Father's social class was the only factor which was significantly related to the oral assessments. This factor made a statistically significant contribution to the explanation of the general performance (holistic), task specific and verbal performance assessments. These three scales were quite highly correlated. Pupils whose fathers were in non-manual work obtained significantly higher scores than other groups (a difference of nearly four points on the holistic measure of general performance, compared with an overall mean of 21.5 points). In contrast, social class was not related to attainment in the lexico-grammatical or non-verbal performance scales.

It appears that, as with other cognitive areas, oral attainment is related to social class background. In terms of general performance, the ability to fulfil the requirements of different kinds of speaking tasks (the specific assessment), and in the use of language, children from non-manual background had rather higher attainments. There were, however, no significant differences in non-verbal performance (the child's ability to involve her or his audience through eye contact and gesturing) or in the structure of speech (lexico-grammatical features).

Teachers' assessments of pupils' ability

There were very marked differences at each assessment, according to father's social class, in the percentage of pupils rated by their class teachers as above and below average ability.

In the autumn of the first year, 48 per cent of the non-manual, compared with only 25 per cent of semi- and unskilled manual group were rated as of above average ability. Only 16 per cent of the non-manual, but 32 per cent of the semi- and unskilled manual group, were rated as below average ability. By the third year, the differences were even greater.

As noted earlier there were marked variations between children of different social classes in terms of their cognitive attainments. Because teachers' assessments of pupil ability were found to be strongly related to performance in reading, writing and mathematics, analyses were conducted to establish whether social class background was related to teacher judgements, while controlling for attainment in these three areas and for other background factors. The results indicated that, once account was taken of reading, mathematics and writing performance, social class background was still related to teachers' ratings of abilities. This effect, it must be emphasized, was small. It was, nonetheless, statistically significant and operated in favour of the non-manual group on each occasion.

It seems, therefore, that although teachers' judgements of ability were largely determined by children's attainments, on the whole, teachers tended to have a slightly more favourable view of those of non-manual backgrounds. Thus, higher teacher expectations may be one factor which contributed to the greater progress in reading and writing made by the non-manual group in comparison with other groups during the junior years. These findings support those identified by other researchers (see the review of the literature concerning teacher expectations by Pilling and Kellmer Pringle, 1978).

Non-cognitive outcomes

Behaviour

Analyses showed that socio-economic factors were highly related to teachers' behaviour assessments of pupils at entry to junior school. Both mother's and father's social class were significantly associated with the behaviour rating in the first, second and third years of junior school. According to their teachers' assessments, children from semi- and unskilled manual backgrounds had a higher incidence of behaviour difficulties in school.

Comparison of pupils who were assessed as having some kind of behaviour disturbance on two or more occasions with those who were never assessed as disturbed, shows that differences between the two groups in socio-economic background were very marked (see Table 7.5). In all, only 10 per cent of disturbed, compared with 24 per cent of non-disturbed pupils, were of non-manual origins. In contrast, 23 per cent of disturbed children's fathers did not live with them, compared with 12 per cent of non-disturbed children. Thus, as with the cognitive outcomes of education, social class also appears to have a strong effect on non-cognitive areas.

Table 7.5 Social class and the incidence of behaviour difficulties **

	Pupils assessed as disturbed on two or more occasions	Pupils never assessed as disturbed
	(N = 164) %	(N = 903) %
Mother's Social Class		
Non-manual	8.5	14.0*
Skilled manual	—	1.7
Semi- and unskilled	14.0	11.3
Not working	47.6	37.5
Absent	4.3	1.6
Not known	25.6	34.0
Father's Social Class		
Non-manual	10.3*	24.2
Skilled manual	27.4	31.9
Semi- and unskilled	20.1	13.4
Not working	6.7	6.3
Absent	23.2	12.1
Not known	12.2	12.1

*   Due to rounding, percentages do not sum to 100.
** Pupils assessed as disturbed on only one occasion excluded.

Attitudes

Background factors accounted for only a very small percentage of the variation in pupils' attitudes towards mathematics, reading or towards school in any year. The analyses demonstrated that attitudes to curriculum areas and to school were related less strongly to pupils' backgrounds than was attainment in the various cognitive areas.

Social class was not related to children's attitudes to mathematics, to 'reading to yourself', or to general attitudes towards school in the first year. By the third year, however, father's social class was related significantly to attitude to reading. Overall, children whose fathers were in non-manual work expressed more favourable attitudes to reading.[13] Children in this category did not, however, show more favourable attitudes to mathematics than did most other groups.

It appears that, amongst primary-aged children, socio-economic factors were less powerful determinants of attitudes towards school or towards curriculum areas, than they were of cognitive attainment. This may be because attitudes are influenced more by teacher behaviour or school organization and atmosphere than is attainment (an argument put forward by Reynolds, 1982). Alternatively, it may simply be that children's attitudes are much more difficult to measure and much less stable than cognitive attainment at this stage in their school careers.

Self-concept

In all, only a very small proportion of the variation in scores on the self-concept measure was explained (in a statistical sense) by background factors, sex and age (3.2 per cent). This figure is of similar size to the proportion of variation in attitudes explained by the same background factors, sex and age. It seems that non-cognitive areas measured by self-report questionnaires were less predictable in terms of pupils' characteristics than were the cognitive outcomes of schooling. There were no significant differences between the social classes in pupils' self-concepts. However, overall, low income (as measured by eligibility for free school meals) did have a small but significant relationship with self-concept. The responses of those children eligible for free meals indicated that they had poorer self-perceptions than children who were not.

Attendance

Overall, background factors were less strongly related to children's attendance than to their attainments (only around 12 per cent of the variation in attendance compared with 24 per cent of the variation in reading attainment, for example, was accounted for by background factors). On the whole, attendance in the junior years for children of all backgrounds was very good. Nonetheless, attendance in the first year of junior school was related significantly to social class. Children with fathers in non-manual work were absent for the least time, whilst those whose fathers were unemployed, economically inactive or absent, missed the most school time in the first year. However, those from semi- and unskilled manual homes were not absent for a significantly greater proportion of time than those of non-manual backgrounds (see Table 7.6). This is in contrast to relationships in the cognitive areas described earlier.

Table 7.6 *Average percentage of time absent from school in years 1, 2 and 3 by father's social class*

	% Time Absent					
Father's Social Class	*Year 1*	*N*	*Year 2*	*N*	*Year 3*	*N*
Non-manual	7.4	(361)	8.3	(343)	7.0	(302)
Skilled manual	8.4	(516)	8.5	(493)	7.9	(447)
Semi- and unskilled	7.8	(229)	9.5	(218)	8.8	(164)
Not working	11.2	(125)	9.8	(117)	9.8	(105)
Father absent	10.6	(246)	11.1	(234)	10.2	(201)

Mother's occupation was also related significantly to attendance. There was a tendency for children whose mothers were economically inactive or unemployed to be absent for a higher percentage of time than was the case for those whose mothers were in employment. This may reflect the difficulties working mothers have in obtaining time off work, which could explain why they were less likely than non-working mothers to keep children at home.

Children from low income families were also more likely to have poor attendance records than were other children. Those eligible for free meals were absent for around ten per cent of the time, whereas those not eligible were absent for only about eight per cent of the time.

Mother's social class did not make a significant contribution to the explanation of attendance in the second or third year, although father's social class and eligibility for free meals remained of importance. Taking into account all other background factors, in the third year, children with fathers in non-manual work were absent for around one per cent less of the time than others, compared with a mean of 8.3 per cent.

Overall, the results of the Junior School Project indicate quite clearly that children of non-manual backgrounds attained more highly in the majority of cognitive areas. They also made greater progress than other groups in reading and in writing. A small but significant difference was found in teachers' assessments of ability, in favour of the non-manual group. Children whose fathers were in semi- and unskilled manual work, and those whose fathers were absent, were significantly more likely to exhibit behaviour difficulties in school.

There was little evidence of differences according to social class, however, in attendance, attitudes or self-concept. Those from families where the father was absent, or not working, had poorer attendance records. The findings indicate that, for junior-age pupils, socio-economic factors were related to only certain of the measures of adjustment to (or alienation from) school. Furthermore, attitudes and self-concept were less affected than behaviour or attendance.

Differences according to sex

The relationships between sex and cognitive and non-cognitive educational outcomes were investigated in the same way as differences according to age and social class.

Cognitive outcomes

Both variations in attainment and, where possible, progress, were explored for each of the cognitive outcome measures.

Reading

There were marked differences between the two sexes in terms of average reading scores at each assessment (see Table 7.7). Only 17 per cent of girls, compared with 33 per cent of boys, obtained scores in the bottom quarter of the distribution at entry to junior school. In contrast, 31 per cent of girls, compared with 19 per cent of boys, obtained scores in the top quarter of the distribution. At the end of the third year, a very similar pattern was identified, 19 per cent of girls obtained scores in the bottom quarter of the distribution, compared with 31 per cent of the boys. Moreover, 31 per cent of girls and only 21 per cent of boys obtained scores in the top quarter of the distribution.

Table 7.7 Mean raw reading scores at each assessment by sex

	Girls	N	Boys	N	Difference
Year 1 (autumn)	50.8	900	41.4	867	9.4
Year 2 (autumn)	67.5	870	59.1	832	8.4
Year 3 (autumn)	43.7	754	37.0	725	6.7
Year 3 (summer)	55.7	732	48.1	691	7.6

Analyses at the individual level showed that, taking into account all other factors, the raw scores of girls were significantly higher, and those of boys significantly lower than the average, at each assessment. In the first year, for example, this represented a difference of about five months in reading age in favour of girls.

In terms of the fourth year London Reading Test results, a similar pattern of sex differences was identified. Girls were much less likely than boys to score below 35 points (the 'cut off' recommended for special needs screening at secondary transfer). In all, 19 per cent of girls, compared with 32 per cent of boys obtained LRT scores of below 35. These results, therefore, provide no evidence of a significant closing of the gap in reading achievement between boys and girls during the junior years.

This finding concerning the importance of sex as a factor influencing reading attainment supports the APU Language Survey (1981) which also indicated, in a national sample, that girls' attainment was superior to that of boys.

Analyses of progress in reading, however, indicated that sex did *not* have a significant effect on progress in addition to the effect on reading attainment. Thus, when account was taken of reading attainment at entry, girls did not make greater or less progress in reading over the junior years than boys. The reasons for the differences between the two sexes in reading attainment are not easily explained. It is possible that girls enjoy reading activities more than boys and that this causes them to spend more time than boys in private reading at home or at school (see APU, 1981, for details of reading preferences). Alternatively, girls may perceive reading as an area in which it is acceptable to excel, or they may receive more adult encouragement in their reading than boys. In the sub-section on non-cognitive outcomes, the behaviour and attitudinal data are examined to test whether differences in behaviour and in attitudes to reading were also associated with pupils' sex.

Mathematics

Figures in Table 7.8 show the average raw scores in mathematics for the two sexes at each assessment. In contrast to reading, sex was not related significantly to mathematics attainment at entry to junior school. Taking into account other background factors in the individual level analyses, very little difference in attainment was identified in any assessment except that made in the summer of the third year. At this stage, however, sex had some effect on mathematics attainment, although the differences between the two groups just failed to reach statistical significance ($P < 0.06$). Although small (just over one raw point) the difference in mathematics attainment in the summer of the third year was in favour of the girls. These results provide no evidence, therefore, that girls' mathematics performance *declines* with age, at least during the junior years. If anything, girls had marginally higher achievement than boys in the later junior years.

Table 7.8 Mean raw mathematics scores at each assessment by sex

	Girls	N	Boys	N	Difference
Year 1 (autumn)	24.6	902	24.0	870	0.6
Year 2 (autumn)	24.5	885	24.0	832	0.5
Year 3 (autumn)	29.4	800	29.2	795	0.2
Year 3 (summer)	27.5	768	25.8	774	1.7

Interestingly, given commonly held beliefs about girls' under-achievement in mathematics, it was found that, when initial attainment was controlled, sex had a statistically significant impact on progress in mathematics ($p < 0.02$). This difference was in favour of girls, who made slightly *more* progress than the boys over the first three years in junior school. This result indicates that girls were not under-achieving in mathematics during the primary years and, in terms of mathematics attainment, they did not transfer to secondary school disadvantaged in comparison with their male peers.

Visio-spatial skills

Sex was not related significantly to performance in the Ravens assessments of visio-spatial skills conducted in the first and second years. When progress in this area was analysed over the first to second year, sex did not make a significant contribution to the explanation of variations in pupils' progress. Thus, sex did not appear to be an influential factor in determining visio-spatial skills amongst the sample. This finding is in contrast to results from research with older age groups which have suggested that boys tend to do better than girls in tests of visio-spatial skills (see Hutt, 1979).

Writing

Sex was related highly significantly to the length of children's writing in the first year of junior school. The differences between the sexes in the length of stories written was 21 words (compared with the average of 88 words) in favour of the girls. More importantly, the work of the two sexes differed significantly in the first year, in terms of quality of language and ideas. The difference was more than half a point (compared with an average of 6.4 points). Overall, in the first year only 20 per cent of girls' writing was assessed as below average in terms of quality of ideas and language. This compares with a figure of 33 per cent for the boys. A very similar result was found in the third year. In all, 19 per cent of the girls', compared with 27 per cent of the boys' writing, was assessed as below average on this occasion. There were also significant sex differences in some of the technical measures concerned with legibility and the use of punctuation. In all cases the differences favoured the girls.

As with reading, therefore, the girls' attainment in writing was markedly better than that of the boys. This again confirms findings by the APU (1981, 1982) that girls tend to achieve more highly than boys in language-based areas.

In both the second and third year writing assessments, girls' writing was found to be significantly longer than that of the boys and was again assessed more highly in terms of quality. It appears, therefore, that girls' initial superiority in writing performance was maintained during the junior years. In terms of progress, however, although on average girls' writing was significantly longer than that of boys (by 34 words compared with a mean of 246), in the summer of the third year sex did not make a significant contribution to the explanation of this variation in length, when account was taken of the length of a child's writing in the first year and background factors. Similarly, sex was not related to progress in terms of quality of third year writing (when quality of first year writing and background factors were controlled). Therefore, girls did not make greater or less progress than boys in creative writing over three years, although differences in attainment remained apparent.

Practical mathematics

No sex differences were identified in any of the three years in which practical mathematics assessments were conducted, either in overall performance, or in the specific skills measured by the different areas covered by the test. Therefore, in neither written nor practical tasks was there any evidence of under-achievement by girls in mathematics during the junior years.

Oracy

Sex was not related to performance in any of the five scales used to assess children's oral skills. Moreover, no significant differences between the sexes in their performance in different types of speaking activity were identified. Therefore, although girls had higher achievement than boys in two of the language assessments (writing and reading) they did not have superior attainments in *all* language-based activities. Again, this result supports the conclusions reached by the APU's work on oracy (see Gorman *et al.*, 1984).

Figure 7.3: Percentage of pupils assessed as a) above, b) below average ability by pupil sex (years 2 and 3)

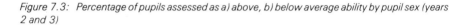

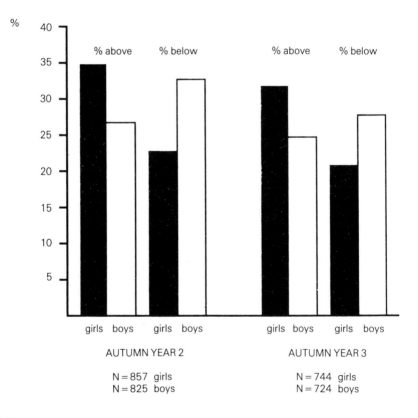

Teachers' assessments of pupils' ability

Overall, a higher percentage of girls than of boys were assessed as above average ability by their teachers at each assessment (see Figure 7.3). Analyses of the relationships between children's attainments in cognitive areas and teachers' ratings of ability, indicated that reading, writing and mathematics performance were strongly related to teachers' judgements. As has been demonstrated, girls were achieving significantly more highly than boys in reading and in writing. When account was taken of children's attainments in these three areas, no significant difference between the sexes in teachers' assessments of ability were identified. However, it is interesting that when account was taken of attainment, the small difference between the two sexes in teachers' ability ratings was consistently in favour of the boys (though these results were not statistically significant).

Non-cognitive outcomes

Relationships between sex and behaviour, attitudes, and self-concept were investigated whilst controlling for the effects of other background factors (using the same methods as employed for analyses of the influence of age and social class discussed earlier).

Behaviour

Analyses of the behaviour data indicated that sex was highly significantly related to teachers' assessments of children's behaviour in school. Girls tended to receive lower assessments of behaviour disturbance than boys. This relationship remained pronounced on each occasion that behaviour was assessed. The results of these analyses support findings of differences between the sexes in the incidence of behaviour difficulties reported by Chazan and Jackson (1974) and Varlaam (1974).

A comparison of pupils who were assessed as having disturbed behaviour on two or more occasions with those who were never assessed as disturbed, revealed marked differences between the groups in terms of the percentages of girls and boys (see Table 7.9). Thus, of those assessed as having behaviour difficulties on two or more occasions, the percentage of boys was much higher than that of girls. In contrast, of pupils who were never rated as disturbed by their teachers, a higher percentage were girls (56 per cent) than boys (44 per cent).

Therefore it appears that sex is related to non-cognitive outcomes, such as behaviour in school, as well as to children's cognitive attainment. As noted earlier, attainment and behaviour were quite closely related. It is possible that part of the relationship between sex and behaviour may be due to boys' poorer attainment in certain cognitive areas. If poor attainment has an adverse impact on behaviour, boys' poorer achievement may account for their greater risk of behaviour disturbance. Alternatively, if poor behaviour has a detrimental impact on later attainment, then boys' poorer behaviour may account for some of the differences in cog-

*Table 7.9   The incidence of behaviour difficulties by pupil sex *

	Pupils assessed as disturbed two or more occasions	Pupils never assessed as disturbed
	(N = 164)	(N = 903)
	%	%
Girls	37	56
Boys	63	44

* Pupils assessed as disturbed on one occasion excluded.

nitive outcomes between the sexes. However, what is particularly interesting is that, despite higher attainment and better behaviour, there was no evidence of over-expectation of girls' ability by their class teachers.

Attitudes

Analyses revealed no significant relationship between sex and pupils' attitude to mathematics in any of the three years for which information was obtained. Thus, there was no evidence that girls have a less positive view of mathematics than boys during the junior years.

Sex was not related significantly to attitude to reading in the first or the second year. By the third year, a small but statistically significant difference between the two sexes in attitude to reading was apparent ($p < 0.03$). Girls had a marginally more favourable view than boys at this stage. Both groups, however, had a generally positive view. Given the absence of a relationship between attitude to reading and sex in the first and second years, it seems unlikely that differences in attitudes between the two sexes could explain the markedly higher reading attainment of girls compared with boys in those years. There were no differences between the sexes in attitudes to writing.

In contrast, sex was related highly significantly to the attitude to school expressed by children in each of the three years ($p < 0.0001$). In each year, boys expressed a much less positive view of school than girls. At the junior level, therefore, it is clear that boys are more likely than girls to be disenchanted with school.

The reasons for sex differences in attitudes to school are not clear. Although poor attainment by boys might be expected to lead to less favourable attitudes to school work and to school in general, sex differences in attitudes to curriculum areas were weak or non-existent, as noted above. It is possible that the tendency for boys to have a higher incidence of behaviour difficulties may have affected their attitudes to school. But it is equally possible that less favourable attitudes to school led to behaviour problems. However, amongst the whole sample, relationships between behaviour and attitudes to school and to work were rather weak.

Attendance

Sex was not found to be related to attendance in the first, second or third year of junior school. The generally higher attainments of girls in certain cognitive areas were not due to better attendance at school. Moreover, although boys tended to have poorer behaviour and less favourable attitudes to school, they were no more likely to be absent from school than were girls. Amongst the junior age-group, alienation from school is apparently more likely to be expressed in terms of attitude to school rather than by poor attendance.

Self-concept

As with attitudes to school, girls were found to have significantly more positive self-concepts in relation to school than boys. This may reflect the nature of some of the items relating to naughtiness included in the questionnaire. The boys were more likely than the girls to admit to naughtiness and irritability and also were more likely to think that the teacher perceived them as being naughty. However, they were less likely than the girls to rate themselves highly on items concerning personal anxiety. As noted in the discussion of behaviour, there was a highly significant difference between the two sexes in teachers' assessments of behaviour in school. Overall, in each year, teachers assessed a higher proportion of boys than of girls as having behaviour problems.

In summary, for this age group, there were striking sex differences in both pupil achievement and adjustment. Marked differences were identified between girls and boys in reading and writing attainment, but not in *progress*, throughout the junior years. In mathematics, however, although differences in attainment were slight, girls made greater progress than boys over the junior years. There were no sex differences in oracy. Girls tended to have more positive attitudes towards school and more favourable self-concepts. Marked differences were identified by class teachers between the two sexes in behaviour in school. Boys were more likely than girls to be assessed as having behaviour difficulties.

Differences according to race

Relationships between ethnic background, pupils' fluency in English and their attainment and progress in various cognitive and non-cognitive areas were investigated in the same manner as were the effects of age, social class background, and sex.

Cognitive outcomes

Reading

Results of analyses of the effects of ethnic background and fluency in English upon reading attainment at entry to junior school indicate that both factors were highly significant ($p < 0.0001$). Thus, children who were not fully fluent in English (according to their class teacher) obtained markedly lower reading scores than those who were fully fluent. The effect of being a beginner, or at the second stage of fluency in English, was a reduction in reading scores by between 14 and 23 raw points (in relation to the overall mean of 46).[14]

The effects of ethnic background were more complicated. Even where fluency in English and other background factors had been controlled, certain Asian groups performed differently from others. For example, those who spoke Gujerati performed better than average in the reading test, whilst those speaking Punjabi had poorer reading attainment.[15] Children of Caribbean, Greek and Turkish family backgrounds obtained lower reading scores than those of English, Scottish, Welsh or Irish (ESWI) backgrounds. Those of Chinese family backgrounds (only 17 in all) had higher scores than those of other ethnic groups, when all other background factors had been taken into account.

In analyses of the second year and the third year reading assessments, ethnic background and fluency in English remained highly significant. Therefore, there was no evidence that the impact of these factors decreased over the junior years. For reading attainment, the pattern of initial differences between the ethnic groups remained fairly stable over time.

Relationships between ethnic family background, language fluency and childrens' *progress* in reading over three years were explored. It was found that both factors had a statistically significant impact upon progress. Children of Caribbean backgrounds and those of Asian backgrounds made significantly poorer progress than other groups, even when account was taken of initial attainment. Children who were not fully fluent in English at entry to junior school also made significantly poorer progress in reading over the three years.

The poorer progress of minority ethnic groups in reading supports the results of previous research (see Rampton, 1981 or Mabey, 1981) which indicated that the gap in attainment between English and Caribbean children increased over time. Amongst the present sample, however, it also appears that Asian children as well as Caribbean children made poorer progress in reading over the junior years. The size of these differences are given in Table 7.10.

Table 7.10   Effects of ethnic background and fluency in English upon reading progress over three years *

	Effect in Raw Score Points
Caribbean	− 3.4
Asian	− 4.5
Incomplete fluency in English	− 3.7
N = 1101	
Overall mean = 53.8	

* Analyses adjusted for other background factors (including age, sex, social class, initial attainment, test reliability and the clustered nature of the sample). Due to the small sample of Asian pupils it was not possible to examine separately the *progress* of different language sub-groups.

Mathematics

For mathematics attainment at entry, analyses also identified highly significant relationships with ethnic background and with fluency in English. Again, there was variation in the achievements of different sub-groups of Asian children. Those who spoke Bengali tended to have lower scores than those who spoke Gujerati (a difference of 5.5 raw points compared with a mean of 24.3). Children who were of Caribbean and of Turkish origins also tended to obtain lower scores (2.6 and 1.5 points respectively below the mean). A consistent pattern of differences between the different ethnic groups in mathematics attainment was also identified in analyses of assessments in later years. Thus, as a group, in the summer of year three, Caribbean children's attainments were 4.5 points below the mean of 26.8 raw points, and Turkish and Greek children were nearly two points below the mean. In contrast, the Gujerati-speaking Asian pupils (a small group) scored nearly three points above the mean. This pattern of ethnic differences was very similar to that identified in the first year.

Although the gap in mathematics attainment remained marked throughout the junior years for children of different ethnic backgrounds or with different levels of fluency in English, there was no evidence of an ethnic or fluency effect on progress in mathematics. Controlling for initial attainment, neither Caribbean nor Asian children made significantly poorer progress than their ESWI peers. In other words, differences in the performance of children from different ethnic backgrounds do *not* increase over the junior years in mathematics, in contrast to the results for reading.

Visio-spatial skills

Fluency in English, but not ethnic origin, was related significantly to performance in the assessment of visio-spatial skills in the first year of junior school. In the second year, however, both fluency in English and ethnic origin were related significantly to performance. Although this assessment was chosen to give a measure of performance not dependent upon language, it is apparent that language fluency in fact was related to children's performance in visio-spatial activities.

Thus, children not fully fluent in English obtained raw scores of three points below the mean of 28.5. In contrast, when the effects of other factors were taken into account, Chinese children and Asian children of Bengali, Gujerati and Punjabi-speaking backgrounds obtained higher scores than average and those of Caribbean background lower scores. In terms of progress over one year in visio-spatial skills, those not fully fluent in English made poorer progress than those fully fluent in English. Caribbean children also made poorer progress than other groups.

Writing

There was no significant relationship between ethnic background and writing performance in the first year in terms of quality or length. In contrast, fluency in

English was highly significantly related to both length and quality of writing. In the summer of the third year, however, it was found that ethnic background was related significantly to the length of writing, with the various Asian groups, those of Caribbean and those of Turkish backgrounds tending to produce shorter pieces of work. There were, however, no significant differences between ethnic groups in terms of quality of ideas and language expressed in their written work. Again, fluency in English was related significantly to quality, but no longer had an independent impact upon length of writing.

When progress in the quality of writing was analysed, no relationship was found with ethnic background, although the effects of fluency in English just reached significance ($p < 0.04$). Thus, taking account of first year writing quality, children who were not fully fluent in English made slightly poorer progress over the three years than did children who were fully fluent (by around half a point on the ten point quality scale). For progress in the quantity written over three years (controlling for length of first year writing), it was found that ethnic background did not have a statistically significant effect.

These results indicate that, in terms of quality of writing, ethnic background was not related to attainment or to progress during the junior years. This is in contrast to the findings for reading and for mathematics attainment. As might be expected, however, children not fluent in English are disadvantaged in attainment in writing as well as in reading and mathematics.

Practical mathematics

There were few significant relationships between achievement in practical mathematics tasks and either ethnic or language background. Children of Asian background performed slightly less well than other groups in the volume tasks. Fluency in English was only related to attainment in activities related to work with sets. Overall, however, the relationships were not strong.

Oracy

As stated earlier, the oracy assessments were designed to judge the communicative effectiveness of children's speech activities, and assessors did not penalize pupils who used non-standard English. Results from the analyses indicated that ethnic background was *not* related to performance in any of the five scales used to assess oracy.

Interestingly, fluency in English (as assessed by teachers) was not related to pupils' speaking skills. The reason for this may be due to an improvement in pupils' abilities to speak English over the junior years (the fluency assessment was made in the first year of junior school, whereas the oracy assessments took place in the fourth year). Alternatively, the results suggest that the ability to use standard English forms may be more closely related to reading achievement than to oral skills.

The project findings show that in some language areas — oracy and quality of writing — there were no significant diffences between children of different ethnic backgrounds. For reading and mathematics attainment and for *progress* in reading, differences were identified. The reasons for differences between the measures of attainment and of progress in reading, rather than in other areas of language, are not yet clear.

Teachers' assessments of pupils' ability

At each assessment, a higher percentage of English, Scottish, Welsh and Irish than of other pupils were assessed by their class teachers as of above average ability, and a smaller percentage as of below average ability.

For example, in the autumn of the second year, nearly a third of ESWI pupils were assessed as above average, compared with around a quarter of Asian and less than a fifth of the Caribbean group. In contrast, over 37 per cent of the Caribbean, compared with around 27 per cent of the Asian and under 25 per cent of the ESWI group were rated as below average by their class teachers.

Amongst the whole pupil sample it was found that class teachers' ability ratings were related strongly to children's attainments in reading, writing and mathematics. Individual analyses of ability ratings, once other background factors (including sex, age and father's social class) and attainment in these three areas had been controlled, indicated that ethnic background was *no longer related* to teachers' ability ratings. This is in contrast to the findings reported earlier in the section on social class. It appears, therefore, that teachers' expectations were more heavily influenced by pupils' social class than by their ethnic background or sex.

Non-cognitive outcomes

Behaviour

Overall, there was a higher incidence of behaviour difficulties in school (according to class teachers' assessments) amongst the Caribbean than amongst other groups. Thus, using the criterion of being assessed highly in terms of the behaviour scale (where a high score signifies greater difficulties) in two or more of the three years, nearly 20 per cent of Caribbean, compared with 12 per cent of Asian and 11 per cent of ESWI pupils, were highly rated. The most common form of behaviour difficulty identified for all groups was associated with learning behaviour problems, rather than aggression or anxiety. In all, nearly 14 per cent of the Caribbean, compared with only 5 per cent of Asian and 8 per cent of English, Scottish, Welsh and Irish pupils were rated highly on the learning difficulties sub-scale.

Much of the relationship between ethnic background and behaviour was accounted for by other factors (it was found that father's social class, sex and eligibility for free schools meals made a significant contribution to the statistical explanation of variations in behaviour ratings). Nonetheless, taking a combined measure of behaviour over three years, analyses at the individual level indicated that, when controlling for the influence of all other background factors, Caribbean pupils were assessed as having greater behaviour difficulties. [16]

It is likely that the higher incidence of behaviour difficulties in school (as assessed by teachers) amongst Caribbean pupils may be due, in part, to the significant link between attainment (especially reading) and behaviour identified for the pupil sample as a whole. Analyses indicated that the Caribbean group had significantly lower attainments at each assessment than ESWI pupils (though not in comparison with Asian pupils). Controlling for first year reading attainment removed the relationship between race and behaviour ratings. It thus appears that lower attainment was related to behaviour, especially learning behaviour difficulties, and that the higher incidence of behaviour difficulties identified amongst Caribbean pupils in the sample over a three year period was possibly attributable to this factor, rather than to race. Thus, although controlling for attainment eliminated the relationship between ethnic group and behaviour, it did not remove the significant relationships between sex, free meals, and father's social class and behaviour. These factors continued to have a statistically significant impact.

Attendance

Very marked differences in attendance were identified during the junior years according to ethnic background. In each year, children of Caribbean background were present for a higher percentage of the time than the English group whilst children of Asian backgrounds were, on average, absent for a higher percentage of time (see Table 7.11).

Table 7.11 Average percentages of time absent in years one, two and three by ethnic background

	% time absent		
Ethnic Group	Year 1	Year 2	Year 3
Asian	11.7	11.6	10.6
Caribbean	7.1	8.2	6.1
ESWI	9.1	9.5	9.0

Asian   N = 112 year 1; 104 year 2;   89 year 3
Caribbean N = 230 year 1; 221 year 2; 212 year 3
ESWI   N = 1047 year 1; 990 year 2; 889 year 3

Taking into account all other background factors, sex and age, analyses at the level of the individual pupil indicated that these differences in attendance were highly statistically significant for the Caribbean group, and were largest in the third year. At this stage, Caribbean children were absent for 3.3 per cent less time than the average for the sample as a whole (8.3 per cent). This represents just over a week's extra attendance in the school year. Although Asian children, as a group, tended to have the poorest attendance, this trend was not statistically significant when other background factors were taken into account.

Attitudes

Overall, very little of the variation in children's attitudes was accounted for by background factors, sex and age in any year (as reported earlier). Nonetheless, there were a few statistically significant differences in the attitudes of children from different ethnic backgrounds. Asian children tended to have more favourable attitudes towards mathematics in the second and third years and towards school in the first and second years. For those of Caribbean backgrounds, more favourable attitudes towards mathematics were identified in the first year, and more favourable attitudes towards reading in the third year.

Self-concept

As with the measures of attitudes, only a small proportion of the variation in children's perceptions of themselves in school was accounted for by background factors, sex and age. Asian children rated themselves significantly more favourably at the end of their third year in junior school than other children. There was, however, no evidence to suggest that Caribbean children had poorer self-concepts in relation to the school environment. (This finding is in contrast to some earlier research which suggested that black children had poorer self-concepts than their white peers — see, for example, Wylie, 1963; Proshansky and Newton, 1968).

In summary, the results of analysing differences in educational outcomes according to race indicated that there were significant differences in some areas of cognitive attainment (specifically reading and mathematics) both at entry to junior school and in later years. Moreover, there were small but significant differences in progress in reading, with the Caribbean group making poorer progress than predicted by first year attainment. Differences, however, were not identified for writing or oral skills.

It also appears that the effects of ethnic background varied for the non-cognitive outcomes of education. The incidence of behaviour difficulties was higher (though still recorded only for a minority) amongst Caribbean children in their class teachers' assessments. This relationship, however, was apparently due to poorer attainment (behaviour and attainment being closely linked). In contrast, the Caribbean group had better attendance and Asian pupils poorer attendance during the junior years. On the whole, attitudes varied little, but the Asian group tended to have more favourable attitudes to school and to mathematics, while Caribbean children had more favourable views of reading. There was no evidence that minority groups had less positive self-concepts than their white peers (the Asian children actually had more favourable views of themselves in school than others).

Relationships between pupils' educational outcomes during the junior years

A variety of analyses were conducted to explore the links between children's attainment in the different cognitive assessments in each year and over time, and to examine the links between the different non-cognitive outcomes.

Cognitive areas

As might be expected, there was a strong relationship between children's attainments in both reading and writing in each year. (The correlations ranged between 0.69 and 0.74.) Children who obtained high scores in reading also tended to produce writing which was assessed highly in terms of the quality of language and ideas. (It should be pointed out that the writing was assessed by independent markers who were unaware of the children's reading performance.) In the third year summer assessments, for example, children whose writing was of *below* average quality had an average reading score of only 31 raw points. Those whose writing was *above* average quality had a mean reading score of nearly 71 points.

Oracy was also quite strongly related to reading and to writing attainment. Thus, for example, in considering attainment in the third year summer reading assessment and that in oracy (assessed one term later), it was clear that the communicative effectiveness of speech was positively correlated with reading attainment ($r = 0.63$). The correlation between communicative effectiveness of speech and the quality of children's writing was $r = 0.57$. The lexico-grammatical features of speech were, however, less closely related to reading ($r = 0.48$) and to writing ($r = 0.43$), in line with the findings noted earlier.

These results suggest that, in general there were relationships between children's attainments in different aspects of language usage, but the associations were stronger between reading and writing than between speech and reading, or speech and writing. This may be because oracy is not usually treated as part of the 'formal curriculum' and some very effective speakers do not perform well in reading and writing tasks in the classroom.

There were also positive correlations between mathematics and oracy, but these were weaker than relationships between reading and oracy ($r = 0.59$ for the general measure of communicative effectiveness and mathematics attainment).

Children's performance in the written and practical mathematics assessments were quite closely related, in each school year. The relationships were stronger in the second and third years than in the first year ($r = 0.55$ in the first year, compared with $r = 0.69$ in the autumn of the third year). It seems that the relationship between practical and written mathematics was more marked amongst older pupils; earlier test results were less strongly related.

There was also a strong relationship between attainment in reading and in the written mathematics assessment. This relationship remained stable in each year (correlations ranged between 0.70 and 0.82). This association was especially marked by the summer of the third year ($r = 0.81$). Mathematics and writing achievements were rather less closely related (correlations ranged between 0.55 and 0.60).

Performance in practical mathematics and reading and writing, however, were only weakly related in the first year ($r = 0.43$ between practical mathematics and reading, and $r = 0.28$ between practical mathematics and writing). In later years the correlations were rather higher but still not very strong. These results suggest that performance in practical mathematics is less closely tied to writing or reading abilities (especially for younger children) and may be a function of the oral administration of the practical assessments. Furthermore, although information about oracy and practical mathematics performance was only obtained for a small number of pupils (because both assessments were conducted on sub-samples), the results suggest that performance in these two areas tend to be related ($r = 0.58$; $N = 68$).

These findings indicate the value of educational assessments which do not require pupils to possess high levels of competence in reading and writing. Such assessments may reveal children's strengths in cognitive areas which are not always apparent in reading and writing-based tasks. The findings clearly have important implications for the ways in which pupils are assessed in school.

Non-cognitive areas

There was a weak but significant relationship ($r = 0.29$) between self-concept and behaviour. Comparing similar items on each scale, the highest relationship ($r = 0.35$) was found for the item assessing pupil happiness. Generally, items which related to aspects of pupils' learning showed the highest correlations, and those relating to the child's personality, the lowest correlations. The anxiety subscales related less well ($r = 0.10$) than the aggression and learning difficulty subscales ($r = 0.25$, and 0.28 respectively).

The child's attitudes to school, and to aspects of school, were also weakly related to self-concept (correlations with all self-concept items were below 0.3) and to the aggression subscale of behaviour (correlations with the aggression items were all below 0.21).

Children who were assessed by teachers as disturbed on the aggression subscale in both the second and third years differed significantly from those not assessed as disturbed in either year on two aspects of their self-concept. These were: their poorer assessment of their own behaviour; and their more negative view of their teacher's perception. Those who were assessed as disturbed also had significantly more negative attitudes to school. However, they did not differ in their attitudes to other aspects of the school, or in their attitudes to relationships with the teacher.

Attitude to school was not related to school attendance in any year.

Relationships between cognitive and non-cognitive outcomes

Correlation techniques were used to establish whether any relationships existed between the cognitive and non-cognitive outcomes. The results of these provide a detailed picture of the links between different measures of achievement and adjustment to school for this age group.

Relationships between behaviour and attainment

Assessments of pupils' behaviour and of reading and mathematics were carried out on four occasions: in the autumn of years one to three, and in the summer of year three. Table 7.12 shows the correlation between the overall rating on the behaviour scale and the reading and mathematics assessments on each occasion. For both reading and mathematics attainments, the correlations with the overall behaviour rating reduced over time. The correlations with reading were higher than the correlations with mathematics on all occasions except the last.[17] The stronger relationship between behaviour and attainment in the earlier years (found for reading and mathematics) show that behaviour and attainment were more closely linked for younger children.

*Table 7.12 Correlation between behaviour (overall rating) and reading and mathematics attainment over the four occasions **

	Behaviour and reading	N	Behaviour and mathematics	N
Year 1 (autumn)	−0.55	1717	−0.50	1719
Year 2 (autumn)	−0.50	1650	−0.46	1663
Year 3 (autumn)	−0.46	1328	−0.43	1436
Year 3 (summer)	−0.44	1275	−0.44	1285

* A high score on the behaviour assessment denotes poorer behaviour.

Writing length and writing quality showed a similar decrease in their relationship with behaviour over time. Writing quality showed comparable, though slightly lower, correlations with behaviour than mathematics (decreasing from 0.48 in the summer of year one to 0.42 in summer of year three). For writing length, the correlations with behaviour were lower than those for either reading or mathematics, decreasing from 0.36 to 0.28 over that time period.

The behaviour subscales (learning difficulties, anxiety and aggression), when examined separately, showed differing correlations with each of the cognitive attainments. In each case, the learning difficulties subscale was more closely related than the other two subscales, the aggression subscale showing the smallest relationship. Table 7.13 shows the correlations with reading over the four occasions.

For these attainments, the reduction in the association with the overall behaviour rating over the three years was mainly due to the decreasing correlation with learning difficulties. Writing quality and length were also related most closely to the learning difficulties subscale and least closely to the aggression subscale. For writing quality, these correlations showed a systematic decrease over time.

Oracy, as measured by the 'general assessment' scale, had a correlation (again

Table 7.13 Correlations between behaviour subscales and reading attainments over the four occassions *

	Learning Difficulties	Anxiety	Aggression
	r	r	r
Year 1 (autumn)	− 0.58	− 0.35	− 0.27
Year 2 (autumn)	− 0.50	− 0.37	− 0.22
Year 3 (autumn)	− 0.49	− 0.29	− 0.26
Year 3 (summer)	− 0.45	− 0.34	− 0.23

* A high score on each of the behaviour sub-scales denotes poorer behaviour in that area.

corrected for reliability) of 0.35 with the overall behaviour rating (in summer of year three), of 0.39 with the task specific rating and 0.43 with the verbal rating.

The correlations reported, whilst giving evidence of a link between cognitive attainments and behaviour, are not sufficient in themselves to allow investigation of the causal relationships, if any, between the two measures. It is likely that learning difficulties are antecedents to lower than average progress on cognitive attainments, and equally, that low attainment would reinforce a low rating on any of the behaviour subscales, and in particular, on learning difficulties. Alternatively, the association between the two measures could be an artefact of a common relationship of both the measures to aspects of the pupils' background. (For example, it has been shown earlier in this chapter that both reading and writing were related to pupils' social class and sex, that mathematics was related to social class, and that behaviour — and in particular learning difficulties — was related to social class and sex).

To explore the relationship between reading and learning difficulties in more depth, statistical techniques based on the use of structural equations methods were used.[18] Reading was found to affect the assessment of a child's learning difficulties subscale a year later, given the learning difficulties measured in the previous year. This relationship was found to be identical within sex and social class groups and was constant over both periods (from year one to year two, and year two to year three). Thus, lower reading attainment tended to result in greater learning difficulties at a later age. However, no relationship was found between these measures over a period of more than a year.

Learning difficulties were also found to affect reading attainment a year later, when account was taken of initial attainment (in the same year). The relationship was again found to be constant over both periods — year one to year two, and year two to year three. Learning difficulties tended to affect later reading performance but no relationship between measures was found over a period of more than a year.

Overall, therefore, there is evidence that pupils with a higher rating in learning difficulties in a given year tend to make less progress in reading over the following year. Similarly, pupils with lower reading scores in a given year tended to show an increase in the severity of learning difficulties in the following year. These findings suggest that pupils' reading attainment and behaviour in school are linked, in a complex way; each influences the other. Poor reading tends to encourage poor behaviour and poor behaviour leads to poor reading attainment.

Relationships between attitudes and attainment

Attitudes to reading, mathematics and writing had very small but positive relationships to the attainments measured in the same year. There was a slight increase in the strength of these relationships between the first and third years. Of the curriculum areas studied, the highest relationships between attitudes and attainment occurred for writing and reading, the maximum correlation (in each case, in the third year) being 0.11.

These data indicate that the relationships between attitudes and attainment were clearly very much lower than between children's behaviour and attainment. The data also suggest that attitudes were almost independent of attainment for junior age pupils.

Relationships between attendance and attainment

In the first year, children with high absence rates from school had generally lower attainments in reading ($r = -0.20$), mathematics ($r = -0.15$) and in writing (for writing quality, $r = -0.12$ and writing length, $r = 0.22$). These relationships, though highly significant, were nevertheless small. In later years the relationships became weaker, showing some tendency to reduce from the second to the third year. Amongst the junior age-range, not surprisingly, poor school attendance appears to impact on cognitive attainment.

The relative importance of school and background

There is strong evidence that schools vary considerably in the areas they serve and the background characteristics of their pupils. This is especially true at the primary level. The sample of junior schools in the Junior School Project was no exception. Marked variations in the initial attainments, behaviour and background characteristics of pupils forming the intakes to the sample schools were identified (see Mortimore *et al.*, 1986).

The analyses of the links between background factors and pupils' educational outcomes (both in cognitive attainment and progress over time, and in measures of adjustment to school) reported above demonstrated that factors such as age, sex, social class and ethnic background have a powerful impact. This impact is identifiable early in children's school careers (see Blatchford *et al.*, 1985) and is already marked at entry to junior school. Given the strength of background influences it is clearly important to take full account of differences in intakes when comparing the effects of schools on the progress and development of their pupils. Without adequate controls for intake, comparisons of schools can be misleading because of failure properly to compare like with like (see Gray, 1981, 1983; Gray and Jones, 1983).

Due to the extensive collection of data about intakes at the level of the individual pupil, it was possible for the project to employ more sophisticated statistical techniques in analyses of the effects of schools upon pupils' educational outcomes.

Because of the importance of age, sex, social class, race and language background, and family circumstances, the analyses of school effects took into account each of the background factors identified as influential in a series of preliminary screening analyses. Membership of an indivudal school was included as an additional characteristic for each child, because it was hypothesized that school attended could have an impact upon a child's progress and development. In this way the effects of background characteristics and of school membership were identified and separated out, whilst controlling for the effects of all other factors simultaneously. All analyses were conducted at the level of the individual pupil (for further details see Mortimore *et al.*, 1988b).

The effects of school membership on pupils' progress in the three 'Rs' (reading, mathematics and writing) and upon pupils' attainments in the oracy and practical mathematics assessments were identified.[19] The effects of school membership were measured by the amount of variation in pupil progress explained (in a statistical sense) by the school. This method allows a comparison of the strength of school effects in general, with those effects due to background factors. In addition, variations in the effect on pupils of being a member of a particular junior school were also explored.

School effects upon pupils' non-cognitive outcomes (attitudes, attendance, behaviour and self-concept) were also examined. Clearly, a simple concept of progress cannot apply to some of these measures of adjustment to, or alienation from, school (attendance and behaviour, unlike reading, for example, should not be expected to improve automatically over time), although it is possible to investigate whether change has occurred.

School effects on pupil progress

As has been noted earlier, children differed very markedly at the point of entry to junior school in their attainments in reading, mathematics and writing skills, and because of this it was essential to take account of attainment in such areas at entry in any comparisons of school effects on their pupils. In the analyses of schools' effects on their pupils, the focus of the Project was upon the amount of progress (or change over time) pupils made in reading, mathematics or writing. It was possible to establish this because of the longitudinal nature of the research and because data were collected at the level of the individual pupil. For each child, therefore, attainment at entry was the *baseline* against which progress during the junior years was measured.

The results of the analysis of pupils' progress in reading, writing and mathematics describe the impact upon a child's progress over three years of being a member of one particular school in the Project sample, rather than of the other schools.

School membership was found to have had a significant impact upon the amount of progress children made in the three 'R's. When account was taken of pupil initial attainment at entry to junior school (the essential baseline against which progress can be measured) it was found that the school had a much larger impact upon progress than background factors.[20] Thus school attended accounted for nearly 24 per cent of the variation in pupil's reading progress, whereas all background factors taken together only accounted for around 6 per cent, for example (see Table 7.14).

Table 7.14   The percentage of variance in pupils' progress accounted for by school and by background factors

	% variance due to school	% variance due to background factors
Reading	23.6	6.1
Mathematics	23.1	2.4
Writing quality	19.7	3.0

As with reading progress, the analysis of mathematics and writing progress confirmed the overall importance of school. Indeed, the relative importance of school for the explanation of variations in pupils' progress in mathematics and writing was greater than for progress in reading. Although it was not possible to analyse the impact of school upon pupils' progress in oracy or practical mathematics, the results of analyses of attainment in these areas also indicated that the impact of school was greater than that of background factors.

School effects on non-cognitive outcomes

As well as being a major influence upon pupils' cognitive achievements, the research demonstrated that school attended also made a significant contribuiton to children's non-cognitive outcomes.

Table 7.15 illustrates the percentage of variance in the assessments of attitude to school, attendance, behaviour and self-concept due to school and the percentage due to background factors. It can be seen that for attitudes, attendance and self-concept the school had a greater influence than background factors. Only for behaviour in school was background more important than school attended.

Table 7.15   The percentage of variance in attendance, attitude to school, behaviour and self-concept accounted for by school and by background factors

	% variance due to school	% variance due to background factors
Attitude to school	8.7	5.0
Attendance	5.6	3.9
Behaviour in school	9.8	12.9
Self-concept	8.4	3.2

The results indicate that school plays a major part in determining pupils' educational outcomes during the junior years of education. Indeed, for *progress* in cognitive areas, and for all measures of adjustment to school (with the notable exception of behaviour) the school had a stronger effect than background factors. Thus, although background characteristics such as age, sex, social class and ethnic group are important influences on, and predictors of both cognitive and non-cognitive outcomes, the importance of relationships between background and measures of children's achievement and adjustment to school should not be allowed to obscure the crucial role which the school also plays in promoting pupils' progress and development.

When the size of the effects of individual schools upon their pupils' outcomes were compared, the results revealed that the differences between the most and the least effective schools were striking. In some schools pupils made far greater progress than would be expected given their initial attainment at entry. In others, however, pupil progress was much poorer than predicted given attainment at entry. For example, over the three years the difference between the school with the most positive and that with the most negative effect on reading was a striking 25 raw points. This compared with an overall average of just under 54 raw points on the third year summer reading test, and a range of possible scores of 0 to 100 points.

There were also very marked differences between individual schools in the sample in terms of their effects on pupils' non-cognitive outcomes. Because the scales used for each of the outcomes was different it is difficult to make valid comparisons between schools' effects on each of the outcomes. However, Table 7.16 expresses the differences between the most and the least effective school as a percentage of the overall mean for each outcome separately. The difference between schools in their effects on pupil attendance, though highly significant, only reached nine per cent. Thus, pupils in the most effective school in terms of effect on attendance were present for nine per cent more time than those in the least effective school on this outcome. In contrast, differences in schools' effects on attitude to school or behaviour were far larger.

Table 7.16 *The most and the least effective schools*

	% difference from the overall average	
	Most effective	Least effective
Reading	+28	−19
Mathematics	+21	−21
Writing	+27	−21
Oracy	+27	−23
Self-concept	+14	−12
Behaviour	+32	−15
Attendance	+ 5	− 4
Attitude to school	+38	−41

In order to establish whether some schools were more effective than others at promoting a variety of pupils' educational outcomes, further analyses were undertaken. Schools varied in the number of cognitive and in the number of non-cognitive outcomes on which they had had a positive impact. Giving each school a score of one if it had a positive effect on any areas and zero if it had a negative effect, a scale was constructed to record the total number of outcomes on which each school had a positive effect. The maximum possible score was four (good effects on progress in reading, mathematics and writing and attainment in oracy) and the minimum zero (negative effects on all).[21] Overall, five schools had a positive effect on all areas whereas four schools scored negative effects on all areas.

A similar procedure was adopted for the non-cognitive outcomes. A total score was calculated for each school to record the number of non-cognitive outcomes on which it showed a positive effect. The maximum score possible was seven (positive effects on behaviour, self-concept, attendance, attitude to school, attitude to mathematics, attitude to reading and attitude to writing). The minimum possible was zero.[22] Overall, five schools had a positive effect on only one of the seven areas. In contrast, two schools recorded a positive effect on all seven areas, and five a positive effect on six.

These results demonstrate that some schools were more effective in promoting pupils' cognitive outcomes than others. Likewise, some were better at fostering non-cognitive development. Of particular interest is the question of whether some schools were more effective at promoting both achievement and adjustment in a broad range of outcomes. By cross relating the total number of cognitive and non-cognitive areas upon which each school had had a positive impact, this question could be addressed. Overall, it was found that fourteen schools had positive effects on three or more of the cognitive and four or more of the non-cognitive outcomes. In contrast, five schools had positive effects on only one or more of the cognitive, and on only two or fewer of the non-cognitive areas.

Thus, amongst the sample of schools included in the Junior School Project there were striking differences in effectiveness. Moreover, the results indicate that it is possible for schools to be effective in promoting a variety of outcomes — both cognitive and non-cognitive. In particular, it is clear that in order to promote pupils' progress it is not necessary to neglect the non-cognitive outcomes of education. Similarly, schools which fostered the non-cognitive outcomes related to pupil adjustment did not do so at the expense of promoting pupil achievement in academic areas.

Conclusions

Because of the wealth of data relating to individual children collected at different points throughout their junior education, and the combination of analyses related to both background and school effects, the Junior School Project research helps to illuminate current understanding of pupil achievement and adjustment in the junior school.

Important differences were identified in children's educational outcomes during the junior period. Such differences in outcomes were found to be related significantly to a number of background characteristics. Age, social class, sex and race had an important impact on cognitive outcomes. In most cases, marked differences in attainment were identified at entry to junior school and continued throughout the junior years. Differences in progress were less notable, though reading progress was related to father's social class and to race. Children of non-manual origins made greater progress than expected and those of Caribbean background made less progress, given their initial attainment.

Differences in pupil's non-cognitive outcomes also varied according to age, social class, sex and race. These differences, however, were not always in the same directions as for cognitive outcomes. In particular, poor behaviour in school was related to age, sex, social class and race. There was also evidence that behaviour and cognitive attainment were strongly inter-related.

These findings demonstrate that certain background characteristics increase the 'risk' or probability that particular groups of children will have low attainment and exhibit poor adjustment to school. Awareness of the existence of such risk factors may help teachers to be more sensitive to the possible special needs or extra support which may be required by such children. Because under-achievement and poor adjustment also provide important indicators of the likelihood that pupils will become alienated from school, it is clear that teachers should maintain detailed individual records of attainment, progress and adjustment for all pupils. In this way they will be able to monitor children's educational outcomes more effectively, and will be better placed to identify children whose achievement and adjustment may indicate the need for special consideration. The JSP research indicates that behaviour difficulties were strongly associated with poor cognitive attainment in reading and mathematics. For junior-aged pupils, this suggests that records of these areas may provide teachers with particularly useful indicators of possible adjustment difficulties and problems associated with alienation from school.

However, although background factors were found to be important determinants of pupil attainment and adjustment, the JSP research indicated that the school also played a very important role. School membership made a significant contribution to the explanation of variations in pupils' progress over three years in reading, writing and mathematics and to attainment in oracy. School was also very important for pupil adjustment as shown by measures of attitudes, attendance, self-concept and behaviour.

The results indicate that the school to which a child belongs during the junior years of schooling can have a beneficial or a negative effect on his or her progress and development. The importance of school in explaining variations in pupils' progress is a major finding of the JSP, because previous research for this age group has tended to concentrate only on the influence of background while neglecting the vital role of the school.

Amongst the sample of schools, striking differences in effectiveness were identified. Some schools had positive effects on their pupils' progress and development in several areas. Others had a negative impact on most outcomes. The implication of these findings is clear. For the pupil, the particular school he or she joins at age 7 can have a highly significant impact upon future progress and development. The effects of junior schooling are likely to be carried forward with the child at secondary transfer and may well have a long-term influence on later educational success and employment prospects.

Acknowledgements

The JSP research was directed by Peter Mortimore and coordinated by Pamela Sammons. The Project team included Louise Stoll, David Lewis and Russell Ecob. Thanks are due to a number of teachers who made a significant contribuiton through their work as field officers on the Project — Mary Hunt, Jennifer Runham, Dick Cooper, Pamela Glanville and Cathy Bunch. Thanks are also expressed to past and present colleagues at the Research and Statistics Branch, in particular Audrey Hind, Kate Foot, Andreas Varlaam, Brian Clover, Christine Mabey, Anne-Marie Hill, Colin Alston, and Adrian Walker. Pat Wood, Shirley McGillick and Barbara Andrews provided excellent support by their efficient word-processing throughout.

It would not have been possible to carry out this study without the continued support of all the headteachers, teachers, pupils and parents involved. The team are extremely grateful for the cooperation of all the schools included in the research.

Appendix

The characteristics of the pupil sample

In 1980, a sample of 50 schools was selected randomly from 636 ILEA primary schools containing junior pupils. Analyses have confirmed that the sample was representative of junior age pupils in the Authority as a whole. In comparison with children nationally, however, the sample was bound to reflect the characteristics of children in an inner city area. Thus, the percentage of children from one parent families, ethnic minority groups, those using English as a second language, and those receiving free school meals, were probably higher than figures for the country as a whole.[23]

The characteristics of the sample at the start of the Project in terms of sex, ethnic group, language, parental occupations, family size and eligibility for free school meals are shown in Table 7.17.

Table 7.17   The characteristics of the sample of pupils at the start of the Project

Ethic and Language Background

		% *
Ethnic Group	African	2.9
	Asian	6.5
	Caribbean	12.9
	Chinese	1.0
	ESWI	60.6
	Greek	1.7
	Turkish	1.5
	Other	12.9
Child's First Language	English	84.4
	Not English	15.6
Fluency in English	Not fully fluent	7.7

Parental Occupations (Registrar General's Classification)

			Mother's	*Father's*
Non-manual	I		0.9	2.6
	II		5.8	13.9
	III		11.8	8.1
Manual	III		3.3	35.0
	IV		10.1	8.2
	V		5.7	7.3
Long Term Unemployed			0.8	6.1
Economically Inactive			59.2	2.1
Absent			2.3	16.8

Family Size and Structure

Family Size	Only child	15.8
	Two children	42.5
	Three children	23.6
	Four or more children	18.1
Child's Position in Family	First born	40.2
	Second born	32.5
	Third born	16.1
	Fourth born or later	11.3

Income

	Free meals received	30.5

N of pupils = 1823

* Pupils for whom information was not known were excluded in the calculation of percentages for the characteristic concerned.

Notes

1.   The tests used were: the Edinburgh Reading Test; the NFER Basic Maths Test; and Ravens Coloured Progressive Matrices.

2.   Many analyses were undertaken to investigate the strength of relationships between family factors (family size, position in the family, parental language, one parent status) and pupil attainment and progress in cognitive and non-cognitive outcomes. These relationships (wherever they were found to be statistically significant) were taken into account during the analyses of progress and school effects. Moreover, all background factors found to be important in previous studies were included when addressing the separate effects of age, sex, social class or race on pupils' attainment and progress. Other home-based factors were also investigated for the sub-sample of pupils involved in a home interview study. The results of this work were reported by Sammons *et al.*, 1985 and Varlaam *et al.*, 1985.

3.   Attainment at entry was used as the baseline against which to assess progress in mathematics over the following three years. As would be expected, initial attainment accounted for the majority of the variation in progress (53 per cent) but the figure is lower than that for reading, indicating that mathematics performance is more susceptible to change over the junior years than is reading performance.

4.   Unsurprisingly, the quality of writing produced in the first year was the most important predictor of later attainment in writing. Nonetheless, it accounted for only 32 per cent of the variation in third year attainment. For length of writing, first year length accounted for 15 per cent of the variation in length of third year stories. These figures, though highly significant, are considerably weaker than those identified for reading or mathematics progress. Writing performance appears to be more susceptible to change over the junior years than performance in reading or mathematics.

5.   The oracy assessment was only conducted for a sample of pupils (N = 379) due to the 'one to one' nature of the administration of the tasks employed.

6.   It is, of course, highly likely that age would be related to performance in a sample of pupils of more varied age.

7.   The combined measure employed the sum of behaviour ratings in the autumn term of years one, two and three as the dependent variable.

8.   In considering the relative importance of age and length of schooling, Russell and Startup (1986) have noted that in practice it is a little difficult to tell which of the two theories is better supported by the data. This is because in Britain, length of schooling is highly related to age.

9.   In considering the relative influences of the mother's and the father's social class the high percentage of mothers who were not in paid employment (59 per cent of those for whom data were avilable) needs to be borne in mind. Moreover, the proportion of children for whom no occupational information was known was much higher for mothers (25.5 per cent) than for fathers (17 per cent). The fact that only just over a quarter of mothers had an occupation-related description reduces the potential of this variable for the explanation of children's attainments, since it is likely that mothers classified into the economically inactive (not in paid employment) group may have had very different employment histories.

10.   All analyses adjust for test reliability and the clustered nature of the sample.

11.   Although social class was not significantly related to progress in mathematics, one socio-economic measure (eligibility for free school meals, an indicator of low family income) did have an impact upon both reading and mathematics progress. Children eligible for free meals made poorer progress than predicted given their initial attainment in both reading and mathematics.

12.   As with progress in other cognitive areas, those children eligible for free meals made poorer progress in writing quality from the first to the third year — a difference of a quarter of a point in terms of the ten point assessment.

13.   Children who were eligible for free school meals also expressed rather less favourable attitudes to reading in the third year.

14.   For a description of the stages of fluency in English, see Kysel, (1982).

15   Because the numbers of Asian children in different language groups were often small (e.g. Gujerati = 14 in year 1, Punjabi = 10) results on differences *between* sub-groups of Asian children should be treated with caution.

16   This effect, though statistically highly significant, was nevertheless small in comparison to the effects of pupil sex, father's social class or eligibility for free meals.

17   All correlations were corrected for measurement error for all the cognitive variables and for the overall behaviour scale.

18   The method of analysis — structural equation modelling — is described in further detail in the technical appendices of the main report by Mortimore *et al.*, 1986.

19   It was not possible to investigate progress in oracy because only one assessment of oracy was made. For practical mathematics, the assessment did not measure a unitary aspect of attainment. For this reason it was not statistically appropriate to assess pupils' progress over time in practical mathematics.

20   The effects of background characteristics upon pupils' progress (change in attainment over time) in cognitive areas is lower than the effect upon attainment at any one point in time because, as has been described earlier in this chapter, characteristics such as age, sex, ethnic background and social class, are strongly related to the level of children's initial attainment at entry to junior school.

21   Because the practical mathematics assessment was conducted on a sample of children in only 20 schools, effects on this outcome were not included. One school left the Project in the third year therefore forty-nine schools were involved in the calculations.

22   The total number of schools included in these calculations was forty-seven because one school left the Project, one school did not conduct the behaviour and another school did not conduct the attitude assessments in the third year.

23   Unfortunately, it was not possible to compare the sample with national figures directly except for the free meals factor because such data are not collected on a national basis. At the start of the study 30.5 per cent of the pupils received free school meals, compared with 20.7 per cent nationally (CIPFA figures for 1980/81).

References

Assessment of Performance Unit (APU) (1981) *Language Performance in Schools*, Primary Survey Report, No. 1, London, HMSO.

Assessment of Performance Unit (APU) (1982) *Language Performance in Schools*, Primary Survey Report, No. 2, London, HMSO.

Blatchford, P., Burke, J., Farquhar, C., Plewis, I. and Tizard, B. (1985) 'Educational Achievement in the Infant School: the Influence of Ethnic Origin, Gender and Home on Entry Skills', *Educational Research*, 27, 1, pp. 52–60.

Bunch, C. (1984) *Attitudes Revealed in Children's Stories*, Research and Statistics Branch, ILEA.

Chazan, M. and Jackson, S. (1974) 'Behaviour Problems in the Infant School: Changes over Two Years', *Journal of Child Psychology and Psychiatry*, 15, pp. 33–46.

Ecob, R. and Sammons, P. (1985) *Oracy and its Relation to Other Cognitive Attainments and Socio-economic Characteristics of Pupils: some results from the ILEA Junior School Study*, Paper presented to the British Educational Research Association Conference, University of Sheffield, August 1985.

Eggleston, S.J., Dunn, D.K. and Ajjali, M. (1985) *The Educational and Vocational Experiences of 15–18 Year Old Young People of Ethnic Minority Groups*, Department of Education, University of Keele.

Essen, J. and Ghodsian, M. (1980) 'The Children of Immigrants: School Performance', *New Community*, VII, pp. 422–429.

Essen, J. and Wedge, P. (1982) *Continuities in Childhood Disadvantage*, London, Heinemann.

Freyman, R. (1965) 'Further Evidence on the Effect of Date of Birth on Subsequent Performance', *Educational Research*, 8, 1, pp. 58–64.

Goldstein, H. (1980) 'The Statistical Procedures', in Tizard *et al. Fifteen Thousand Hours: A Discussion* (Bedford Way Papers 1), University of London Institute of Education.

Gorman, T.P., White, J., Hargreaves M., MacLure, M. and Tate, A. (1984) *Language Performance in Schools: 1982 Primary Survey Report*, Assessment of Performance Unit DES, London, HMSO.

Gorman, T. and Hargreaves, M. (1985) *Talking Together: NFER/ILEA Oracy Survey*, Slough, NFER.

Gray, J. (1981) 'Towards Effective Schools: Problems and Progress in British Research', *British Educational Research Journal*, 7, 1, pp. 59–69.

Gray, J. (1983) 'Questions of Background', *Times Educational Supplement*, 8 July, p. 4.

Gray, J. and Jones, B. (1983) 'Disappearing Data', *Times Educational Supplement*, 15, July, p. 4.

Hunter, J., Kysel, F. and Mortimore, P. (1985) *Children in Need: The Growing Needs of Inner London Schoolchildren*, Research and Statistics Branch, RS 994/85, ILEA.

Hutt, C. (1979) 'Why do Girls Under-achieve?' *Trends in Education*, 4, pp. 24–28.

Kysel, F. (1982) *Language Census 1981*, Research and Statistics Branch, RS 838/82, ILEA.

Kysel, F., Varlaam, A., Stoll, L. and Sammons, P. (1983) *The Child at School — A New Behaviour Schedule*, Research and Statistics Branch, RS 907/83, ILEA.

Mabey, C. (1981) 'Black British Literacy: A Study of Reading Attainment of London Black Children from 8 to 15 years', *Educational Research*, 23, 2, pp. 83–95.

Mabey, C. (1985) *Achievement of Black Pupils: Reading Competence as a Predictor of Exam Success among Afro-Caribbean Pupils in London*. PhD thesis, University of London.

MacCoby, E. and Jacklin, C. (1980) 'Psychological Sex Differences', in Rutter, M. (Ed.) *Scientific Foundations of Developmental Psychiatry*, London, Heinemann.

Marjoribanks, K. (1979) *Families and their Learning Environments: An Empirical Analysis*, London, Routledge and Kegan Paul.

Marks, J., Cox, C. and Pomian-Srzednicki, M. (1983) *Standards in English Schools*, London, National Council for Educational Standards.

Marks, J., Cox, C. and Pomian-Srzednicki, M. (1986) *ILEA Examination Performance in Secondary Schools*, London, National Council for Educational Standards.

Mortimore, J. and Blackstone, T. (1982) *Disadvantage in Education*, London, Heinemann.

Mortimore, P. (1983) *Achievement in Schools*, Research and Statistics Branch, RS 829/82, ILEA.

Mortimore, P., Sammons, P., Stoll, L., Lewis, D. and Ecob, R. (1986) *The Junior School Project*, Main Report (4 volumes), Research and Statistics, ILEA.

Mortimore, P., Sammons, P., Stoll, L., Lewis, D. and Ecob, R. (1988a) *School Matters: the junior years*, Wells, Open Books.

Mortimore, P., Sammons, P., and Ecob, R. (1988b) 'The effects of school membership on pupils' educational outcomes', *Research Paper in Education*, 3, 1, pp. 3–26.

Piers, E.V. and Harris, D.B. (1964) 'Age and other correlates of self-concept in children', *Journal of Educational Psychology*, 55, 2, pp. 91–95.

Pilling, D. and Kellmer Pringle, M. (1978) *Controversial Issues in Child Development*, London, National Children's Bureau, Paul Elek.

Proshansky, H. and Newton, P. (1968) 'The Nature and Meaning of Negro Self Identity', in Deutsch, M., Katz, I. and Jensen, A. (Eds) *Social Class, Race and Psychological Development*, New York, Holt.

Radical Statistics Education Group (1982) *Reading Between the Numbers: A Critical Guide to Educational Research*, London, BSSRS.

Rampton (1981) *West Indian Children in our Schools: Interim Report of the Committee from Ethnic Minority Groups* (The Rampton Report) London, HMSO.

Reynolds, D. (1982) 'The Search for Effective Schools', *School Organization*, 2, 3, pp. 215–237.

Russell, R. and Startup, M. (1986) 'Month of Birth and Academic Achievement', *Personality and Individual Differences*, 7, 6, pp. 839–46.

Rutter, M. and Madge, N. (1976) *Cycles of Disadvantage*, London, Heinemann.

Sammons, P., Kysel, F. and Mortimore, P., (1983) 'Educational Priority Indices: A New Perspective', *British Educational Research Journal*, 9, 1, pp. 27–40.

Sammons, P., Mortimore, P. and Varlaam, A. (1985) *Socio-economic background, parental involvement and attitudes, and children's achievements in junior schools*, Research and Statistics Branch, RS 982/85, ILEA.

Strachan, V. and Sammons, P. (1986) *ILEA Junior School Project: The Assessment of Creative Writing*, Research and Statistics Branch, ILEA.

Swann Committee (1985) *Education for All: The Report of the Committee of Inquiry into the Education of Children from Ethnic Minority Groups*, London, HMSO.

Thompson, D. (1971) 'Season of Birth and Success in the Secondary School', *Educational Research*, 14, pp. 56–60.

Thorndike, R.L. and Hagen, E.P. (1969) *Measurement and Evaluation in Psychology and Education*, London, Wiley International.

Tizard, B., Burgess, T., Francis, H., Goldstein, H., Young, M., Hewison, J. and Plewis, I. (1980) *Fifteen Thousand Hours: A Discussion*, (Bedford Way Papers 1) University of London Institute of Education.

Varlaam, A. (1974) 'Educational Attainment and Behaviour', *Greater London Intelligence Quarterly*, 29, pp. 29–37.

Varlaam, A., Woods, J., Mortimore, P. and Sammons, P. (1985) *Parents and Primary Schools*, Research and Statistics Branch, RS 987/85, ILEA.

Williams, P. (1964) 'Date of Birth, Backwardness and Educational Organisation', *British Journal of Educational Psychology*, 34, pp. 247–255.

Wylie, R.C. (1963) 'Children's Estimates of their Schoolwork Ability as a Function of Sex, Race, and Socio-Economic Level', *Journal of Personality*, 31, pp. 203–24.

8
Two Steps Backwards, One Step Forwards?: The Implications of Testing and Assessment for the Primary School

Colin Conner

Introduction

> This school is smart and effective. It doesn't push you too much. You go at your own pace . . . if you stumble . . . well, you get up somehow. You learn a lot because it's so relaxed. I was at a Prep School before. You had tests and exams all the time. All it proved was that you were either good or bad at tests. They never tested what you had learned. I couldn't stand the pressure. I was made to feel a failure every time I asked a question . . . here we talk all the time . . . too much some times.

In the above comment, which comes from a recent Advanced Diploma study (Crowley, 1988), you see a ten-year-old who has already experienced what failure can be like. All that tests had proved to him was that you were either good or bad at them. Fortunately, he is now in a supportive environment where his talents are being developed more fully. But does all testing need to be so negative? With the introduction of national testing with the Education Reform Act, 1988 are we in danger of developing disenchanted and alienated individuals at a progressively earlier age? Nuttall (1987), for example, has commented that:

> The dangers of reinforcing failure from an early age are particularly acute for the disadvantaged, those with special educational needs and generally for those aged 7 (or thereabouts) . . . . The experience of testing such young children with national tests is negligible.

This chapter proposes to consider the implications of testing and assessment in the primary school. It opens with a discussion of the increasing trend toward bureaucratization in education of which assessment is a central feature. This is then followed by some reactions to testing generally as a preliminary to a consideration of the implications for primary education. The discussion concludes with a review of some of the more positive features which might arise and which have particular relevance for teaching and learning. For as Murphy and Torrance (1988) emphasize, it is important to recognize that assessment, learning and teaching are inextricably linked:

> Wherever learning takes place, or it is intended that it should take place, then it is reasonable for the learner, the teacher and other interested parties to be curious about what has happened both in terms of the learning process and in terms of any anticipated or unanticipated outcomes . . . Good education, by definition encompasses good assessment.

Education, accountability and bureaucracy

Without doubt, we live in an age of increasing accountability. More than ever before, education is likely to be evaluated in terms of its cost-effectiveness and the extent to which pre-specified objectives are achieved. The consultation document, *The National Curriculum 5–16* (DES, 1987a), was a culmination of this movement and laid the basis for the 1988 Education Act. In a *Times Educational Supplement* article in September 1987, Maurice Holt commented that the entire consultation document:

> . . . is steeped in the mechanistic assumption that schools can be run like biscuit factories; providing the skills and technology are there, backed by clear objectives and precise assessment, the right product will roll off the assembly line.

But we all know that schools are not like that and that the purpose of education, especially in primary schools, is not merely to prepare children for the work force.

At a DES conference on Evaluation and Appraisal in 1986, Peggy Marshall, a former Chief HMI questioned the 'production line' mentality current in the thinking of many politicians. She suggested that, as national economies have weakened and money has become tighter, there has been an increased demand internationally for greater accountability in education, and given the size of the bill, she believes this is reasonable:

> Often, though, it has been argued in the cost-effective terms of manufacturing industry, with pupils regarded as products off the school assembly line, and their assessed achievement as indices of how far public money has been properly spent. (Marshall, 1986)

But such a model, she argues, is inappropriate because, unlike manufacturing industry, which seeks to provide, at minimum cost, a standard product conforming to exact specification with as little variation as possible, schools are trying, within the time and resources available, to develop each individual as fully as possible: 'the more successfully it does so, the more divergent, beyond certain basic competencies, the pupils are likely to become'. It has been argued, however, that a major problem to be faced is whether 'we are giving so much freedom to each individual school that continuity for our pupils in a mobile society is ignored' (*Schools Council Working Paper* No. 33, 1971), and that 'there is a need to improve relations between industry and education' (editorial in *Education*, 22 October, 1976).

Tremendous changes have taken place in the world of work since the mid 1970s and this has had a profound effect on education, especially in the secondary sector. We cannot be sure, however, exactly what kinds of employment children currently in primary schools will undertake, or even if they will have full-time employment at all. Issues of this kind strike at the very purpose of education: should it give children a good general foundation or should it prepare them for specific careers?

The Secretary of State for Education at the North of England Conference in January 1987 described the English education system as one of those institutionalized muddles that the English have made peculiarly their own! He went on to introduce the well-known comparison with our European competitors:

In England we are eccentric in education as in many other things. For at least a century our education system has been quite different from that adopted by most of our European neighbours. They have tended to centralise and standardise. We have gone for diffusion and variety.

In another speech in January 1987, this time to the Society of Education Officers, Kenneth Baker introduced a criticism of those professionally involved in education:

I realise that the changes I envisage are radical and far reaching and may, therefore, be unwelcome to those who value what is traditional and familiar and has often served well in the past. But I believe profoundly that professional educators will do a disservice to the cause of education, and to the nation, if they entrench themselves in defence of the status quo. More and more people are coming to feel that our school curriculum is not as good as it could be and needs to be, and that we need to move nearer to the kind of arrangements which other European countries operate with success, but without sacrificing those features of our own traditional approach which continue to prove their worth.

Yet not everyone agrees with the suggested advantages of the education systems of our European competitors. In their comparative study of French and English School systems, Broadfoot and Osborn (1987) found French primary schools were typified by 'a dull, repetitive and harsh pedagogy' and they suggest that teaching to a prescribed curriculum and national tests would lead to the loss of 'that warm and creative learning environment that has made English primary schooling the envy of many parts of the world'. It is also the case that in France attempts have been made to introduce devolution in the government of education, motivated by the need for 'more flexible, locally relevant, educational provision at a time of significant social and economic change' (Broadfoot, 1988). Broadfoot also suggests that a history of centralization in France has created teachers who are conservative and have no enthusiam for, or experience of, teacher-led development at a time when this is felt to be urgently needed.

Similarly in the West German system, so much admired by the Department of Education and Science, Chisholm (1987) reminds us that: 'pupils are under great pressure to achieve demonstrably and continuously . . . children gradually learn to see grading as a process of personal affirmation'. In such a situation, the able survive but there are significant numbers who do not.

Even the United States, where testing is used extensively, 'appears to be moving away from such reductionism towards promoting the culture of the individual school, a more liberal approach to curriculum experience and a more professional highly paid and liberally-educated teaching force' (Holt, 1987).

There clearly seems to be a difference of opinion between those who are professionally involved *in* the system at present and those who have a bureaucratic responsibility *for* the system.

Chitty (1988) describes the differences between these two groups as follows. The professional approach, he suggests:

> reflects a genuine concern with the quality of the teaching process and with the needs of individual children. . . . It requires teachers who are well-motivated, well-trained and skilled in identifying any specific learning problems for individual pupils. It is wary of any system geared to writing off large sections of the school population as failures.

The bureaucratic approach, on the other hand:

> is concerned with the efficiency of the whole system and with the need to obtain precise information to demonstrate that efficiency. It is concerned with controlling what is taught in schools and making teachers generally more accountable for their work in the classroom.

Chitty goes on to describe more specific differences between these two models. Whereas the professional approach emphasizes the quality of input and the skills, knowledge and awareness of the teacher, the bureaucratic approach concentrates on output and testing. The professional approach is based on individual differences and the learning process, but the bureaucratic approach is associated with norms and bench marks, norm-related criteria and judgements based on the expectations of how a statistically-normal child should perform. Lastly, he argues that the professional curriculum is concerned with areas of learning and experience, whereas the bureaucratic curriculum is pre-occupied with traditional subject boundaries. As Lawton (1987) suggests, attainment targets have bureaucratic advantages through the presentation of statistics that allow comparison between teachers and schools.

But is any of this increased bureaucratization of education likely to have any effect on primary schools? Evidence suggests that even the Plowden report was not as significant an influence on primary schools as many critics of primary education would have us believe (Simon, 1980). Yet, because it is centrally prescribed and enshrined in legislation, the impending National Curriculum *is* likely to be significantly more influential, and has raised many concerns in primary quarters particularly in relation to the narrowing of the curriculum, the increasing emphasis to be placed on testing and assessment and the potential alienation of children. As has been explained, this chapter proposes to focus upon the implications of the 1988 Education Act for practice in primary schools — particularly in relation to proposals for assessment. Clearly what I have to say has to be seen as tentative, even speculative; but as far as possible it will be based upon evidence derived from the work of those currently addressing the issues involved.

Assessment and the National Curriculum

As Broadfoot (1988) has recently argued, a major feature of the increasing bureaucratization of education is the centrality of assessment in Government proposals. The National Curriculum document (DES, 1987a) emphasized this, by including assessments at 7, 11, 14 and 16 years, the purposes of which will be to assess the extent to which children have reached attainment targets in the core subjects of English, Maths and Science and seven other foundation subjects. The main purposes of such assessment will be to show what a pupil has learnt and mastered and to enable teachers and parents to ensure that adequate progress is being achieved.

Much of the assessment at 7, 11, 14 and 16 years (for non-examined subjects) will be done by teachers as part of normal classroom work:

> But at the heart of the assessment process there will be nationally prescribed tests done by all pupils to supplement the individual teacher's assessment. Teachers will administer and mark these, but their marking — and their assessments overall — will be externally moderated. (DES, 1987a, para. 29)

More recently, however, in the Supplementary papers of the Task Group on Assessment and Testing (DES, 1988) we are informed that in the moderation process teachers' assessments will need to conform to patterns which emerge from the analysis of pupils' performance on the nationally prescribed tests, which implies a devaluing of teachers' assessments. All of which confirms Broadfoot's (1988) view, that at the centre of the Government's proposals is the assumption that 'standards can be raised by the pervasive influence of comparison and competition', and that 'accountability will lead to increased efficiency and hence productivity in education'. All of this, of course, is untested at present.

General reactions to national testing

Hopkins (1988), a critic of wholesale national testing, has offered four main concerns about the Government's proposals. Firstly, he believes that national testing will inevitably lead to divisiveness in schools. A national testing system, of necessity, separates pupils into high and low achievers and creates a system which confronts children with failure at regular intervals during their school lives.

The Task Group report (DES, 1987b) has attempted to remedy this by an emphasis on criterion referenced assessment, in which

> an award or grade is made on the basis of the quality of the performance of the pupil irrespective of the performance of other pupils; this implies that teachers and pupils be given clear descriptions of the performances being sought. (DES, 1987b)

This is not the full story, however, because the assessments which emerge are then subject to moderation. This implies norm referencing, whereby it is expected that children will be compared with their peers in the immediate locality. The results for an individual school are also likely to be subject to comparison with schools nationally.

The second criticism offered by Hopkins is that national testing trivializes the nature of knowledge, which might lead teachers to teach to the tests which by implication leads to a narrowing of the curriculum and reduction in its overall breadth and balance:

> Introducing a hig profile national system of standardised testing linked to a national curriculum is tantamount to making a public statement to the effect that a pupil's education is successful to the extent that he or she scores well on a range of narrowly defined tests.

If this is all that is valued in education it is a narrow and impoverished view, and certainly contradicts the aims and intentions of many primary teachers. In this context, Simons (1988) has commented that:

> 'breadth and balance', so regularly intoned by ministers in justification of the foundation curriculum . . . is . . . fatally undermined by subjection to conventional achievement tests, which depend upon narrowly stipulative domains of learning.

A third criticism offered by Hopkins is that national testing neglects the process of education. Current research on the effectiveness of schools emphasizes teacher professionalism, where collegiality, shared decision-making, and school-based in-service is central. This fits uneasily with a role for teachers as transmitters of a nationally prescribed curriculum content. This is an issue comented upon recently by Simons (1988):

> In the plethora of critique that has accompanied the National Curriculum consultation document relatively little attention has been paid to the professional role of the teacher and the loss to our education system of the pedagogical and curriculum developments that have taken place over the past twenty-five years . . . . The implication . . . is that there will be no room for curriculum development other than that related to the national curriculum and only then by schools chosen by the Secretary

of State . . . . Testing and schemes of work will confine pedagogy to what is conducive to publicly comparable performance and the responsibility for curriculum experimentation, development, growth and change — the hallmark of educational professionalism — will no longer be the concern of teachers, schools or localities. They are destined to become the implementers of curricula, judged nevertheless by the success of treatments they no longer devise.

Lastly, Hopkins believes that there is evidence that systems of national testing just do not work. He describes a recent study in the United States which suggests that standardized teaching and learning results in short-term increases in test scores at the expense of boredom and failure. A four-year research project on the Madeleine Hunter 'Follow Through' programme in California reports short-term positive effects but no lasting changes. In fact there were decreases in student scores in the final year of the programme. The researchers involved concluded that such assessment-led approaches to teaching and learning cannot sustain teacher or pupil interest, and teaching in this way restricts the generation and exchange of ideas. Kenneth Baker argues, however, that he has recognized the inhibiting influences of a national curriculum and the potential reduction of innovation, and believes that these limitations can be avoided 'by designing the system so as to encourage flexibility. I intend to ensure that schools will be perfectly free to adapt their teaching to new opportunities as they become available' (*Times Educational Supplement*, 25 September 1987).

Reactions from the primary sector

With regard to assessment and testing in primary schools, critics of the current state of primary education are to be found in the higher echelons of Her Majesty's Inspectorate. At the Conference on Evaluation and Appraisal mentioned earlier, Eric Bolton, the Chief HMI, made a significant contribution to the debate on assessment at the primary level when he suggested the following:

> Much of the work on assessment and evaluation to date is biased towards the secondary phase. We lack broad agreement about how to describe and scrutinize the primary curriculum. The absence of clarity and agreement about what children should be capable of at various stages of their primary education leads to a distinct lack of information about standards of pupil achievement in individual primary schools and a consequent difficulty of establishing any standards of achievement as a basis for an assessment of performance. (Bolton, 1986)

This was closely followed in October 1986 by Kenneth Baker who said he wanted to establish attainment targets for children of different ages because a child's full potential can be developed only if his or her progress is fairly and reliably assessed at stages along the way.

Criticisms of this view have been vehement in primary circles. They have probably been most forcibly presented by Armstrong (1988), a strong advocate of progressive primary practice. Tests, he argues, whether of the more formal pencil and paper variety preferred by Mrs Thatcher, or of the kind advocated in the Task Group Report on Assessment and Testing, 'measure no more than the SHADOW of achievement'. The role of tests, he suggests, is peripheral to assessment. He admits that sometimes they help in the diagnosis of weaknesses, the identification of gaps in knowledge and understanding and provide an indication of unevenness in development. They can also be used to demonstrate children's competence in a limited range of specific tasks. However,

> ...when the shadow is mistaken for the substance — when nationally prescribed tests are placed at the CENTRE of a school's assessment of its pupils and become the chief criterion of comparison between children, teachers and schools — then children's individual accomplishments will at best be caricatured and at worst be altogether denied.

To describe children's achievements adequately, Armstrong believes we require 'a critical account of their most significant pursuits'. These should include:

> their stories, their paintings, their scientific investigations, their mathematical speculations, their historical researches and especially of the work on which they have lavished the greatest care and enthusiasm.

To offer a detailed critical analysis of activities of this kind requires professional commitment, developed observational skill, reflection, and knowledge of the child whose achievement is being considered:

> In the end individual achievement is incommensurable. The act of measurement is inevitably an act of reduction and rejection — an act which deprives many children of the value of their own accomplishments. (Armstrong, 1988)

Yet, as Gipps *et al.*, (1983, 1987) remind us, a great deal of testing already goes on in primary schools. In two surveys undertaken to investigate the extent of testing routinely undertaken with all or any part of the primary age group, Gipps and her colleagues found a considerable range of testing already in existence at the ages of 7, 8 and 11 in particular. If this is the case, why are the new proposals so threatening?

In a more recent article, Gipps (1988) suggests that there are three ways in which the new proposals are different from the existing use of tests. First, the tests currently most in use are standardized group tests for reading, reasoning and mathematics and not specifically related to the curriculum. In the new proposals, testing, as we have seen, is central to the national curriculum, their purpose being to see that the curriculum is being properly taught. Secondly, results from tests currently used have often been part of the process of identification of children with special educational needs, or have been made available to the next teacher or school or used by local authorities in their monitoring of standards, so their significance was fairly limited. Under the new proposals Gipps believes children are likely to be classified much more formally than in the past, right from the start of their junior education. Also, because results have to be made public, teachers will feel under pressure to get good results. The third concern Gipps expresses is the very nature of the tasks which are expected to be 'differentiated', which means that the children will be classified according to how they perform. At present children can complete their primary education without a sense of failure, but, 'under the new examining system . . . there is a return to competitiveness and emphasis on individual effort . . . encouraged as part of a plan for economic recovery'. This leads Gipps (1988) to the rather depressing view that:

> . . . the disadvantages associated with the proposed system of national assessment at primary level outweigh the possible positive impact. Primary schools under the new arrangements will be a good deal more like secondary schools in being under the influence of exam board constraints (who have the responsibility for moderation). More ability banding, more competition, formal teaching relationships and methods, stricter subject boundaries . . . .

One step forwards?

With such a depressing scenario, pupil alienation might seem a real possibility. But are there any advantages to be gained? I would like to think that there are and that national testing, properly conceived, could indeed serve to increase the motivation of primary school children.

One central feature of the Task Group proposals is the emphasis upon *formative* assessment, which means that the results of any of the testing will provide information to the teacher which should influence the organization and structure of future learning both for individual children and the class as a whole.

A second important element of the proposals is that assessment should be concerned with finding out *what children know and can do*. As the Task Group report (DES, 1987b) comments:

> The Assessment system being proposed differs from most of the standardized testing that is now used in many primary schools and some secondary schools. Those tests are not related closely to what the children are being taught, and when they identify children likely to have difficulties they give little indication of the nature of their problems. Their purpose is to compare children with each other and with samples of children with whom the tests were originally developed, often many years ago.

Such tests are described as '*norm-referenced*'. As mentioned earlier, what the Task Group recommends are assessments which are *criterion referenced*, much more like the assessments teachers make about children every day. So, it is intended that each child's progress is viewed primarily in relation to him or herself, and that he/she is provided with information on what the assessment is about to allow them to perform at their best.

How will this form of assessment be organized? The National Curriculum now includes eleven foundation subjects of which the first three are to be core subjects (i.e. English, Maths, Science, Technology, History, Geography, Art, Music, Physical Education, a Foreign Language, and more recently, Religious Education). Some of these will have a Working Group to consider what attainment targets should be set for each of the assessment ages. If detailed assessment were undertaken from the above list of subject areas, teachers would be spending all of their time in assessment. To overcome this, the Task Group have recommended:

> ...that the best balance between precision in detail and overall comprehensibility will be found if attainment targets are clustered by subject working groups so that each group identifies about four subdivisions of the subject (never more than six) for reporting.

The Task Group describe these sub divisions as *profile components*. As examples of three profile components in the assessment of science, attention might be given to children's competence in *observation, the identification of hypotheses*, and *the setting up of an experiment to investigate a hypothesis*. Initially, at age 7, each of these would be extremely generalizable and not necessarily science specific. They would become increasingly 'science oriented' when investigated at the ages of 11, 14 and 16. As a result, some of these components would be appropriate to a number of the subjects in the National Curriculum, while others could be much more specific. In Geography, for example, one of the profiles might be concerned with 'Graphicacy', the development of children's competence in dealing with information presented in diagrammatic form, as in mapwork.

It is envisaged that initially there will be a limited number of profile components at age 7, but the Task Group anticipate the need to introduce new profile components as the children progress. At the first reporting age of 7, components would tend to be more general than subject specific, but would be the basis from which later subject components might emerge.

To investigate competence in each of these profile components the Task Group recommends the use of *standardized assessment tasks*. For 7-year-olds and largely also for 11-year-olds it is suggested that these should be related as far as possible to the work that it is already going on in the classroom. They will be designed so that they look like pieces of work that the children normally undertake. In the process of doing them children will be able to demonstrate a range of competence which teachers can monitor by *observation* of the children's activity, the processes they engage in as well as the products they produce, whether they be artistic, written or oral. It is anticipated that these teacher assessments will employ standardized procedures and that their results will be subject to *moderation*, where teachers from a group of schools will compare and contrast their analyses of their children's responses to the set tasks as well as their own general assessments of children's attainments. (As was suggested earlier, there is still some uncertainty about the relationship between moderation of these tasks and teachers' own assessment of children's competencies via their general classroom work.)

The tasks will be designed and tested in trials to be sure that they can be attempted by the whole age group. Teachers will then be able to select from a 'bank' of tasks those that are suitable for the background and interests of their children, as well as consider the extent to which they relate to their current learning activities. The suggested advantage of the approach is:

> . . . that children are much more likely to show what they can really do when involved in activities which for them are normal and have a clear purpose . . . and because children are more likely to do full justice to themselves in contexts which are familiar and interesting.

It is also the case that there are potential advantages in the emphasis placed upon the central role of *observation* and the *moderation* process within the assessment procedure. As the digest of the Task Group report commented:

> Teachers make frequent judgements about children's peformance to decide whether they are ready to go on to new work. Sometimes the decision can be settled quickly, at other times *much detailed observation* is needed so that a teacher can be sure or can discover more precisely what is restricting progress.

We are reminded in the Parliamentary Select Committee report on the primary school (House of Commons, 1986) that the greater proportion of judgements made by the teacher are subjective in the sense that they have to reached quickly without going through a set of systematic procedures. Their quality depends upon close observation and the capacity to apply knowledge and experience. It is also suggested that such skills need training and refining:

> The fact that these judgements are vital to children's progress and inescapable, suggests that much of initial and in-service training should be directed at helping teachers to make them effective. (para. 7.24)

The experience of preparing for and implementing the new assessment proposals might contribute significantly to developing teachers' skills in this area. Evidence from teachers already engaging in such observational activity (e.g. Cambridge Action Research Network, The Ford Teaching Project) serves to demonstrate the extent to which the knowledge gained feeds back into teaching and thus improves the quality of children's learning experience. As Rowland (1984) has commented:

> From my experience of working on my own in a classroom, I had begun to realise that whenever I looked really closely at what children were doing, the choices they were making and the forms of expressions they were using, then a picture began to build up of a child who was, in some sense, more 'rational' than I had previously recognised. It seemed that, the closer I looked, not only the more I saw, but the more intelligent was what I saw.

In addition to benefits of individual teacher's observations of children at work in their classrooms, Dean (1983) emphasizes the benefits of looking at situations in discussion with other teachers:

> Perhaps the really important point to note here is that skill in observation is one of the most important skills a teacher can have and it is a skill which teachers need to be working to improve all the time. One way of improving observation is to look at children and their work with other teachers, who, because they are different people, will see differently from you and may thus enlarge your seeing.

This is in fact what the moderation process is about, sharing, explaining, and justifying your judgement and in such a context extending your own understanding of individual children's competencies. Again this would feed back into classroom activities. One classic generalization we often state as primary teachers is that 'we start from where the children are'. I sometimes wonder how far the rhetoric matches the reality. Recently a teacher described to me an attempt to put such a premise into practice. He and his colleagues had planned a forthcoming topic for their year group of 8–9 year olds and had begun to organize tasks and identify and select resources. They were well on the way to completing their planning when the teachers decided to find out what knowledge, experience and understanding the children already had of the theme to be addressed. Much to their surprise, the children had a great deal of experience to build upon, much of which was not anticipated by the teachers involved.

As far as moderation is concerned, Rowland (1986) has a further useful comment about the benefits, one which also recognizes the reality which teachers face daily in primary schools, and thus the context in which assessments will take place:

> Given the real classroom situation with thirty or more children often engaged in a wide variety of activities and only one teacher, much of our interpretation is done very rapidly and on the spur of the moment. The speed with which we have to make decisions on our feet often allows little time for cool reflection. For this reason the interpretations we make in the classroom are likely to be based upon rules of thumb and everyday assumptions about the children and the subject matter which we use uncritically. A more careful investigation of what children's activity really means requires not only time but a certain 'intellectual space', an opportunity to reflect, preferably with others, and to develop and share insights into the children's concerns, skills and understandings. Certainly, we cannot reflect with this degree of intensity upon all of the children's work . . . . Nevertheless, the in-depth study of selected samples of activity from our classrooms can lead us to challenge, modify and at times radically alter those assumptions from which we work when we interact with children in the classroom. It can help us build an understanding of the learning process and of the concerns of children

which are expressed and developed through that process. We must develop such understanding if we are to realise our role as educators rather than merely as purveyors of knowledge. (p. 29)

It strikes me that such a philosophy should underpin our reactions to the national curriculum and national assessment. The security that primary schools provide at present will continue because both children and teachers will be clearer about what is expected of them, and the creativity of the individual teacher will ensure variety in the children's learning experiences, thus ensuring that the potential alienation of primary children is avoided. It is also likely that the procedures advocated will lead to improved interchange between parents and teachers, by providing more detail for parents of their childrens' progress.

The Task Group team were conscious that the model they offer is untenable without the support of teachers and attempted to emphasize the possible benefits for teaching and learning. A digest of the report concludes:

The Task Group knows that many teachers are apprehensive about some possible outcomes of a national system of assessment. In brief, there are worries that some pupils may be disadvantaged; that relations between teachers, pupils and parents may be soured; that schools or teachers may be singled out unfairly; and that the process may unduly constrain the work of a school. In arriving at its recommendations, the Group has aimed to prevent or minimise those possible consequences. It has been in no doubt that a successful system of assessment depends upon teachers' confidence in it and their willingness to take responsibility for it. These requirements make it necessary that the system should support teachers' professional concern for the effectiveness of their teaching . . . . The Group is also in no doubt that the system proposed is practicable and that it should contribute to the raising of educational standards by complementing and supporting the work that teachers already carry out.

We face an uncertain future in education. We need to face it positively and turn opportunities to the advantage of the children in our charge. By so doing, we can further enhance the learning opportunities available for them and reduce the potential alienation feared by the many critics of the changes to be brought about by the implementation of a National Curriculum.

References

Armstrong, M. (1988) 'Popular education and the National Curriculum', *Forum*, 30, 3, pp. 74–6.

Bolton, E. (1986) 'Assessment techniques and approaches: an overview', in *Better Schools* (Evaluation and Appraisal Conference, Birmingham, November 1985), London, HMSO.

Broadfoot, P.M. (1988) 'The National Assessment Framework and Records of Achievement', in Torrance, H. (Ed) *National Assessment Testing: A Research Response*, Paper presented to the British Education Research Association, University of London Institute of Education, pp. 3–14.

Broadfoot, P.M. and Osborn, M. (1987) 'French lessons', *Times Educational Supplement*, 3 July, p. 18.

Chitty, C. (1988) 'Two models of a National Curriculum: origins and interpretations', in Lawton, D. and Chitty, C. (Eds) *The National Curriculum*, Bedford Way Paper 33, University of London Institute of Education.

Crowley, C. (1988) *Primary School Shakespeare: A cross curriculum mode of learning*, Unpublished Advanced Diploma Long Study, Cambridge Institute of Education.

Dean, J. (1983) *Organizing Learning in the Primary School*, Beckenham, Croom Helm.

Department of Education and Science (1987a) *The National Curriculum 5-16: A Consultation Document*, London, HMSO.

Department of Education and Science (1987b) *National Curriculum: Task Group on Assessment and Testing — A Report*, London, HMSO.

Department of Education and Science (1988) *National Curriculum: Task Group on Assessment and Testing — A Digest for Schools*, London, HMSO.

Gipps, C. (1988) 'What exams would mean for primary education', in Lawton, D. and Chitty, C. (Eds) *The National Curriculum*, Bedford Way Paper 33, University of London, Institute of Education.

Gipps, C., Steadman, S., Blackstone, T. and Stierer, B. (1983) *Testing Children: Standardized Testing in Schools and LEAs*, London, Heinemann.

Gipps, C., Cross, H. and Goldstein, H. (1987) *Warnock's 18 percent: Children with Special Needs in the Primary School*, Basingstoke, Falmer Press.

Holt, M. (1987) 'Bureaucratic benefits', *Times Educational Supplement*, September, p. 30.

Hopkins, D. (1988) 'Why national testing is wrong', *Cambridge Institute of Education Newsletter*, 9.

House of Commons (1986) *Achievement in Primary Schools: The Parliamentary Select Committee Report on the Primary School*, London, HMSO.

Lawton, D. (1987) 'Fundamentally flawed', *Times Educational Supplement*, 18 September.

Marshall, P. (1986) 'The role and responsibility of the school: an overview', in *Better Schools* (Evaluation and Appraisal Conference, Birmingham, November 1985) London, HMSO.

Murphy, R. and Torrance, H. (1988) *The Changing Face of Educational Assessment*, Milton Keynes, Open University Press.

Nuttall, D.L. (1987) 'Testing, testing, testing', *NUT Education Review*, 1, 2, pp. 32–35.

Popham, W.J. (1981) *Modern Educational Measurement*, Englewood Cliffs, New Jersey, Prentice-Hall.

Rowland, S. (1984) *The Enquiring Classroom*, Basingstoke, Falmer Press.

Rowland, S. (1986) 'Classroom enquiry: an approach to understanding children', in Hutsler, D., Cassidy, A. and Cuff, E.C. *Action Research in Classrooms and Schools*, London, Allen and Unwin.

Schools Council (1971) *Choosing a Curriculum for the Young School Leaver*, Working Paper 33, London, Evans/Methuen.

Simon, B. (1980) 'Primary education: myth or reality', in Simon, B. and Willcocks, J. (Eds) *Research and Practice in the Primary Classroom*, London, Routledge and Kegan Paul.

Simons H. (1988) 'Teacher professionalism and the National Curriculum', in Lawton, D. and Chitty, C. (Eds) *The National Curriculum*, Bedford Way Paper 33, University of London, Institute of Education.

9
Educational Psychology, Primary Schools and Pupil Alienation

Neville Jones

Young children are capable of making decisions and choices, taking responsibility, and owning their own learning. In fact, without adult interference, that is exactly what they do! (Brandes and Ginnis, 1986)

Introduction

This chapter is concerned with the interface between psychological theory and practice in primary schools, as pursued by educational psychologists, and the task of teachers to provide a climate for effective growth and learning for pupils of primary age. These two aspects have not always, historically, followed a common path in ideology or practice.

The aim is to trace briefly the history of ideas that have determined primary school practice and to adjudge the influence and contribution psychology has made to primary education. With new ideas dictating new approaches, the educational *context* to which academic psychology has been able to contribute, and where educational psychologists practise, has been one of continuing change. The psychology of the time, in whatever period we are looking at, has not always been appropriate to the educational innovation that has determined ethos and practice in the schools. As a consequence, as we shall see, educational psychology has been, for the most part, a marginalized service, dealing mainly if not completely with pupils who already have been regarded by teachers as not fulfilling the ideals of learning and development at primary level. Too often, therefore, educational psychologists have failed to address the problem of pupil alienation until too late. Their role has been reactive, treating pupils who are already alienated from the school system, rather than preventative, thus helping teachers to manage classroom learning and behaviour in such a way that pupil alienation is less of a problem.

Psychology and education

Within educational psychology itself there have been, and still continue to be, divisions so that in certain aspects academic child development only 'relates weakly to what actually occurs in the classroom' and educational psychologists 'have their roles defined for them largely by whatever problems the system throws at them' (Bolton, 1989). This is as true for other phases in the system as it is for the primary phase in education. Bolton, in his analysis, does not lay this failure of communication solely at the door of psychology but sees the problem as:

> symptomatic of a more fundamental malaise which is characterised, on the one hand, by the incoherence of educational theory and, on the other, by the multiplicity of therapeutic intentions....The major foundational disciplines of education, by which I mean Psychology, Philosophy and Sociology, have failed to relate to one another.... They exist almost entirely in isolation from one another, so that there is no genuine, interdisciplinary basis for educational theory and practice.

Because of the lack of a unified theory of education there is now a particular political setting within which changes can be brought about in the education service. This is exampled by new organizational strategies and management practices — market forces and open competition — embraced within the legislative instruments of the 1988 Education Act. We shall look in more detail later in this chapter at this new departure for primary practice creating as it does a new *context* for applied educational psychology. It is this context within which educational psychologists work, and indeed secure their professional identity and image, that pre-occupies Bolton who would like to see applied psychology in school moving 'away from functionalism and reductionism towards reciprocal determination in viewing learning as a shared concern within a social context . . . he indicates that curriculum development is a proper concern for educational psychologists' (see Jones and Frederickson, 1989).

The period of theorizing

Adelman (1989) has drawn attention to the fact that 'we cannot understand the idea of child-centred education', characteristic of much applied primary education in the 20th century, 'out of the fragmentation of the present practices in primary education today'. Part of the reason for this is that for many who work in the education service, or maybe as a national phenomenon, there is a reluctance to take up and debate any particular theory or theorist that actually dictates practice, in this case in the classroom. Lester Smith, writing in 1957, was able to claim that:

> in education we are certainly much more receptive of new ideas than we used to be, but we continue to dissemble our interest in them by associating them with movements.... A glance at the list of educational

societies in *Whitaker's Almanack* or at the annual programme of the *Conference of Educational Authorities* will provide continuing evidence of our tendency to sample, discuss and promote various theories by promoting groups for that purpose.

This was so in the nineteenth century, an era of great theorists like Newman, Spencer, Arnold and Huxley, when the pre-occupation of those concerned with the education service was with the structural fabric of schools, i.e., with buildings and equipment. Educational philosophers, like Rousseau, Pestalozzi and Froebel, have all contributed to the thinking and practice of education in our primary schools, but in the latter half of the nineteenth century when such ideas were active in Germany and America, the 'vast mass of English teachers or educationalists were totally ignorant of it' (Peterson, 1952). This did not mean that there were not those who were active in propagating new ideas as was seen in the setting up of the Home and Colonial Society, the Froebel Society, and the educational movement that became known as The New Era.

It was only towards the end of the nineteenth century that psychology, detaching itself from its roots in philosophy, began to emerge as a new discipline centred on the 'scientific' study of behaviour. Both these factors have yet to be finally analyzed, the break with philosophy and the need for the emerging psychology, to be recognized as part of the realm of the natural sciences. But there is now a substantial body of opinion that these two factors alone created a gulf between the base discipline of psychology and the practice of education. It is one thing to attempt to apply the methods of science to things educational, but limiting educational psychology in this way has meant that a true school psychology — arising from the craft of teaching — has not been allowed to emerge, and teachers and their pupils have equally been deprived of a knowledge area that could have made a greater contribution to education than it has done (Jones and Sayer, 1988; Jones and Frederickson, 1989).

Although teachers in training were, and are still, intrigued by some of the ideas emanating from eminent psychological theorists, they have found the content of much academic psychology 'a dull subject, consisting of talk of concepts, images, and precepts. Children did not enter into it at all' (Weddell, 1955). Making the connections between academic psychology and how teachers experience pupil growth, thinking and development in the classroom, has also been a problem for educational psychologists when called upon to advise, from a psychological standpoint, on matters relating to educational issues in terms of teaching and pupil learning. The educational psychologist learns his or her craft of applied psychology *in schools*, having completed an academic training, and when the psychologist enters the classroom in partnership with the teacher. Where there is no partnership there is impasse. There have, of course, been a number of able academics who have in part portrayed 'a sympathetic interpretation of psychology and able to show its relevance to the daily business of school' (Smith, 1957).

The new era in primary education

Rousseau, in his novel *Emile* had begun to think about education afresh. Nothing was to be taken for granted — a fresh and untrammelled mind abandoning precedent and tradition. He came to the view that 'nature would have children be children before being men — childhood has its own ways of seeing, thinking and feeling' (p. 54). It was in this tradition that ideas developed through such educational luminaries as Pestalozzi, Herbart, Froebel, Montessori, the McMillans, Caldwell Cook, and John Dewey. The methods developed are now familiar: the Dalton Plan, Play Way and Projects. The nature and quality of teacher-pupil relationships in present day primary schools are but the outcome of these approaches to the education of young children, whereby teachers moved from the strict and conformist roles of instructors to that of guiding pupils in the ways of knowledge based on methods of activity and experience.

In the abandonment of pre-determined curriculum this did not mean that the commonplace pedagogy of today, learning by doing, and expressed through the two ideas of *nature* and *freedom*, were always understood. In looking to *nature* Rousseau did not advocate a free-for-all approach to learning where there was little or no intervention on the part of adults; rather he believed in a guided experience for children and a 'well-negotiated liberty'. Young children needed to be 'formed by their educative experiences, not least because there cannot be dependence entirely upon human instinct nor the processes of growth and development'. But whereas Rousseau's ideas gradually permeated primary education in Britain, particularly in the 20th century, there were those in the 'progressive' movement who experimented with self-governing communities in the belief 'that freedom with social responsibility has power to regenerate individuals who have previously been at variance with society and with their own higher selves' (Wheeler, 1922, p. 76). Examples are the work of 'Daddy' George in America (George, 1909), Homer Lane in his work with the Little Commonwealth (Wills, 1964, Bazeley, 1948), and the work of A.S. Neil (Hearnshaw, 1979; Neil, 1953), to mention but a few (see Bridgeland, 1971, for an extensive account of early progressive pioneers in Britain).

Bridgeland (1971) points out that 'the principles of the educational movements of those dynamic years [early 20th century] were to be significant . . . and largely pragmatically derived'. Although much of the impetus for change was derived from the teachings of Dewey and the influence of Montessori, many of the early pioneers of this period developed their ideas from empirical insights. These were seen by O'Connor (1958) as:

> more like the empirical insight of the herbalist in the early stages of medicine. Practice comes first; but its theoretical justification has to wait for the scientific development that can explain early success. Thus educational theories which preceded the rise of scientific psychology were more or less acurate guesses at explaining successful practice'. (quoted in Bridgeland, 1971, p. 131)

Bridgeland has pointed out that the pioneers in the progressive movement largely learned from each other, their 'practice adventurous and experimental', and that 'schools which were founded too rigidly on theory tended not to survive, while those which drew their life from a dynamic human being frequently did so. Perhaps theories tend to change and decay rather more quickly than men!'

At this time the psychology that many teachers were looking at, both in progressive schools and in state education, was not so much the scientific psychology referred to by O'Connor, but more the social psychology grounded in the pragmatism of Dewey's thinking, the ideas beginning to circulate from the writings of Freud, and the teaching that was surfacing in the training colleges. In the 1920s and 1930s there were few educational psychologists working in LEA services, the first, Cyril Burt, having been appointed to the London County Council in 1913.

A number of the private progressive special schools established at this time arose because psychiatrists working in clinics were finding that their therapeutic endeavours were severely curtailed by the appalling home conditions of many children coupled with inadequate schooling. Some of the early pioneers were clearly reacting to their own experiences in state education (Wills, 1941, 1945) or because they were disenchanted about the inadequacies of the system, and went off to develop their own ideas as in the work of George Lyward (Burn, 1956).

The psychology that was increasingly influential in education at the turn of this century was that of the German philosopher Herbart (1776–1841) whose ideas John Adams, Principal of the London Day Training College, was expounding through his work in the College and a publication called *Herbartian Psychology Applied to Education*. This was seen as 'the first attempt in this country to put the new psychological theories into a form that would be useful to the practical teacher' (quoted in Smith, 1957).

But these European ideas on educational development were not welcomed by a number of educational thinkers and practitioners in Britain. Central among those at the turn of the century was Edmond Holmes, the Chief Inspector for Elementary Education at the Board of Education. Both Herbart and Holmes drew their inspirational thinking from the earlier writings of Rousseau and Froebel, but Holmes was of the opinion that Rousseau 'left too much to Nature and too little to the teacher' while Froebel 'left too little to Nature and too much to the teacher' (Holmes, 1914). Holmes' reaction to the Herbartian psychology was that the disciples of Herbart, now beginning to exercise considerable influence on teacher training in Britain, were more dogmatic than their philosophical mentor and it was to this dogmatism being introduced into primary education that Holmes most objected. Furthermore, he argued that any theory of educational practice needed to be applied to the context of the time and Herbartian theory of the early part of the nineteenth century was inappropriate in the early years of the twentieth century:

> A philosophical system has its meaning, in part at least, by reference to the context of the life and thought of its own age; and all modifying influences emanating from that context must be duly allowed for, if the ideas that dominate the system are to be set free (Holmes, 1914, p. 8).

The influence of Edmond Holmes

Already then early psychological thinking and practice was becoming seen as something in conflict with child education in schools. The ideas and writings of Edmond Holmes (1850–1936) touched upon generations of students, teachers and administrators. But he was 'a curiously shadowy figure — there is no full-length biography of the man, and there are few modern editions of his books' (Gordon, 1983). His interests were wide, spanning poetry and literature, theology and philosophy. Like many who worked in the progressive school movement of the time, Holmes found his own education at the Merchant Taylor's School in London, less than inspiring. Holmes was appointed HMI of schools in April 1875 at the age of 24 years. He first worked in West Riding, then in Kent and later in Oxford, and became Chief Inspector at the Board of Education. In retirement Holmes reflected on the fact that as a 'dutiful, industrious and almost ultra-conscientious official', as Holmes was, there were difficulties of working and bringing about change in what he saw as the 'administering of a pernicious system' (Holmes, 1922):

> So potent was the pressure of the system under which we all worked that it drove me deeply into the deadly grooves in which it imprisoned the teachers and the children. I saw that the system had many defects, but I regarded these as interest in any and every scheme of education for the masses; and I was well content to play my appointed part in that vast complex of machinery which had been elaborated by the wisdom and was controlled by the authority of Whitehall (Holmes, 1922).

His experiences in West Riding of Yorkshire caused him to report on 'the parlous state of the teaching he had discovered in his schools, where teachers who were suspicious of new ideas, proceeded mechanically along well-beaten tracks and used out-of-date methods (Holmes, 1879). Holmes reflected that this was not the fault of the teachers because 'circumstances are against the teacher from the first to last'. It was only when Holmes moved to Kent that he was able to put into practice some of his own ideas on education. His particular interest was English, how it was taught, and the important part of English that encouraged expression and feeling, particularly poetry.

At this time the methods of reading were considered to be unsound and received less attention than any other subject in the elementary school curriculum. Reading was a subject separate from grammar and poetry and Holmes worked hard to bring these three elements together. He believed that reading was more important than arithmetic, science and geography because 'it cultivates the emotions and appeals to the heart . . . . On these grounds I hold that its educational value is higher than that and all these other subjects put together, provided always that it is equally well taught'.

The problem Holmes found was how to staff the elementary schools 'with progressive teachers able and willing to undertake experimental work'. He put forward the proposal that there should be established local training centres where teachers could have intensive in-service courses and he hoped that these would develop a national system of training colleges. He had found in his Oxfordshire district that only one fifth of teachers had been trained but the Oxfordshire County Council had initiated a four-week in-service training programme. This idea, put by Holmes to the then Vice-President of the Committee of Council on Education, resulted in the Board of Education publishing in 1905 *Suggestions for the Use of Teachers and Others Concerned in the Work of Elementary Schools* (later called the *Handbook of Suggestions for Teachers*). The aim of the Board was to encourage teachers to look towards elementary education with a wider perspective. The *Suggestions* aimed:

1. To encourage teachers to apply teaching methods which were most suitable to the particular needs of the school;
2. To develop a curriculum aimed at preparing children for citizenship, to develop loyalty, to encourage an aptitude for work, and to use leisure intelligently.

But these were innovations well before their time and it was not until the 1950s that we began to see the fruition of some of the ideas that Holmes was putting forward at the turn of the century. At this time, however, the philosophy and educational theory he was advocating began to be merged. He published in 1911 a volume called *What Is and What Might Be* which attracted wide attention partly because of a controversy stemming from a confidential memorandum from Holmes to the Permanent Secretary of the Board, Robert Morant, which had criticized local authority inspectors and been published and widely circulated (Gordon, 1978). In his book Holmes criticized the existing education system with its:

excessive systemization, its emphasis on visible results, such as examinations, competition instead of co-operation, the stress on the mechanical obedience of the child rather than self-realisation, and teaching methods which were inappropriate for the curriculum (Gordon, 1983, p. 21).

Once retired Holmes was free to explore his own ideas about education by visiting the Montessori schools in Italy, where he was encouraged in seeing a system of education 'that allowed infants to develop at their own pace and in an atmosphere of freedom, whilst they made good progress in reading and writing' (see an education pamphlet he wrote called *The Montessori System*, Board of Education, 1912).

Earlier was mentioned the psychological thinking of Herbert whose influence was strong in the teacher training colleges. The publication by Holmes *What Is and What Might Be* was aimed at the system of education at the time, of his ideas of self-realization for pupils, for which he was criticized because of what was regarded as lack of realism (Morris, 1911), because of his views of the place of religious education in the curriculum (Smith, 1911), and as a reaction to what he called 'the complacent dogmatism of the typical Herbartian . . . '. Holmes was concerned that the typical well regulated school in Germany at this time, with pressures for autocratic authority, only 'led to mechanical obedience by the pupils and that of the teaching of patriotism appealed to latent selfishness' (Holmes, 1915). His arguments against what he saw as the pseudo-science of Herbartism psychology of education (called philosophy of education in the nineteenth century) was set out in a book called *In Defence of What Might Be* published in 1914.

The publication of *What Is and What Might Be* in 1911 was an attack on traditional elementary education because of its authoritarianism, rote learning, and the cramming for examinations. As part of the Idealist movement of the period Holmes was concerned to rid the 'system' of its soullessness and to facilitate pupils in their education towards 'self-realization'. Self-realization in Holmes's theory and in philosophical idealism in general was the highest ideal that could be aimed for in human endeavour. Holmes, therefore, is well known as 'an advocate of standing back from the child and letting inner potentialities develop to their fullest extent'. His ideas and work were strongly influenced by the work he had seen in an elementary village school in Sussex where enlightened 'child-centred' education was being pursued by Harriet Finlay-Johnson. This work, he considered, fitted well into his theory of developing the pupils' unborn instincts — towards communication, the dramatic, the artistic, the musical, the inquisitive and the constructive — and where the aim of the teacher is to create the conditions for these instincts to flourish. Only in this way, where such instincts were given free rein, would the pupil be able to reach the ideal of self-realization. Holmes thought that this goal could be reached through educative processes where nature would be the guide to practice, and there was the need to move away from policies and practices that made children egotistic and competitive. It may be thought that Holmes placed too much emphasis on the value of the school in its educative role, but this is an issue that needs to be readdressed some eighty years later with current government policies for primary education and the requirements of the 1988 Education Act. For Holmes the education potential in a school lies, as he observed in the Sussex school, in the teacher becoming 'more significant as an educator at a time when she is learning to abstain from instruction and merely guide the hand of nature' (Gordon and White, 1979).

The new realists

Idealism as an influential movement in British education was at its nadir between 1870 and 1920: between the two World Wars its influence diminished, although idealist thinking reappears from time to time such as with the 1942 Beveridge Report and the 1944 Education Act. Institutions based on idealist philosophy — the new universities, for example, and the Open University — all developed and flourished at a time when traditional idealism had given way to a 'progressiveness' in education that was based on other practices such as scientific psychology. The strands of theory that are now intertwined in contemporary primary school education are such that it is difficult at times to decide which and what philosophical tradition they represent.

The basis for progressive education in primary schools changed in the 1920s. The progressive movement, linked with Holmes and idealism, began to recede in its social and religious aspects leaving self-realization as a residual concept. The way was open for a new realism, whose main exponent at the time was Percy Nunn, who was closely associated with a group known as the New Realists (Passmore, 1957). Nunn (1920) focused on the good of the individual being derived from nature rather than society, the main purpose being to ensure the maximum development of every pupil's individuality. The social improvement of the individual pupil had less credence and value in Nunn's philosophy than with Holmes, but he differed basically from the idealist position in the way he viewed pupils as essentially biological. There were many writers at this time, in the fields of biology, animal psychology and psychoanalysis, who were exploring and advocating ideas related to man's essential animal nature (T.H. Huxley, Darwin, and Freud). This was consistent with a view of the individual child as 'a self-centred entity' and a central plank of the 'child-centred' movement in primary education which has lasted to present times.

Supporting all this was the movement in child study and the beginnings of the testing movement initiated by Alfred Binet in his work with Parisian children in 1904. This had its roots in the writings and philosophies of the eugenics movement, and all this came together in the writings and research of bio-psychologists like Galton, Pearson and Cyril Burt. Later, the researches of Piaget would be built on the same foundation.

Nunn was also an advocate of the view that, while accepting that there are areas of learning that children might instinctively react to and avoid, 'children should be left alone as far as possible to develop by themselves'. Educational thinking had taken a dramatic step in moving away from education that was socially orientated, in terms of the good of social groups in the community, to a view that every pupil was a self-contained entity and education should be developed to secure this to its full potential. The door was wide open for research and practice to follow this line of thinking which was consistent with new psychological techniques being devised to select children for the types of categorization that we would see interpreted in education planning, especially in the tripartite system of education following the Second World War. What was needed was a work-force to apply the tests and develop the techniques — and school psychologists began to be appointed to carry out these tasks which led to a divisiveness in our school populations based on ideas about mental functioning and potential for learning. The mould was set to ensure that all pupils were properly placed in their 'mental' place in the school system, and hence in society, and the new psychology was located in LEAs. In this way 'society will best achieve its nature-given ends if it allows the impeded growth of an intellectual elite'. Educational psychologists are, of course, part of that elite themselves.

Psychological services

The appointment of educational psychologists to LEA services was slow in the beginning and even today there are no more than 1500 working in our schools. But educational psychologists began to play a powerful influence in the education and life chances of a small group of pupils, about 2 per cent of the total school population, who are now categorized as having special educational needs.

Psychology now underpins the whole of the theory and practice of special education in Britain particularly in segregated provision. This also applies to teacher training and in-service work, illustrated by the fact that all major university departments of special needs are run and organized by psychologists (and the same applies to many teacher training colleges). Educational psychologists are seen by many teachers as the only 'expert' source of knowledge on learning and pupil behaviour. All this came about because of the enormous range of research and power originally exercised by Cyril Burt, the father figure of educational psychology services in this country. Burt 'firmly established the psychologist's power-base and projected his subject into a place in the developing special education system, where it has remained quite secure' (Swann, 1982). It is not surprising, therefore, that educational psychologists are now reluctant to give up this power base so that they may work more specifically in mainstream education on matters central to the running of schools.

As early as the 1970s there were indications that not all educational psychologists were happy in their role as 'gate-keepers' for special education and some were becoming critical of the value of IQ testing as part of their work. Additionally, there were those who were beginning to swing back from what might be described as blatant 'individualism' in education. Pupils began to be grouped for co-operative learning, for which teachers began to regard psychological testing invalid when not irrelevant. Furthermore, a new group of teachers began to be appointed to support the ordinary teacher in the classroom. This was a development on the original peripatetic remedial teacher service but it meant that the support teachers were taking on roles which had previously been held by educational psychologists even though much of the 'expertise' offered to schools contained little formal psychology.

Psychologists working in schools were also beginning to find that teachers, partly through in-service work initiated by LEAs, were themselves beginning to become the 'experts' on a whole range of issues relating to education itself and that psychology, particularly in its scientific stance, was becoming remote and irrelevant for classroom practice, particularly in primary schools. Pupils were beginning to be educated with a strong emphasis on being social creatures in a social world and education had a part to ensure that every pupil was prepared to take a responsible role in that social environment. It became difficult for educational psychologists to apply their 'scientific' skills to a context that was changing. By continuing with patterns of work practice built up since the days of Cyril Burt they found themselves becoming increasingly marginalized as far as education in schools were concerned. Continually they were, and are still, thrown back on dealing with pupils who had failed the education system in some way, and educational psychologists in the early 1980s became content with taking up any problem offered to them by teachers. This strongly affected morale in the service, producing lethargy and lack of purpose. This might have continued had it not been for the 1988 Education Act which seems likely to produce a new school context within which educational psychologists can begin to work, but a lack of clarity about the 1988 Act itself i.e. the fact that it is not educationally based or on any sound moral philosophy (Hargreaves, 1989) but on economic and market forces, has only created further problems for educational psychologists.

Need for a partnership with teachers

Education in primary schools is broadly about whole-school management and pupils as people. Educational psychology, in its 'academic' stance, has been concerned with some aspect of pupil learning and behaviour, applying a scientific 'within the child' mode of intervention. Furthermore, the discipline of psychology has restricted its application to schools, in the work of educational psychologists, to a very limited knowledge base of the discipline of psychology itself. Taken together, these two aspects explain why the 'psychology' offered to teachers has been, for the most part, a response to school needs which has been less than appropriate, and when appropriate, too detailed and technically sophisticated for teachers to utilize in their daily work with children.

Many teachers in primary education have resented, and thus not responded to, the way psychological intervention has failed to treat pupils as persons: by labelling and categorizing them, through the use of test procedures, and in the final analysis, helping to create within a school both social and intellectual elites among pupils. This is not to deny that some primary teachers have been glad to participate in this marginalization process especially in relation to pupils who fail to learn or have learned to behave inappropriately. A whole-school philosophy implies an obligation by all who work in the school to all pupils who attend. Some pupils stretch that sense of obligation to breaking point and relief to individual teachers and the corporate body of the school is sought through external (psychological) intervention. This recognition that educational psychologists work from a knowledge base that increases in relevance the more a child is removed from the ordinary classroom — the centre for normalizing and learning promoting influences — produces a paradox. The support service to the teacher is a service that by nature engages in that part of a teacher's professional role and identity which the teacher feels is a failure. This creates a professional ambivalence between teachers and educational psychologists.

Educational psychologists in some LEA services have been trying to break away from the stereotype of interventionists geared to a role of testing and remediation, but leaving the management of pupil needs still in the hands of the teacher. It has been argued that to change this position they will, as a professional group, have to make some very specific decisions about their role as this affects education services (Jones, 1989). For example, at the moment, the school psychological service is still fundamentally a testing agency. Its main client population is in relation to pupils who are failing in their learning (or are seen so by someone in authority, i.e. parent or teacher). The intervention work is mainly in providing a therapeutic response or in the remediation of learning difficulties (this latter task now substantially taken over by LEA teacher support teams either school-based or peripatetic). The infrequency with which educational psychologists visit schools still creates problems for a service that tries to maintain some consistency and continuity from a management point of view. Heads find it very difficult when educational psychologists change their 'client' schools frequently, and become disenchanted when it becomes known that these changes are the result of internal reconstructions of the service for no clear reasons other than those known to the educational psychology service.

Educational psychologists resist strongly any suggestion that there should be an accountable partnership with schools, arguing that they carry out their work more effectively when placed in a professionally neutral role. However, this contradicts the notions of professional partnerships, which educational psychologists put forward with vigour with respect to other professional groups that serve schools (or in school-parent partnerships), and therefore makes this kind of advocacy less meaningful where teachers are concerned.

Perhaps the biggest barrier to effective partnership work with primary schools is that the educational psychologist is seen pure and simple as the person to turn to in relation to pupils regarded as having special educational needs. The specific intervention by educational psychologists with pupils with a special pathology makes it more difficult for the educational psychologist to change in role and task and to become involved in a wider spectrum of activities that are central to the running of a school. Here I am referring to work in schools relating to curriculum planning for all pupils; to questions of staff selection, promotion and self-evaluation procedures, and professional in-service work; to work with other agencies and maximizing the benefits that can accrue with effective involvement of parents in school activities and their own pupils' learning. Perhaps the strongest factor in recent years in securing the work of educational psychologists to special needs has been the 1981 Education Act, with educational psychologists having statutory duties to sustain a system of diversity in schools through the statementing procedures whereby we continue to maintain two categories of pupil — those regarded as normal (unstatemented) and those less than, or other than, normal (the statemented). Educational psychologists therefore support procedures that create educational elites and educational divisions through the activities of testing and assessment, and in meeting legislative requirements.

Unfortunately, few educational psychologists have taken advantage of opportunities to move away from much of the work described above that places them in a segregated role from those working in the mainstream of education. First, an opportunity occurred by virtue of the integration movement so that the disabled could remain in mainstream education and those segregated in special schools be rehabilitated. Educational psychologists could well have developed the managerial expertise on how integration policies and practices might work effectively, and thereby supported schools in a consultancy role. It is worth recalling the fact that the exclusion of every child from mainstream education because of their special needs is a result of the professional intention of an educational psychologist (with others) in the statementing procedures. The managerial expertise, relating not only to planning appropriate curriculum for these pupils, but also to areas like supporting parents during the anxious period when the pupil is returning to normal education, would have been welcomed by headteachers and their staff. It would also have set educational psychologists along a road of acting as consultants to schools in an area which was meaningful to heads who were coping with the problems of integration. Instead, much of this support came from a few heads of special schools who themselves had a vision about how special education could change.

A second opportunity for educational psychologists to move closer to the central activities of schools was lost when the government legislated on the Warnock Report in 1981. Educational psychologists could easily have disassociated themselves from this particular piece of legislation by making clear their opposition to the proposals about statementing before the Act was enacted, and in LEA policies about integration which have affected levels of statementing. Educational psychologists, however, were not united in their views and policies about integration, and hence they became easy servants of the Government's legislation in 1981, as they are likely to become with the national assessment requirements built into the 1988 Education Act. Indeed, in some LEAs the educational psychologists not only engaged actively in setting up the LEA internal procedures for statementing but assumed administrative roles in the preparation and collation of statementing documents.

A new opportunity for educational psychologists to engage more realistically in educational practice in schools has now emerged with the 1988 Education Act. Clearly within this Act there are strong forces at work that can bring about the exclusion of even more pupils from mainstream education than at present. Educational psychologists need to resist completely any participatory role in this envisaged change in educational practice by heads i.e. the excluding of pupils, who are by some national or other bogus criterion, slow learning or behaviourally maladjusted. But there is an opportunity in the 1988 Act procedures whereby educational psychologists can, and should, engage purposefully with headteachers on how psychologists can offer to schools an expertise other than that historically carried out in the management of pupils with special needs. This calls for a close collaboration between heads and psychologists, with a meaningful accountability worked out so as to preserve professional identities, but without creating professional barriers. Educational psychologists will need to keep clear of all activities associated with the Government's plans for the national testing of pupils at 7, 11, 14 and 16 years of age. Consultancy roles, where required and worked out, need to develop out of joint consultation between the teaching profession and psychologists, and for consultancy work to be rigorous and managerially efficient.

A psychology for primary schooling

The form this collaborative role might take was brought out during a series of seminars held in 1986, at the London University Education Management Unit. This brought together headteachers, educational psychologists, those in educational research and administration, to look at why the discipline of psychology was making only a limited contribution to the *management* of schools. The central concerns of headteachers are those of curriculum planning and implementation, appointing and managing staff (linked with teacher professional development), monitoring and evaluating pupil learning and progress, coping with stress, crises and the interminable flow of visitors (professional or otherwise), liaising with the LEA, its school support services and other community agencies, and importantly working with parents. Educational psychology, through the school psychological services, only responds to a few of those areas of central concern to schools, and then often intermittently and in a peripheral way.

The London seminars were directed towards looking at psychology as a central concern for schools, starting where the school is, and appraising what kind of psychology of schooling might emerge when the epicentre for psychological intervention is in the school rather than in the psychological laboratory, as at present. Following a writing conference at Oxford University in the same year, the seminar group produced its first publication called *Management and the Psychology of Schooling* (Jones and Sayer, 1987). Each chapter was an essay exploring some wider aspect of psychological intervention than is touched upon, for the most part, by psychological services at the moment. These included topics like values in schools, classroom management, curriculum planning, community links, school climate and ethos, and pastoral systems. These broadly came under the title of school management. Further chapters were addressed to the specific needs of teachers and pupils: communication skills, managing groups, pupil learning, professional development, work with parents, consultancy work with teachers, in-service and advisory activities.

The group saw its task as one of looking at areas of school activity that would directly relate to the thinking and work of heads on a daily basis. These would include: leadership skills; decision making that was effective; how resources could best be organized; how change could be facilitated without crippling stress to those involved; the issues in providing a broad, balanced, yet appropriate curriculum for all pupils (irrespective of their individual needs); effective systems of liaising with support agencies, parents and industry; and the management of the self and others in one-to-one and group settings. The group was also clear that the task was not to address and evaluate the problem of applying the science of academic psychology to the craft practices of teaching and educating children. It was acknowledged, however, that much of academic psychology related to personnel selection; management of staff or performance appraisal, for example, was not currently offered to schools through the agency of school psychological services, nor was there an expectation on the part of headteachers that educational psychologists would be able to offer advice and expertise in these areas. This present concern, therefore, is not only about the content of the psychology that can enhance classroom and school practice, but the structure of the delivery service, and whether present-day school psychological services are the most appropriate form for effective delivery of a 'psychology of schooling'.

At the moment educational psychologists do not have an employment brief to extend their work beyond that of working with individual 'client' pupils referred to them by teachers. Educational psychologists have, therefore, had to create a space for themselves, usually in close collaboration with their 'client' schools, in order to explore some of the areas of school practice just mentioned. Perhaps most of the effective contributions made to schools in the past 20 years have been where educational psychologists and heads have worked out localized patterns of work and involvement for the educational psychologist to cover a wider spectrum of commitment rather than testing pupils with perceived special educational needs.

The group also recognized that a psychology of schooling was not a wholistic and coherent set of principles and practices — a blue print for future work for all educational psychologists. Some looked to an evolutionary process whereby, through a different form of training and selection of personnel, the educational psychologist of the future would be able to offer heads a specific knowledge and skill related to one of the major areas of school organization and practice. This would be a much more senior position in LEA organization than that of the educational psychologist testing individual pupils and advising in general terms on a broad perspective of issues depending on which particular issues were presented by headteachers.

There was also recognition that there were areas of academic psychology not drawn upon by educational psychologists, in their educational psychology training or practice, and this knowledge was often syphoned off into industry, commerce and central government departments. A broader view of this approach was to recognize that major contributions to school practice can be, and have been, made from other closely allied disciplines like sociology, philosophy, theology and social administration. The way forward in all this has yet to be determined but progress will only be made when there is a sufficient body of practising educational psychologists who have a will as well as the vision to extend their work as indicated, and thus create the means to achieve these new objectives.

As the discussion extends on the future of school psychological services, very much prompted by the uncertainties inherent in the 1988 Education Act, there is need for all concerned, or who want to be concerned, to tease out some basic ideas and to explore what delivery structures are required and how these can be brought about.

A second group of papers has recently been published where there has been an attempt to identify more precisely those areas of work in which educational psychologists of the future might be participants (Jones and Frederickson, 1989). In this volume the areas of work examined are individual pupil learning, consultancy roles in schools, work with parents, communication skills, the importance of learning in groups, systems work and theory, the role for educational psychologists in Government sponsored projects, and educational psychologists' involvement with teacher in-service training.

These new territories can only be explored, and the expertise built up, if educational psychologists are prepared to abandon some of their time-honoured practices related to the testing and assessment of individual pupils. This has the implication that in time psychological practice in schools will be less exclusively concerned with pupils who are failing in their learning and more generally concerned in effective management of learning for all pupils. This means a gradual disengagement from those parts of the education system now referred to as 'special' with all its trappings of deficit-model evaluations. We should look forward in time to when no child is labelled 'special' and all pupils, whatever their needs, are offered as broad a curriculum as they can manage in settings that maximize and secure pupils' feelings of self-esteem in normal school contexts. This would be consistent with viewing pupils in the round and not making important decisions for their future education based on single or multiple tests and evaluations by out-of-school agents or agencies.

It may be the case that educational psychologists will have to examine how far they are going to participate in school practices which, by virtue of goverment legislation, such as the 1981 Education Act and possibly the 1988 Act, ensure that they continue as test agents practising deficit-model psychology. At the moment, as the law stands, all pupils who attend special schools are required to be statemented. Educational psychologists have it in their control not to participate in statementing procedures where the LEA is not developing integration policies and phasing out segregated education for statemented pupils. Educational psychologists need to 'normalize' their own professional image and to do this by developing expertise in the management and schooling of all pupils in ordinary schools. The 1988 Education Act provides a channel in which educational psychologists can become even more marginalized than they are at present, or alternatively, can branch out in a dialogue with heads to see how their time (with acquired new expertise) could be used for the benefit of schools and the pupils that attend them. Educational psychology would then cease to be a disaffected service, as viewed by many teachers and some educational psychologists, and a new collaboration in the context of a psychology of schooling could then emerge.

References

Adelman, C. (1989) 'Children's learning: an historical perspective', in Barrett, J. (Ed.) *Disaffection From School: The Early Years*, Lewes, Falmer Press.

Bazeley, E.T. (1948) *Homer Lane and the Little Commonwealth*, 2nd edit. London, Allen and Unwin.

Board of Education (1912) *The Montessori System*, Pamphlet No. 24, London, HMSO.

Bolton, N. (1989) 'Educational psychology and the politics and practice of education', in Jones, N. and Frederickson, N. (Eds.) *Refocusing Educational Psychology*, Lewes, Falmer Press.

Brandes, D. and Ginnis, P. (1986) *A Guide to Student-Centred Learning*, Oxford, Basil Blackwell.

Bridgeland, M. (1971) *Pioneer Work with Maladjusted Children*, London, Staples Press.

Burn, M. (1956) *Mr Lyward's Answer*, London, Hamish and Hamilton.

George, W.R. (1909) *The Junior Republic*, Appleton and Company, New York.

Gordon, P. (1978) 'The Holmes-Morant Circular of 1911: A Note', *Journal of Educational Administration and History*, January, pp. 36–40.

Gordon, P. (1983) 'The writings of Edmond Holmes: a reassessment and bibliography', *History of Education*, 12, 1.

Gordon, P. and White, J. (1979) *Philosophers as Educational Reformers*, London, Routledge and Kegan Paul.

Hargreaves, D.H. (1989) 'Introduction', in Jones, N. (Ed.) *School Management and Pupil Behaviour*, Lewes, Falmer Press.

Hearnshaw, L. (1979) *Cyril Burt: Psychologist*, London, Hodder and Stoughton.

Holmes, E. (1879) *General Report for the West Riding of Yorkshire*, Report of the Committee of Council on Education 1878–9, 594.

Holmes, E. (1911) *What Is and What Might Be: A study of education in general and elementary education in particular*, London, Constable.

Holmes, E. (1914) *In Defence of What Might Be*, London, Constable.

Holmes, E. (1915) 'Ideals of life and education — German and English', *Nineteenth Century and After*, October, p. 962.

Holmes, E. (1922) 'The confessions and hopes of an Ex-Inspector of Schools', *Hibbert Journal*, 20, July, pp. 726–7.

Jones, N. and Frederickson, N. (1989) *Refocusing Educational Psychology*, Lewes, Falmer Press.

Jones, N. and Sayer, J. (Eds.) (1988) *Management and the Psychology of Schooling*, Lewes, Falmer Press.

Morris, M. (1911) 'Musings Without Method', *Blackwood's Magazine*, August, pp. 265–73.

Neil, A.S. (1953) *The Free Child*, London, Jenkins.

Nunn, P. (1920) *Education: the Data and First Principles*, London, Arnold.

O'Connor, D.J. (1958) *An Introduction to the Philosophy of Education*, London, Routledge and Kegan Paul.

Passmore, J.A. (1957) *A Hundred Years of Philosophy*, London, Duckworth.

Peterson, A.D.C. (1952) *A Hundred Years of Education*, London, Duckworth.

Smith, S.F. (1911) 'The Ideas of a Chief Inspector of Schools', *The Month*, November, pp. 449–61.

Smith, W.O. Lester (1957) *Education*, Harmondsworth, Penguin.

Swann, W. (1982) *Psychology of Special Education*, Unit 12, Open University Course E241, Milton Keynes, Open University Press.

Weddell, M. (1955) *Journal of the Institute of Education of Durham*, January, Durham.

Wheeler, O. (1922) *Bergson and Education*, Manchester, University Press.

Wills, W.D. (1941) *The Hawkspur Experiment*, London, Allen and Unwin.

Wills, W.D. (1945) *The Barns Experiment*, London, Allen and Unwin.

Wills, W.D. (1964) *Homer Lane: A Biography*, London, Allen and Unwin.

10
Disadvantaged Children:
The Community and the Problems of
Junior School Alienation

Paul Widlake

Introduction

There is no doubt that in the last eight years the community has been invited to become more involved in the British state education system. Four major Education Acts have increased parental representation on the governing bodies of schools and have added substantially to the powers of these bodies. About the long-term effects of these far-reaching reforms we can only speculate, with all the dangers attendant upon that occupation. One can take consolation for possible inaccuracy in the knowledge that contenders for the title of World's Worst Prophet include famous names like that of Cyril Connolly, the writer and critic, who remarked to George Orwell on 8 April 1941, as they stood on a roof-top gazing at fires started in the blitz: 'It's the end of capitalism. It's a judgement on us.' Orwell himself was not convinced and merely observed the size and beauty of the flames. A variant of either of these approaches seems appropriate in contemplating the 1988 Education Reform Act and its effects on disadvantaged children.

The questions to be addressed are whether this legislative framework, perhaps contrary to the intentions of those who initiated it, can be useful to that part of the community described as 'disadvantaged'. Since the demon of market forces has been unleashed into the sedate and previously closed world of state education, it makes sense to examine what can be done by those who are NOT white, middle class professionals — the obvious beneficiaries — but who are poor, unemployed, or disadvantaged by reason of class, race, gender, disability or geographical location. As Finch (1984) acutely observed in her study of education as social policy, the history of education in Britain would not support the view that:

> it has been simply imposed from above, because sometimes it has been demanded from below.... The pattern implied is a complex one of struggles, bribes and concessions.... At the same time policies which are

implemented (whether imposed from above or won from below) may
have unintended and unanticipated consequences. (p. 180)

So the strategy might be to examine vigorously whether these new powers actually
exist or are mere shadows behind which the real business of central government is
intended to be transacted. The first example of public parental protest did not
provide an encouraging precedent: the Inner London Education Authority parents
who voted overwhelmingly against its abolition were told off for wasting rate-
payers' money and their petition was ignored.

This legislation seems likely to determine the structure and style of education
provision for a very long time because no viable alternative has as yet even been
formulated by those who might form a future government. Moreover, the record of
the Labour Party towards the involvement of parents has been equivocal, both
during its periods of administration and opposition, and the local parties have not
differed much from their Conservative opponents in their eagerness to award school
board membership to elected representatives. Although the 1944 Act provided for
Boards of Governors to be established in all schools, in some places little was done:
'This was particularly so in regard to the primary schools and the result was that
contact with the schools — and parents — was minimal. It had been hoped that
parents would be included on the Boards, but this rarely happened' (Bullivant,
1981).

The action really began with the appointment of the Taylor Committee and its
report *A New Partnership with Parents* (DES, 1977), which was greeted by the
National Union of Teachers as 'a busybodies' charter' but in time led to the 1980
Education Act. Teachers and parents of pupils were given the right to elect
representatives to the Boards of all maintained schools. Eventually every school was
to have its own Board but it is hard to grasp that this basic right took so long to
appear in English schools. The 1981 Act, which was based on the preceding
Warnock Report (DES, 1978), and was but a pale shadow of the Report, was also a
landmark in special education. It established the principle that as many children as
possible should be educated in mainstream schools and explicitly recognized the
essential role of parents in the assessment and education of their children.

The 1986 Act went further and laid down a new standard composition for the
governing bodies of county and special schools, the largest of which could include
five parents and six coopted members. It gave governing bodies increased powers
over the selection of staff, the right to make a curriculum statement for their school
which the head must take into account, and gave governors a say in the spending of
capitation monies. The Act also provided for the training of governors and, almost
incidentally, abolished corporal punishment in schools! It is worth noting that both
these long overdue decisions should occur under a Conservative rather than a
Labour Administration.

The 1986 Act had barely been enacted, and the newly constituted Boards had
not yet come into being, before the 1988 Education Reform Act arrived. The effects
remain to be seen, but the intention is to introduce significant changes in the
distribution of powers and duties in schools, giving much more to central

government and individual schools, and much less to local education authorities. The legislation grew massively as the Bill progressed through its parliamentary stages, and some of the issues dealt with on the hoof, as it was driven along, generated so much emotion that the original purposes of the Bill have tended to be overlaid. They were two-fold: to give schools more self-control and to prescribe national achievement targets. These are now reflected in the Act's central clauses:

i. The Act provides for local management of schools whereby any school over 200 pupils will have its own delegated budget, with full power over staffing and most other spending. Schools over 300 pupils, though not special schools, will be able to opt out of their LEA.

ii. All children, including those with special educational needs, unless specifically exempted by their headteacher, will follow a national curriculum with testing of their levels of achievement at 7, 11, 14 and 16.

Two other issues which were hotly debated and opposed were the abolishing of the Inner London Education Authority and the strengthening of provisions about religious education and worship along Christian lines. There could be little opposition to the formal establishment of City Technology Colleges since they were already up and running, and their relevance to the present discussion is limited. Their presence may have some backwash effect, however, through adding another layer to the status hierarchy of the secondary schools for which primary schools act as feeders.

Disregarding for the present the political showdown with the Inner London Education Authority (and the spectacle of Labour-controlled Councils scrambling over the carcasse); accepting that the National Curriculum might well bring benefits to hard-pressed primary school teachers; ducking the head to the testing programme as a swimmer might to a spume-tipped wave lashed up by a temporary wind which will soon abate; assuming that the robust common-sense customarily displayed by our admirable headteachers will see them safely over the rocks which the clauses on religion have suddenly brought to the surface, after years of being safely submerged; further assuming that very few primary schools will opt out of local education authority control: having, as I say, thus disregarded, accepted, ducked, assumed and further assumed, it does seem possible that something might be done with the new powers which have been allotted to 'the people'.

It follows that those who regard themselves as disadvantaged by the operation of the education system should look to themselves, as well as to professionals, to make good its deficiencies; and the role of concerned professionals should be to help them to help themselves. Their immediate needs are to become more aware of the mechanics of the education system and more adept at competing for scarce educational resources. It should be known that, outside the legislative framework, parents have been taking an increasingly active role in their children's education over the last three decades, but until recently, have done so on terms dictated by the professionals; they have been helping teachers to achieve goals specified by teachers in ways specified by teachers. As I have argued elsewhere (Widlake, 1986), 'a deeper level of parental involvement is necessary for the regeneration of the British education system in the late twentieth century'. It may be that the local management provisions in the new legislation can be used to this end, and that the knee-jerk antagonism of working class people to 'Tory' inspired schemes, however well founded, does not serve any useful purpose. Better to use the model provided by Wolverhampton's Education Officers and members (from all parties) of the Labour-controlled Education Committee. They literally went 'shopping for parents' in the town centre — trying to recruit them to serve as governors, with the offer of training in the skills required for specialized committee work. Full-page advertisements were placed in local newspapers and leaflets — in English, Punjabi, Bengali, Urdu, Gujerati, Hindi and Polish — were distributed to family groups. The Director, Dr. Chris Saville, is firmly committed to marketing education and had plans for roadshows and possibly an education shop in the town's market.

The leaflets brightly summarized what a parent governor has to do:

> to act as an important link between the community, the school and local education authority;
> to ask questions and seek convincing answers.

Governors are also involved in:

> deciding what is taught;
> helping to set standards of behaviour;
> interviewing and selecting staff;
> deciding how the school budget is spent;
> preparing an annual report to parents.

These activities represent another stage in the efforts to involve parents in schools. It is a great opportunity for those education professionals who care about raising the standards of achievement of working-class children.

But another movement has been conducted in complete amity by parents, teachers and other school staff over the last three decades. Many strategies for involving parents have been explored and recorded (Wolfendale, 1987; Widlake, 1986; Macbeth, 1984). The Education Reform Act has created a new climate and generated a great deal of interest in school administration, but very little is being said or written about *how* to use the skills of working class parents to improve the educational performance of their children.

Language and reading development

Empirical evidence about the efficacy of community involvement programmes was, and still is, hard to come by. An opportunity arose to conduct a survey and follow-up study of eight community primary schools in Coventry. These were schools which, inspired by the Authority's Community Education Project, had been involving parents both formally and informally over a long period. Only one of the schools tested had been officially designated as a community school and was thus able to claim the extra staffing and letting advantages associated with that status.

The others offered models of what can be achieved by dedicated staff in normal primary schools. It proved possible, though extremely difficult because the work was carried out during a very bitter industrial dispute, to gather data on nearly a thousand children. Unfortunately, this still left some gaps, such as the reading scores for Coventry working-class pupils (see Table 10.1). A full account of this survey has been published (Widlake and Macleod, 1984) and attracted considerable press attention at the time of publication. Together with the seminal research conducted by Tizard, Schofield and Hewison (1982), it seems to provide strong evidence about the positive effects of parental interest on educational performance. It is worthwhile to re-present some of the findings in the light shed by the Education Reform Act, if only because of the lasting impression which the schools made on the present writer. At this time, there was such enthusiasm and commitment to the practice of parental involvement, so much verbal interaction between children and adults, so much originality and zip among the teachers, that it was not really much of a surprise that the test results revealed good levels of achievement.

The sample of eight schools was fully representative of deprived urban areas. Data was also collected from a control school in another local authority. Socio-economic profiles compiled from census data and school returns to the local authority left no doubt that the sample schools were placed in areas where the indicators of deprivation were above the average for the city as a whole, and this at a time when unemployment stood at 20 per cent. Spoken and written language and reading were assessed using the Hunter-Grundin Literacy Profile (1982). This comprises four group tests assessing Attitudes to Reading, Reading for Meaning, Spelling, and Free Writing and one individual test assessing Spoken Language. None of these tests takes longer than ten minutes to complete, and together they provide information on a wide spectrum of language skills.

The Hunter-Grundin Profile was standardized as recently as 1982, and therefore provided relevant national norms against which the progress of the Coventry sample could be measured. It was possible, therefore, to assess the value added by the schools, since the Profile also gives a breakdown of the socio-economic status of the school population, using the terms SPS (for special priority school), working class and middle class.

Table 10.1   Mean Standard Scores for Reading for Meaning (Hunter-Grundin Literacy Profile)

	Level 1 (Age 6.4–8.8)			Level 2 (Age 7.10–9.3)			Level 3 (Age 8.10–10.3)		
School category	National norm	Coventry sample	Control school	National norm	Coventry sample	Control school	National norm	Coventry sample	Control school
Social Priority	95	94	—	95	102	—	93	107	—
Working Class	99	88	84	98	112	97	98	—	92
Middle Class	102	—	—	106	—	—	103	—	—

As can be seen from Table 10.1, the mean scores in Reading for Meaning for the working-class Coventry cohort was below the Hunter-Grundin national norms at Level 1 (6–8 years), indicating that this intake was certainly no different in kind from those usually found in such areas; but the Level 2 (7–9 years) working-class cohort and the Level 3 (8–10 years) Coventry SPS children actually scored higher than the national norms for middle-class children, while the control school was below at each Level. This suggested that the educational procedures being followed in these Coventry schools were much more successful than might have been hypothesized from previous research, which concluded:

i. that attainment among children in inner cities is generally low, especially in reading;
ii. that there is a close, and apparently irreversible, relationship between poor achievement and social class as indicated by father's occupation. Mortimore (1983) had written that, 'from a variety of sources it is clear that from the age of seven onwards, there is considerable difference in achievement between pupils from homes where the parent has a non-manual occupation and those who come from what is termed the working class'.

Very impressive results were recorded for free writing at ages eight, nine and ten years. In the last named group, over 90 per cent could write legibly, and nearly as many could write fluently and accurately.

Attitudes to reading were also extremely positive, again quite contrary to what is widely reported and accepted as the inevitable concomitant of living in disadvantaged areas. Of the 116 infant school children who were individually tested, 72 per cent graded at C or higher on a five-point scale; of 636 junior school children tested, 86 per cent indicated a positive attitude towards reading.

In a separate study, three schools were asked to designate children as receiving from their parents (a) very good support, (b) good, average support, or (c) little support. In all schools, for both the years tested, there was a linear, and statistically significant, relationship between parental support and reading scores. These results seem conclusive and would be very easy to replicate. There were also significant differences between schools, which would repay further investigation.

Infant children, and especially those in the school with the highest indices of deprivation, responded very positively to the test requirements on Spoken Language. 81 per cent scored high on *confidence*; more than 90 per cent were categorized as having *intelligible speech*; nearly 80 per cent scored high on *vocabulary*. Whatever sophisticated objections can be brought against the reading data, these findings with young children cannot be ignored. They correspond exactly to what one expected after spending time chatting with the children in schools where teachers and parents were talking purposefully to the children all the time. Capability in language can be characterized as an awareness of the possibilities implicit in language, says Wilkinson (1971): of what language is, of its function in communication and particularly, of its joys. 'The deep and unconscious delight in language is one of the marks of difference between advantage and deprivation; the deprived child is deprived of joy' (p. 151). The Coventry children were being given, perhaps temporarily, the learning environment which 'advantaged' children enjoy, and their language performance began to correspond to the middle-class norms.

There are good reasons why the children in so many schools perform so much worse than in this sample. Getting teachers and parents to work collectively for the common good of the children requires the exercise of immense skills and patience, particularly on the part of headteachers. The aim is to recruit and train people who have not previously had the confidence to accept such responsibilities. I have written elsewhere of a project in Humberside which provided an early example of genuine participation by parents. Women who had not previously been involved in any kind of public work took active roles as Chair, Treasurer and Secretary of a Neighbourhood Centre. They proved quite capable of accepting the responsibility for raising funds and administering them. It is not people's capabilities which are in doubt so much as their willingness to make use of them, especially in a school setting. It is likely that working-class parents will require a good deal of encouragement and support if they are to fulfil the role intended for them in the new legislation.

However, many schools in tough districts have found ways and means of reducing the sense of alienation between schools and parents: the onus is on schools which have not found such means to explain their poor relationships. Let us now look at some of the strategies which community primary schools have used to bring about these good results.

Making contact

Anxiety is still sometimes generated among some teachers at the prospect of working-class parents becoming more involved in school life. The fruitful outcome of such partnership and the friendly relaxed atmosphere which so many schools are reporting should by now be sufficient to reassure even the most doubtful, but making a start can still present difficulties.

We could always ask the parents — they might say 'yes, we are very interested!' A questionnaire completed by 53 parents of nursery children in Salford (Widlake, 1985) showed that 69 per cent were willing to help in school and 92 per cent said they would like to borrow books from school, 56 per cent regularly. 60 per cent said they would like to see more activities for parents (only 25 per cent gave an outright 'no'). Questions and comments parents added were about school holidays, meals, discipline and the work the children would do in school, so that parents could better prepare them for it and help them with it. One parent suggested that parents could watch the children during playtime and playground activities and several commented on how helpful staff had been in giving information:

> I am very grateful to the teachers, who put everything they can into learning each child. It would be a good idea, if in the few weeks before starting school, the children could get to know the school and its teachers.

Primary schools which have nursery or reception classes usually have an abundance of contacts with parents. The headteacher of a Salford nursery school made the point that she saw virtually every parent (nearly all mothers but there were about half a dozen fathers raising children on their own) either in the morning when they brought the children or in the evening when they came to take them away.

Since most of the mothers had part-time jobs — machinists in the revamped garment industry, waiting in restaurants, serving in public houses, working in the school meals service — they had more time to spare in the evenings than the mornings. Since the headteacher and her colleagues knew all the children very well, there were ample opportunities for conversations which often broadened to include discussion of personal circumstances. Since the nursery accepted very young children, mothers were encouraged to come in during the day to feed them and play with them. They were welcome to spend half-a-day playing alongside them and taking a full part in their care, but most were too preoccupied to take full advantage of this offer. A potato-pie supper was one informal occasion which had been held on a Friday evening — all evening meetings were difficult for these parents whose children were only admitted if criteria relating to personal difficulties were met.

Many primary schools allow parents to come and go freely, within certain limits defined by the school. Some are able to allocate a room for parents' use only. Displays of children's work are mounted and continually changed so as to show parents what children are doing in the school. An emphasis on building up trust is generally apparent and parents regularly help with routine activities like duplicating, baking, embroidery, preparing Christmas shows, garden fetes. At a Leicester primary school the organizer noted one December:

> 'Christmas Bazaar'. Fantastic success. Five mothers came in the morning to sort and price. People arriving until 13.30. Fairly chaotic, stalls not completely ready. Willing hands appearing everywhere. Frantic delegation. Amazingly no major disasters. Dinner ladies and staff very supportive. Five of the original six organisers had never done anything like this before but we were ready to start on the next one immediately. They had a great time!

Parents are often asked to attend meetings, such as on the occasion when their children entered school. They also attended special morning assemblies.

Outings tend to arise naturally out of other activities. At a Salford infants school the parents' group was a thriving one going from strength to strength. They organized many social fund-raising events, and helped with the Spring Fayre. They repeatedly said what a benefit the group was to them.

Drop-in groups are widespread. The following are extracts from the diary kept by a Leicester primary school:

> We welcome parents to social gatherings and discussion groups . . . . Our 'drop in' group held eighteen Friday afternoon sessions between October and the following March. There was a total of 41 people on the register, of whom 13 joined in the first three weeks and seven in the last three weeks.

The average attendance was 10, with the largest session attracting 18 and the smallest 3. One mother attended 17 out of 18: 6 attended more than 50 per cent of the time. In general it is very successful, with a core of regulars who did not know one another before and new members arriving every week.

Home visiting was an important way of enlisting parental involvement:

> ... visited one Bangladeshi family, purely socially. Mrs V. had been asking me for a long time now. She prepared a Bangladeshi sweet dish for me (like milk pudding) and we talked for over an hour ... her husband was very forthcoming and it was a very friendly visit.

Some teachers who took part in visits associated with a paired reading scheme found that they were nervous because they were not sure they possessed the necessary skills and so were uncertain of their reception. These worries were easily overcome, providing the teacher was otherwise well disposed, by a practical demonstration on the part of the organizer:

> Made a home visit to Mrs D. to involve her in a paired reading programme. Mrs N. the class teacher went with me. She is not a chatty person so the visit was rather business-like. I felt it was an achievement to have got her into the home. The child is being pushed a lot at home by an elder brother who gives him spelling lists to learn for an hour every evening. We suggest that he stop and just do the five minute exercise.

Teachers who felt that the comparatively new ground of making home visits to Asian families required testing out ensured that there was someone within the family group who could provide communication. These cautious opening gambits enabled them to establish strengths and weaknesses. Soon visits included most parents and the organizing teacher was well pleased with the scheme though, as she put it, she had had to lead many teachers by the hand to parental homes. Home visiting was also undertaken by the head of a nursery unit for children who were due to start their education. On each occasion she took a 'Ready-for-school' pack. It was received with pleasure and adequately occupied each child who received it. Mothers were able to talk about their concerns, and she was able to reassure them on several points.

One class teacher cut through the objections which are raised about visiting parents in their homes by arranging to go home with one child each evening, until all had been visited. Most of the children lived within easy walking distance, it is true, but the same would apply to other schools who seem to find the difficulties insuperable.

There are other, well-tried and non-threatening ways of bringing the community into the school. A primary school in Coventry had an active adult education programme and published a lively magazine which encouraged parents to join in:

> Education can make you more aware of what is going on in the world

around you. It can give you the confidence to sort out some of those 'all important' problems. For example, if you are plagued with damp housing, a good strong Tenants' Association could help overcome the problem. In short, a good education can make life a little easier. If you are an adult, with second thoughts about studying, why not give it another try? To start with, you could attempt a couple of 'O' levels . . .

Thus exhorted, parents did take advantage of the many classes and meetings which were made available.

Visitors to the school would have been aware of the presence of parents, both as enthusiastic learners and as helpers in their children's learning. Sometimes these processes were combined, as in a session on oral history where elderly members of the community were being interviewed. Trainee teachers from a College were helping to organize this work, which would eventually provide an excellent teaching resource on local history. Many threads of community education were thus being held together involving adults both as learners and as facilitators of learning. They helped to refocus the curriculum towards the immediate environment, its history and people's lives. All this raised the consciousness of the people from the many different age groups who participated in a learning process as well as explicating the principle of life-long learning.

In Coventry and in London, parents wrote stories for their children, which were published and shared in the schools. The London project (reported in Bloom, 1987) began in Thomas Buxton school, an inner-city school where many of the children had mother tongues other than English, though the project was not confined to them. The school staff wanted to acknowledge and use this linguistic richness and also to involve the parents, bringing home and school closer. The class teacher in the school approached parents, mostly mothers, and suggested that the stories might be based on the child, the family or the parents' memories of childhood. Parents and teachers edited the writing and added illustrations while other members of the family made contributions. Eventually the book would be typed, a photograph included of the child for whom it was written, an autobiographical note on the author added, and the whole distributed. If the book was in a language other than English, a second copy would be produced in English, and many written in English were translated into other languages. Other copies were produced for home or library use.

Adults in Partington, an overspill town near Manchester produced 'Lifelines' (Manchester Polytechnic, no date), joint biographies which get close to the realities of working-class life. This seems a very good way for teachers to become more familiar with the people in the community which contains their school. Sarse, born in Ireland, but living in Partington for fifteen years, said:

You've got this sort of tradition, where only so many in a family can stop at home, and the rest have to go. It's like a hammer hitting a nut, and the bits go everywhere — there's some of my family in America, some in Australia, some in Singapore . . . . And then you get there, and other problems roam along. You're never in command of anything . . . . But I feel it's not only me in this position but a lot of working-class people. They're just pushed by circumstances, don't have any choice about what they do.

Parents and the curriculum

We have seen the powerful effects parents can exert on their children's language and reading development and considered some of the techniques used by schools to create favourable learning environments. Other aspects of the curriculum can similarly be enhanced.

Mathematics is of particular concern to parents, the subject of the well-publicized Cockcroft report and more recently, the subject of recommendations from the DES (1988) Task Group on Assessment and Testing. This will certainly be one of the areas in which parent governors will want to ask questions, and these are likely to have a high emotional content because of the fears which have been generated about pupils' poor attainments in mathematics. The Secretary of State appeared personally on television to re-assure parents that paper-and-pencil methods of doing long-division would not be threatened by the Task Group's advocacy of calculators in primary classrooms! Obviously, teachers must give high priority to convincing parents that they believe in children memorizing number facts, while pointing to some of the limitations of this form of learning. A really outstanding guide to primary school mathematics, published by the ILEA (1988), deals specifically with parents' fears, identifying as possible concerns: calculators, expectations about workbooks and textbooks, the problem solving role of mathematics in other curriculum areas and indeed in life generally, and parents' expectations about recording mathematics. The ILEA guide is addressed to mathematics coordinators and warns that staff as a whole will have to be prepared to discuss standards with parents and 'real or perceived shortcomings in the overall teaching in the school'. In *Better Mathematics* (Ahmed, 1987), yet another excellent report, this time from the Low Attainers in Mathematics Project, it is pointed out that:

> The relationship between teachers and parents is complex. Both groups have a strong commitment to the same children. Both parents and teachers have strong memories of their own schooling. Both groups are vulnerable and easily threatened. (p. 74).

These relationships will not be acrimonious if strategies for facilitating parental involvement have been followed. Many schools hold maths workshops for parents, where they are encouraged to do some work for themselves, set up displays and arrange times for parents to visit and observe teaching, or even join classes to work with groups of children. Others have invited pupils to explain the work to parents, making clear how much thinking and problem solving had gone into the work; sent work home to be done by the pupils with their parents; asked parents who are already involved to run sessions and involve others; encouraged local community centres such as libraries and leisure centres to host exhibitions. *Better Mathematics* stresses that effective and useful communication can only be achieved by parental involvement on a regular basis — one-off activities will not do.

Nowhere is the need to compete more urgent than in *Information Technology*. Even the comparatively low technology currently available to schools is sufficient to force a reconsideration of all conventional forms of instruction. We can effectively eliminate many of the usual explanations of learning failure, such as poor concentration, lack of attention to task, low self-esteem as a learner.

These improved student behaviours usually result in a measurable increment in, say reading scores, but much more interesting is that computers are tools enabling the user to achieve high levels of cognitive functioning through the exercise of relatively low level skills. Computers already offer to primary and secondary schools, word processing, desk top publishing, electronic communication systems, databases, spreadsheets and control technology at very low cost and through software which is more and more 'user-friendly'. By mastering a simple sequence of key presses, the user can organize and re-organize text, create complex graphics, download material from Australia to incorporate into a newspaper produced in a single day within an ordinary primary or secondary school, eliminate the requirement to carry out lengthy mathematical computations, produce musical compositions, maintain records of business transactions, control robots: as we all know, the prospects are endless. Gardner (1983) has reminded us that a computerized society has less need of the linguistic skills which have been so central a feature of traditional schooling: 'The individual can now perform much of his work purely through the manipulation of logical and numerical symbols'. Since schooling in its present form has been so disadvantageous to pupils from deprived backgrounds, this shift in emphasis could present an excellent format for re-organizing their learning opportunities.

Policy-makers pay lip service to their intentions of using the present atmosphere of change for the benefit of *all* pupils but the reality may be rather different. The politics which determine allocations of IT hardware between schools are vibrant; possession of recent technology imparts status; schools without IT will be seen as of low status and will be likely to become unpopular in the great competition for pupils. Moreover, whole-school policies for the use of IT across the curriculum draw in every member of staff, demand the reassessment of every aspect of school life and its relationship with the community. Disadvantaged pupils and their schools must feature on the agenda in all these discussions, for there will be even more reasons than usual for them to be ignored. The systems themselves are classless, but knowledge of how to use them and deploy them is accumulating in the hands of middle-class professionals and could still further widen the gap between disadvantaged groups and others in the community. Parent governors could perform a very great service to their schools by becoming knowledgable about computers and IT, and honing their skills as managers on this whet-stone.

The climate of change provides opportunities for disadvantaged parents to take some control of their schools. Parents now have the right to ask for explanations if they are not satisfied, and it will be extremely interesting to observe whether some ethnic groups who have been expressing extreme dissatisfaction with schools take the opportunity of opting-out. One profoundly hopes not, and that the spirit of cooperation which has prevailed in the schools described, and which has produced such good results, could grow to encompass all. Unfortunately, the conflict model — so much in the ascendant — is quite at odds with these ways of working. This dichotomy is deeply perturbing, yet not inevitable: mindful of the distinguished example of Cyril Connolly, I have presented a well-tried framework for action, but offer no prophecies.

References

Ahmed, A. (1987) *Better Mathematics: A Curriculum Development Study*, London, HMSO. (Based on the Low Attainers in Mathematics Project).

Bullivant, B. (1981) *School Governor's Guide*, Sheffield, Home and School Council.

Bloom, W. (1987) *Partnership with Parents in Reading*, London, Hodder and Stoughton.

Department of Education and Science (1977) *A New Partnership for Our Schools,* (Taylor Report), London, HMSO.

Department of Education and Science (1978) *Special Educational Needs* (Warnock Report), London, HMSO.

Department of Education and Science (1988) *National Curriculum Task Group on Assessment and Testing*, London, HMSO.

Finch, J. (1984) *Education as Social Policy*, London, Longman.

Gardner, H. (1983) *Frames of Mind: The Theory of Multiple Intelligences*, New York, Basic Books.

Inner London Education Authority (1988) *Mathematics in ILEA Primary Schools*, London, ILEA Centre for Learning Resources.

Macbeth, A. (1984) *The Child Between: A Report on School-Family Relations in the Countries of the European Commission*, Brussels, EEC.

Manchester Polytechnic Institute of Advanced Studies (undated) *Near the Witching Hour: Lifelines 5*.

Mortimore P. (1983) 'Underachievement: a framework for debate', *Journal of Community Education*, 2, 2.

Tizard, J., Schofield, W.N. and Hewison, J. (1982) 'Collaboration between teachers and parents in assisting children's reading', *British Journal of Educational Psychology*, 52.

Widlake, P. (1985) *Report on the Parental Involvement Project in Salford and Leicester*, Coventry Community Education Development Centre.

Widlake. P. (1986) *Reducing Educational Disadvantage*, Milton Keynes, Open University Press.

Widlake, P. and MacLeod, F. (1984) *Raising Standards: Parental Involvement Programmes and the Language Performance of Children*, Coventry Community Education Development Centre.

Wilkinson, A. (1971) *The Foundations of Language: Talking and Reading in Young Children*, Oxford, Oxford University Press.

Wolfendale, S. (1987) *Primary Schools and Special Needs: Policy, Planning and Provision*, London, Cassell.

11
Alienation in the Junior School: The Case for Gifted Children

John Welch

Many highly gifted children sail through their junior school years without a problem. They are happy and fulfilled. Their needs and expectations, and the needs and expectations of their parents and teachers, are satisfied. Their performance in all sorts of school activities seems to match their early promise. Their behaviour at school and home is such as to delight many and offend none.

There is another group of children whose behaviour offends no one but whose needs and expectations are not met. This group normally consists of clever but conforming girls who do what they are asked quickly, quietly and tidily. They then spend the rest of their lesson time ornamenting their exercise books with beautiful illuminated scrolls. Their work is much prized by their teachers for open days and for decorating corridors.

A third group, in this case often boys, also keep very quiet about their talents. Their gifts and the need for their fulfilment do not obtrude. They slide quietly into mediocrity because of their wish to conform to their friends' performance in the peer group. Since the school offering is frequently aimed at a hypothetical average child, these bright boys take the easy way out and do no more than they need to keep their heads above water and below the parapet. Occasionally they reveal their talents in end-of-term tests in which they score highly without any apparent effort.

It is a fourth group of children whose unhappiness often persuades their parents to join the National Association of Gifted Children (NAGC). They are the children whose social, educational and emotional needs are not met in the junior school. In the Association's survey on these issues (NAGC, 1987), Susan Leyden is cited as suggesting that problems arise whenever discrepancies exist between a child's expectations and the responses of the institution. The children in this fourth group do not lapse into beautiful but pointless repetitive ornamentaion, nor do they sink into anonymous torpor. Their alienation from the system results in much more obvious and destructive behaviours. Their lives are riddled with conflict: conflict with themselves because their own expectation of themselves is not matched by their performance; conflict with their parents, who, because they are often aware of their potential, sometimes hold unrealistic expectations and make undue demands; and conflict with, and resentment of their teachers because their offerings do not, in any sense, provide for their needs.

It is often pointed out that the resentment and social and emotional maladjustment of thwarted gifted children match the resentment and frustration of slow learning children. Insofar as both the least able and the most able deviate considerably from the average in their demands of the school curriculum, and since frustration and boredom accrue from the discrepancy between their needs and this offering, both groups see the school as a threat to their own security, to their self-respect, to their self-image and to their self-development. In other words, the universal human needs described by Abraham Maslow (1954) are not fulfilled, and dire consequences result.

I am suggesting that the needs which are not met in gifted children are those common to all human beings, and that the alienation which accrues stems from the absence of appropriate care and provision in those schools where the needs of the average child are taken as paramount. Singer (1978) has pointed out that the positive experiences of surprise, interest, joy, and liveliness which enhance good learning are conditional upon the learner's ability to control the flow of in-coming information. When information comes too quickly for the child to assimilate, it is accompanied in by a feeling of anxiety; and when it comes too slowly or repetitively, it produces feelings of boredom, possibly giving way to irritation, frustration and anger. I would suggest that inadequate identification of high potential and talent, coupled with poor provision, is the major cause of alienation amongst the most able.

In most literature on the subject four main attributes are described as typical of giftedness. They are normally presented in the following order:

i. a very high IQ;
ii. high powers of creativity;
iii. high powers of performance;
iv. high powers of social leadership.

I wish, however, to discuss the last two characteristics first.

High powers of performance

It is in the demonstration of performance that the least alienation is reported by parents in the NAGC. This is perhaps because exceptional performers are easily identifiable, most commonly accepted as deserving special attention, and most often provided for by teachers and local education authorities.

Nearly everybody agrees that any person whose artistic or gymnastic performance is manifestly better than the general run of the population is gifted. We readily acknowledge and admire the gold medallist, the best runner, the best violinist, the best gymnast, the best dancer. It is very noticeable that even those people in authority who are normally hostile to making provision for the academically gifted, seem to be perfectly happy to make special resources available for high performers in musical, athletic, dramatic and gymnastic arts. The gladiatorial classes, the circus performers, Shakespeare's 'all licensed fools' can become the privileged darlings of society. Perhaps it is because, as the entertainers of the world, they have no political clout and pose no threat to institutions.

There are possibly other reasons for the apparent willingness to provide for giftedness in these areas. Most of the performing arts demand teachers who are themselves skilled performers and practitioners. The teacher/pupil relationship resembles the master/apprentice contract, and a common feature of training is the achieving of a high degree of skill. In many fields the mastery of the skill is achieved through the demonstration-imitation technique, when the master craftsman demonstrates and the student-apprentice emulates. The learning takes place as an initiation into a mystery which will eventually result in the student-apprentices' achieving an outward and visible sign of proficiency. They will in fact have become master craftsmen themselves.

Now, for the most part, politicians and junior school teachers (all teachers for that matter) are themselves not privy to the esoteric understanding of the mystery and do not feel competent or sufficiently knowledgeable to criticize or to prevent a child's following the mystery. Every Tom, Dick and Harry feels competent to criticize English and mathematics courses in schools; very few are prepared to chance their arms on gymnastics, or violin-playing unless they are themselves knowledgeable and skilled gymnasts or very good violinists, in which case they will feel pre-disposed to support the achievement of high standards among their pupils by the very method by which they themselves were made good performers.

Another strong incentive to supporting high performers is their high motivation and the fact that parents are prepared to make great sacrifices to help the children, looking for tuition out of school if necessary. It may seem cynical to comment that these twentieth century junior gladiators also provide valuable publicity at school concerts and speech days and in winning local competitions.

There are powerful lessons to learn from this phenomenon, lessons which might profitably be used to support children gifted in other ways. The first is the role of the teacher in initiating the child into the mystery: the teacher is aware that he too was once in the child's situation and empathizes with it. The second is the enthusiasm of the teacher who is also a practitioner; the teacher is himself continuing as practitioner to strive for excellence in the skill, or is so expert that he has a vested interest in preserving the status of the skill. The third is the place of different sized groupings which make for effective teaching; sometimes the appropriate relationship is one to one, sometimes it is a small group; sometimes it is a large one. The fourth lesson is the tolerance of mixed aged groups in performing arts classes as opposed to the mania for age-locking in typical mainstream junior schools; the unifying factor in good 'performance' classes is not the age of members but their skill or talent. Old men and women play and learn alongside young people in orchestras, choirs and evening classes. Lastly there is the esteem in which 'content' is held, as well as the process whereby skills are transferred. The importance of process learning must not be underestimated, yet many children and their parents become frustrated when a content or body of knowledge is trivialized. Teachers may be accused of encouraging 'the pooling of ignorance' if they reject any sort of content input. There is a satisfaction in mastering a body of knowledge as well as in developing the skills to acquire it.

It is of course essential in these situations that teachers are aware of the child's interests and needs. Dr. David George of Nene College tells an interesting story to highlight this fundamental requirement of knowing what the child is interested in. He observed a boy who had clearly opted out of an elementary electronics lesson in which the other children were soldering their own circuits. He spoke to the bored and disgruntled pupil who told him he had done this stuff years ago at home with his dad. He had opted out because the work was too easy. At home he was a skilled radio ham and spoke animatedly to Dr. George about his hobby.

After the lesson Dr. George talked to the teacher, who was worried about the boy's alienation but could find nothing in which to interest him. The final twist of the screw came when Dr. George told the teacher that the boy was in fact an expert radio ham: 'I don't believe it,' said the teacher, 'so am I'. The simple lesson is of course that somehow or other all teachers must learn more about their pupils, and, having learned more, be prepared to provide for their manifest needs and interests.

Records of achievement and progress are valuable so long as they are read *before* the children join a new class; reports by previous teachers are invaluable so long as they are treated seriously. (There is a dotty school of thought which refuses to read children's records 'so that our views will not be tarnished by the prejudices of others'. This is about as sensible as a GP saying that he will not read a new patient's notes).

Although teachers' reports are valuable they too frequently contain only the products of 'teacher-in-school-observation'. In the case of the radio ham boy described above, and in the case of children involved in performing arts out of school, teachers may not actually know anything about the child's interests. A strong case can be made out for teachers' and parents' collectively devising an interest check list or questionnaire for use at a child's entry to junior school. Such a list should generate a thorough, serious, if time-consuming dialogue with all new parents, somewhat on the lines of a health visitor's screening programme. It would require a mutual trust that many parents do not experience in their relationships with teachers. It is very important that both teachers and parents see their roles as co-workers in a child's education rather than as experts and tolerated laymen; or even worse as experts and interfering, pushy and unknowledgeable nuisances.

Forty years ago some London junior schools had a line drawn across the playground and a notice which said 'No parents allowed beyond this line without appointment'. The notices have gone but the psychological attitudes which generated them are still occasionally to be discovered.

High powers of social leadership

The leadership characteristics of gifted children have been discussed more in the USA than in the UK; but they merit very serious attention, not least for their place in the identification process. In the NAGC survey, referred to earlier, it was found that 61 per cent of the children invented games for others to play; 33 per cent were described as natural leaders, and 30 per cent wanted to be leaders but did not really succeed. L. B. Terman (1926), in *The Genetic Study of Genius*, which continues his mammoth study of highly gifted children, reveals how the school profile for his 'A' group confirms that most were 'joiners' of clubs and other groups and that many became freely acknowledged leaders. This was a group of high achievers who went on to exhibit a highly disciplined life-style and joined the highest salary group.

Kippy Abroms (1985), in a summary of recent current thinking on this issue, refers to a scale called 'Activities for Talent Identification', developed by Karnes and Shwedel in 1981. Used as a screening instrument, the measure helps to identify giftedness through such items as: (a) shows an awareness of the needs of others; (b) seems to enjoy being around other people: is sociable and prefers not to be alone; (c) tends to influence others: generally directs the activity in which he or she is involved; (d) assumes responsibility beyond what is expected for his or her age.

Despite the lack of attention paid to this issue in the UK, a large number of enquiries and requests for help to NAGC suggests that it is this sort of behaviour which is a possible source of conflict between gifted children and their teachers.

The classic case is of the organizing, bossy child who sets to control others in games and classroom activities. Conflicts arise when the teacher decides to use the bright pupil as a substitute teacher, as a surrogate in a monitorial role. In the early stages the child can enjoy this leadership position. However, the leader may well not possess the mature emotional qualities necessary to sustain the organizational role, especially when younger children refuse to accept the rules and conditions set by the bright child. The commonest occurrence is when the very bright child organizes a game in which young or less bright children break the rules. Typically the leader becomes agitated or angry, and equally typically the teacher intervenes with 'Don't be silly dear, it's only a game!'. It may not be only a game for the very bright child, however, but may represent a much more significant encounter between chaos on the one hand and children's need to reduce the chaos, to find a pattern, and to bring about order and structure.

It is a commonplace of conflict between teachers and very bright children that, having registered that the bright children can perfrom to high levels of cognitive activity, teachers may well demand of such children higher standards of moral and social behaviour than they are capable of. The alienation occurs when the children fail to live up to demands and expectations of the adults. The gap is between the teacher's projection of the child's intellectual age as compared with this fairly primitive social behaviour. Teachers need constantly to remind themselves that they are dealing with young children who, while high performers in some aspects of their life, have the emotional and social needs of their chronological age group.

The problem is not, of course, solely the responsibility of the teacher. The gifted child needs to learn his or her own responsibilities to other children. There is undoubtedly a place for the teacher to draw the child's attention to the need for considering other people's points of view and feelings in social situations. Arrogance, feelings of superiority and intolerance are besetting temptations for the gifted, and unless they learn to cope with them, gifted children can become rejected and alienated from their peers. They need to develop habits of compassion from observing the behaviour of sympathetic adults and from being reminded when they behave ungenerously.

The Bullock Report (DES, 1975) summarizes the seminal role of literature-teaching in developing empathy:

> In Britain the tradition of literature-teaching is one which aims at personal and moral growth, and in the last two decades this emphasis has grown. It is a soundly based tradition, and properly interpreted is a powerful force in English teaching. Literature brings the child into an encounter with language in its most complex and varied forms. Through these complexities are presented the thoughts, experiences and feelings of people who exist outside and beyond the reader's daily awareness. This process of bringing them within that circle of consciousness is where the greatest value of literature lies. It provides imaginative insight into what another person is feeling; it allows the contemplation of possible human experiences which the reader himself has not met. It has the capacity to develop the empathy of which Shelley was speaking when he said; 'A man, to be greatly good, must imagine intensively and comprehensively; he must put himself in the place of another and many others; the pains and pleasure so his species must become his own'. Equally, it confronts the reader with problems similar to his own, and does it at the safety of one remove. He draws reassurance from realising that his personal difficulties and his feelings of deficiency are not unique to himself; that they are likely to be the experience of others. (DES, 1975, para 9.2)

The exercise, in junior schools pupils, of recreating imaginatively the feelings of others has much to commend it as a means of developing effective role-taking.

High intelligence and high creativity

We are now in a position to consider the potential for alienation in the possession of a high IQ and high powers of creativity. Most gifted children are highly intelligent and quick on the uptake. The quality that intelligence demonstrates is essentially the capacity of individuals to process information. It sets out to relate new experiences and information to past experiences and information, to find the common threads and connections that link them. This is sometimes described as 'detecting the uniformities'.

In processing new information children make generalizations about their experience; they induce laws of behaviour. They use these generalizations to understand new experiences and to solve problems. In the simplest terms, intelligence is the capacity to benefit from past experience and to apply the lessons to future problems.

Highly intelligent children can solve problems logically more quickly and efficiently than others who are less intelligent. Given certain information they can draw on their past experience and predict accurately the meaning of the new information. They frequently predict solutions and meanings from inadequate, incomplete or 'degraded' information. This capacity for prediction manifests itself in a number of ways in junior schools. The teacher can set a problem and ask for a solution; in effect the teacher is providing a set of information which is incomplete but is made complete by the solution to the problem.

Highly intelligent children can solve logical problems very efficiently. They 'complete' the problem by predicting its solution. Sometimes the teacher in a didactic lesson sets out to provide a complete explanation to a class and finds that before the explanation is finished the very intelligent child has latched on to its significance, interrupted the teacher, and spoiled the whole performance by answering the question which has not yet been asked. Such behaviour is never very popular with teachers, and causes tension. Perhaps this explains why many gifted children complain that, although their hands are always up, they are never asked to give answers to questions.

The capacity to predict effectively is increased when the child has become 'expert' in a particular subject, that is to say, has actively worked on the skills involved in a particular field for a long time. The expert can see at a glance what others need time to analyze, and develops instant recognition of a large number of patterns or schemata. It is sometimes said that experts have developed scripts which enable them to come to conclusions very quickly. The development of an expertise, in, say, scientific method, goes with a deep and early interest from the age of six or seven, and is accompanied by the development of persistence, independence and confidence, the hallmarks of high motivation. Unfortunately, alienation develops when children with this gift for prediction and expertise interfere with the routines of the normal pedagogic methods used by most teachers.

The quality of effective reasoning seems to be a function of the conscious mind. It deals with and analyzes information and then makes logical decisions as a consequence. Much junior school practice, including that developed for intelligent children, places a good deal of emphasis on providing an input of experiences which have then to be received and elaborated by the children, in which the test for the understanding of those experiences is rather to have them regurgitated by the children than to have them demonstrated in the solution to further problems.

Since many intelligent children seem to skip the stages of reception and elaboration and are not concerned with regurgitating facts, teachers can become disturbed and angry at what appears to be deliberate insubordination. It should not be forgotten that this sort of confrontation is much more likely when the teacher sets out to deliver the lesson and asks the whole class to respond. It is much less likely to happen when the classroom organization involves groups working collaboratively to solve problems.

The potential for confrontation between a teacher and a highly intelligent child may well be exacerbated when the pupil is a highly creative thinker. To avoid this, the teacher needs to understand how creative ideas occur and how the act of creation can be fostered and encouraged.

Arthur Koestler's (1964) view is that the act of creation takes place when two apparently unconnected, disparate ideas or trains of thought are brought together for the first time, when they are synthesized in a new concept. He calls this 'bisociative' or 'bi-polar' thinking. It is most obviously demonstrated in the good joke. It is rather similar to the creative process described by E. W. Sinnott in his essay *The Creativeness of Life*:

> The creative process that must be taking place in the unconscious may not be different from those in the conscious mind. A scientist, faced with a problem, marshals all the facts he can find that bear on it. Many relations among them seem meaningless, and such he rules out. Others have significance and finally, by rearranging and organising the facts, he is able to build a consistent pattern of ideas and to form a theory. Many psychologists believe that something not unlike this is taking place in the unconscious mind. Among the throng of random images and ideas, the unconscious mind rejects certain combinations as unimportant or incompatible but sees the significance of others. By its means, order — intellectual, aesthetic, perhaps spiritual order — is here distinguished from randomness. Thus, the unconscious mind is able to solve problems and lay at least the foundation for the construction of a poem or a work of art. These are new creations. They might have been produced by the conscious mind, and often have been, through sheer force of mental labour; but the reason that such a frontal attack often fails seems to be that the free association, present in the unconscious, is blocked in various ways and then really creative new relationships therefore are not seen.
>
> One must recognise the operation in the unconscious of such an organising factor, for chance alone is not creative. Just as the organism pulls together random, formless stuff into the patterned system of structure and function in the body, so the unconscious mind seems to select and arrange and correlate these ideas and images into a pattern. The resemblance between the two processes is close. (Sinnot, 1959, pp. 26-7)

If you accept this view you agree that creativity starts with a careful analysis of experience (data) and an active intention to solve a problem in a new way. In other words, the creative thinker has to do his/her homework first. There is no half-baked suggestion that creativity demands no hard work.

It is, however, important for the creator to look for new perspectives and to try to free himself from old prejudices. This is why it is particularly appropriate to encourage children to generate new ideas: they do not have the heavy constraints of logical prejudice of older people, and good schools are places where you can take risks without risking serious damage.

The creative personality seems to exhibit certain characteristics:

i. A willingness to take risks;
ii. An ability to compromise (i.e., nonauthoritarian, non-fundamentalist);
iii. A tolerance of ambiguity (i.e., a psychological capacity to accept that there is often no absolute interpretation of words or experience);
iv. A liking for complexity;
v. Non-conformity.

This sort of personality will not flourish nor will it demonstrate its creativity in an environment that squashes individuality or pours scorn on non-conformity. It will not thrive when teachers are concerned only to preserve their own dignity and insist that they are always right. It will not happen where there is no humour. As Dickens splendidly describes in *Hard Times*, it is destroyed in a society concerned only to 'teach 'em facts'.

Junior teachers who wish to encourage and develop creativity will realise the importance of finding and formulating problems. The capacity to do this, it is said, marks the difference between the scientist and the technician, the artist and the copyist.

Problems, according to Getzels (1982), are of three types:

i. The 'presented' problem, common in school tests, given by teachers to pupils with a clear format and acceptable answer.
ii. The 'discovered' problem: investigated by the discoverer who formulates the problem where the solution is as yet unknown.
iii. The 'created' problem: as when a scientist decides to investigate the nature of light or an artist creates a new still life, where no such problems occurred before or where no such arrangement of objects existed before.

The 'discovered' problem and the 'created' problem can provide additions to the sum of human knowledge. The 'presented' problem does not, although it must be said that practice in this sort of problem-solving can give you insights into flexible habits of thought and the analysis of experience.

Such eminent practitioners as Edward de Bono (1970) are convinced that some very intelligent children are extremely limited in their ability to think productively because their solution to complex problems is blocked by their tendency to stick to logical sequences of solutions. His courses encourage students to examine problems from different perspectives which he calls 'lateral thinking'. In much of the discussion 'lateral thinking', 'creative thinking', 'divergent thinking', 'imaginative thinking' are regarded as similar, different from 'logical thinking' or 'convergent thinking'. It should not be thought that one is better than another; each has its special place.

In encouraging creativity, the role of the parent or teacher is not to let children loose without any preparation or structure, nor is it to bind them tight with shackles of 'nothing but facts'. Creativity needs a sound foundation of knowledge and critical evaluation, but in a school climate of constant testing of assimilation of facts, creativity is not likely to flourish.

It is not always easy in a large class to cope with the unsolicited interruption of a very creative child offering divergent solutions to problems when the teacher is in full flight down a predetermined path. It is unsettling for a teacher when creative pupils detect unintended puns or humour in situations and insist on broadcasting their perceptions to the multitude. Good teachers and good parents of creative children need more than their fair share of tolerance and humour. They must be wary of repressing unintended mutiny or chaos too promptly or they may find themselves unwittingly responsible for what I can only call 'subversive creativity'.

Fred Speed and David Appleyard (1985) sum up the problems in their excellent book *The Bright and the Gifted*:

> Every teacher has experienced the so-called divergent or lateral thinker who interjects a new idea that is seemingly unrelated to a topic or who suggests what at first appears to be an outlandish approach to a problem. The contributions of lateral thinkers often interfere with the flow of conventional teaching, which usually involves the release of new knowledge in sequential or logical steps. The teacher must bend a little to acknowledge the deeper significance of a thought-provoking question or a shrewd observation that switches discussion from the usual well-beaten path. The effect of not appreciating the contributions of a divergent thinker and forcing the student to adhere to a set or rigid system of learning may be that the student either switches off or becomes rebellious. Bright, rebellious students are difficult to handle because they are capable of challenging a teacher's knowledge on the basis of their rich storehouse of information gained by voracious reading.
>
> The science teacher operating within a methodology which places a premium of formal laboratory skills may be often challenged on the 'best' way of carrying out an investigation. Since a new way of carrying out an experiment may be better than the accepted way, the teacher should let the innovative student try this method. If a tried and true method happened to yield better results than an approach suggested by a student, then the student is complimented on his or her imagination but encouraged to consider the time-conserving method. Similarly, a challenge made by a student will be accepted, provided the claim can be substantiated by reference to up-to-date research in the field. Thus the student is not intimidated but encouraged to seek new ways of thinking about or doing things. (Speed and Appleyard, 1985, p. 11)

In the past two or three years, I have been increasingly concerned with a particular problem that presents itself to very intelligent children who are also creative. Because they are so intelligent and learn very quickly the information presented to them by books or adults, it seems natural for them to assimilate the closed ideas presented by convinced authors or speakers. The act of remembering them and learning them can confirm the child in his/her acceptance of well-proven theories. The speed and efficiency of the learning can, in a way, involve the child in an unquestioning acceptance of theories.

Confronted by this propensity in children, the teacher should, at all stages, be at pains to persuade the child that all is not necessarily gospel merely because it is spoken by a teacher or written in a book. However, in a very busy classroom, it is unlikely that the teacher will be able to put up with incessant questioning from children.

Importance of practical work

Another possibility suggests itself to lessen the dangers. It is hinted at in Feynman's (1986) book *Surely You're Joking Mr Feynman*. The author describes how he, as a child, earned a good deal of cash on the side by mending other people's broken gadgets. He had no specific engineering training but he learnt by trial and error to put radios right and gain for himself an enviable reputation as a miracle worker. He brought to bear his considerable intellect on diagnosing the weaknesses in machines but then had to try, pragmatically, to solve the problems with which he was presented. Colleagues will know that he went on to win the Nobel Prize in Theoretical Physics and spent a good deal of time in technology associated with the first atomic bomb. I am suggesting that his creative, flexible approach to problem-solving was encouraged by this practical work in mending, taking to bits and putting together machinery as a child. The nature of this activity is to forecast a solution and then try it out, finding, as in all pragmatic affairs, that sometimes the solution is not the right one. This is essentially different from the business of accepting the adult's solution as necessarily right, which is one of the dangers of the highly intelligent child's convergent response to teachers and books.

It is still far too common in schools for practical design work to be regarded as somehow less important than the so-called academic pursuits. I am suggesting that it is not only as important but even more important if we are to encourage a combination of cognitive and creative activities. I am also suggesting that good, constructional toys may indeed be excellent ways of encouraging this sort of creativity but that the real work of designing and mending machinery may be of greater significance.

Practical implications for the teacher

The possession of high intelligence or high creativity does not tell us anything about particular behaviour or needs or expectations of individual gifted children; but a knowledge of their likely influence on behaviour can alert junior school teachers to identifying those who possess them. The identification is the first stage towards making provision in which these gifts and their possessors can flourish. Once children have been identified, alienation can be avoided by the use of compassion, commonsense and the practical application of sound general principles.

Take the specific example of the gifted eight-year-old mathematician. If he/she is so precocious mathematically that the class teacher cannot cope with the child's needs, alternatives can be explored:

i. He/she can be made to do more of what the others are doing — more of the same in other words.
Good or bad? Bad.

ii. He/she can be given more advanced work in a corner or in the corridor.
Good or bad? Better than (i) but not very good. Children need their peers.

iii. He/she can be withdrawn with a small group of his/her peers to work at more advanced maths or a related subject like statistics/astronomy/computers.
Good or bad? Good, if there is adequate staff.

iv. He/she can be accelerated to a higher class for maths, returning to base for other subjects (partial acceleration).
Good or bad? Good.

v. He/she can be accelerated for the whole of his/her work.
Good or bad? Good, provided he/she is emotionally and physically up to it.

In the field of gifted education, more than most, I warn readers of the dangers of accepting doctrinaire solutions and vast philosophical generalizations. The whole thrust should be to assess the needs of individuals and then to make a humane, caring attempt to cater for them. A rich, varied and demanding curriculum is the best defence against the possibility of alienation in junior schools.

Ten hints directed at teachers may prove useful in conclusion:

i. Be prepared to change your institutional practice if necessity demands.

ii. Strive not to be too sensitive to criticism, especially from parents.

iii. Use parents without fear.

iv. Do not leave the gifted in isolation with good resources or rely on private study.

v. Give the able, at best daily, at worst weekly, a chance to work with intellectual peers of any age. This will mean some sort of setting/withdrawal/support organization.

vi. Offer psychological support/counselling to help the very able cope with their differences. The fewer of them there are, the more necessary this is.

vii. Give yourself a chance of success with short-term pilot modules or out-of-school short courses.

viii. Use all available expertise, and encourage skilled enthusiasts to support children's interests.

ix. Use all the resources outside the school — museums, etc.

x. Do not be afraid to approach the inspectorate, colleges or universities for help.

References

Abroms, K. I. (1985) 'Social giftedness and its relation with intellectual giftedness', in J. Freeman (Ed) *The Psychology of Gifted Children*, Chichester, John Wiley.

De Bono, E. (1970) *Lateral Thinking: Creativity Step by Step*, London, Harper and Row.

Department of Education and Science (1975) *A Language for Life* (Bullock Report), London, HMSO.

Feynman, R. and Leighton, R. (1986) *Surely You're Joking Mr Feynman!: Adventures of a Curious Character*, London, Unwin.

Getzels, J. W. (1982) 'The Problem of the Problem', in R. Hogarth (Ed) *New Directions for Methodology for Social and Behavioural Science*, San Francisco, Josey-Bass.

Koestler, A. (1964) *The Act of Creation*, London, Hutchinson.

Maslow, A. (1954) *Motivation and Personality*, New York, Harper.

National Association for Gifted Children (1987) *The Social and Educational and Emotional Needs of Gifted Children*, London, NAGC.

Singer, J. L. (1978) *Intra-Personal Psychoanalysis*, New York, John Wiley.

Sinnott, E. W. (1959) The Creativeness of Life, in H. H. Anderson (Ed) *Creativity and its Cultivation*, New York, Harper.

Speed, F. and Appleyard, D. (1985) *The Bright and the Gifted*, Toronto, Ontario, University of Toronto Guidance Centre, Faculty of Education.

Terman, L. B. (1926) *Genetic Studies of Genius, Volume 1: Mental and Physical Traits of a Thousand Gifted Children*, Stanford, California, Stanford University Press.

Notes on Contributors

Colin Conner taught in middle schools before joining the staff at Homerton College, Cambridge, where he had particular responsibility for the Post-Graduate Certificate in Education for intending primary teachers. He is now Tutor in Education for Primary and Middle Years at the Cambridge Institute of Education, teaching on the Advanced Diploma course 'Education for Children 3–13' and coordinating the MA course in Applied Research. His main interests and research areas are children's learning, assessment and evaluation. He is currently working on *Assessment and Testing in Primary Schools* for Falmer Press, is acting as a consultant on assessment and testing, and is helping to evaluate a local authority GRIST scheme.

David Coulby is Head of the Faculty of Education at Bath College of Higher Education. Before this he taught in East London. He has written extensively on inner-city education, and is co-author of *Urban Schooling: Theory and Practice* (Cassells, 1985) and *Preventing Classroom Disruption: Policy, Practice and Evaluation in Urban Schools* (Croom Helm, 1985). He is also co-editor of *Producing and Reducing Disaffection* (Open University Press, 1986) and has recently written (with Lesley Bush) *The Education Reform Act: Competition and Control* (Cassells, 1988).

Jacquie Coulby was until recently headteacher of Mowlem Primary School in Bethnal Green, London. Before this she was Acting Headteacher of Redlands Primary School in Stepney. Her particular interests are multicultural and multilingual education in the infant and junior years.

Jim Docking was until recently Principal Lecturer in Education at the Roehampton Institute, London, where he has also been Chairman of the School of Education. He is now a part-time lecturer and educational consultant. He taught at schools in Yorkshire and Coventry before joining the staff of Whitelands College, where he became Head of Education. He is author of *Control and Discipline in Schools:*

Perspectives and Approaches (Harper and Row, 1987), *Primary Schools and Parents: Rights, Responsibilities and Relationships* (Hodder and Stoughton, forthcoming) and various articles on pupil behaviour.

Peter Gurney is Senior Administrator in the University of Exeter School of Education, where until recently he was Senior Tutor for the BPhil/MEd course in Special Educational Needs. Previously he had been deputy head of a junior school. He has been Research Editor for the *British Journal of Special Education* and National President for the Association for Behavioural Approaches with Children. Besides editing volumes on special educational needs and behaviour modification in the University of Exeter's *Perspectives* series, he had recently written *Self-Esteem in Children with Special Educational Needs* (Routledge, 1988).

Peter Kutnick is Lecturer in Education at the University of Sussex. His research interests are social and moral development, cooperative learning, and education in the Caribbean. Besides chapters and articles on these subjects, he has written *Relating to Learning* (Allen and Unwin, 1983) and *Relationships in the Primary School* (Paul Chapman Publishing, 1988). American by origin, he has held lectureships at California State College and the University of the West Indies.

Neville Jones is Principal Educational Psychologist for Oxfordshire. He has written widely on aspects of management and services for pupils with special educational needs, having a special interest in pupils with behaviour difficulties. Between 1971 and 1976, he was a member of British Delegations visiting Boston, Canada, Holland, Israel and Sweden to study community services for the mentally disabled. He has been a member of the Council and Executive Committee of the National Children's Bureau, member of the Executive Committee of the National Association for Mental Health, and member of the Consultative Committees on the Schools' Council projects on Disturbed Pupils and Gifted Pupils. He has co-edited *Teacher Training and Special Educational Needs* (with J. Sayer, 1985); *Management and Special Needs* (with T. Southgate, 1989); *Management and the Psychology of Schooling* (with J. Sayer, 1988) and *Refocusing Educational Psychology* (with Norah Frederickson, 1989). He is Editor of the series *Special Educational Needs Review* No. 1 (1988) and No. 2 (1989) and of *School Management and Pupil Behaviour* (1989). He is Tutor in the Oxfordshire region for the Open University Courses on Special Educational Needs E241 and the Advanced Diploma. Currently he is engaged in directing the Oxfordshire Programme on Pupil Disaffection.

Peter Lang is Senior Lecturer in Education at Warwick University, having been a primary teacher for seven years. His main areas of interest are personal and social education, pastoral care, and parental involvement, both nationally and internationally. He has edited *Thinking About Personal and Social Education in the Primary School* (Blackwell, 1988) and was co-editor (with Michael Marland) of *New Directions in Pastoral Care* (Blackwell, 1985). He is coordinator of the

National Association for Pastoral Care in Education, based at the University of Warwick, and is Features Editor of the NAPCE journal *Pastoral Care in Education*.

Peter Mortimore is Professor of Educational Research and Director of the School of Education at the University of Lancaster. Before that he was an educational administrator and Director of the Research and Statistics Branch of the Inner London Education Authority. He is co-author of two of the main British studies on school effectiveness, *Fifteen Thousand Hours* (with Micheal Rutter *et al.*, Open Books, 1979) and *School Matters* (with Pamela Sammons *et al.*, Open Books, 1988). He has written widely on educational issues, including *Behaviour Problems in Schools* (Croom Helm, 1984) and *Secondary School Examinations* (Bedford Way Papers, 1986) and, most recently, with Bob Moon, *The National Curriculum: Straightjacket or Safetynet?*, an Educational Reform Group Ginger Paper.

Colin Rogers is Lecturer in Education in the Department of Educational Research at the University of Lancaster. Before that he was a researcher at the universities of Leicester and Surrey. His special interests are in the social psychology of education, pupil motivation and teacher expectations, on which he has written many articles. He is author of *A Social Psychology of Schooling* (Routledge and Kegan Paul, 1982).

Pamela Sammons is Senior Research Officer in the Research and Statistics Branch of the Inner London Education Authority. She has special interests in school effectiveness and the determinants of pupil progress, the process of secondary transfer, the construction and use of educational priority indices, and freedom of information in education. With Peter Mortimore she has recently published *School Matters: The Junior Years* (Open Books, 1988), based on the extensive ILEA Junior School Project.

John Welch is Director of the National Association for Gifted Children, a member of the Committee on Marked Aptitudes for the Inner London Educational Authority, and a member of the Clwyd Centre for Educational Development and Research. After wartime service, he taught in junior schools in London, Dulwich College and Tulse Hill Comprehensive School for Boys before joining the ILEA inspectorate. His publications include 'Special Needs for Gifted Children' in *Support for Learning* (1987).

Paul Widlake is a part-time teacher, freelance educational consultant and writer. Besides teaching in schools he has been Research Officer for the Community Education Development Centre in Coventry, Principal Lecturer in Education at Manchester Polytechnic, Adviser on Special Needs in Wolverhampton and a Senior Research Associate at the University of Birmingham. He has written extensively on educational disadvantage, special needs and community education. His most recent books are *Raising Standards* (with Flora Macleod, Community Education Development Centre, 1984), *How to Reach the Hard to Teach* (Open University

Press, 1983), *Reducing Educational Disadvantage* (Open University Press, 1986), and *The Special Children Handbook* (Hutchinson, 1989).

David Winkley is Head of Grove Junior School in Handsworth, Birmingham, and Director of the National Primary Centre at Westminster College, Oxford. He has a special interest in special educational needs, language development and educational management. He is author of *Diplomats and Detectives* (Cassell, 1986), a study of local authority advisers and management.

Index